This book is for

the growing number of people who recognize that mass food production has created many nutritionally empty as well as boring foods. It is also for those who find that meat, fish and poultry have become prohibitively expensive. Here is a way to eat baked goods as an alternative to meat as well as to enjoy bread as a valuable food and not just a starchy luxury.

About the Author

The *Complete Book of High-Protein Baking* was conceived in a big red farm house in the Hudson Valley a few miles from an old, but still working grist mill. There, with friends who were professional bakers, Martha Ellen Katz developed many tasty whole-grain recipes that were not as heavy as the usual "healthy" fare.

Ms. Katz received her M.S. in nutrition from the Institute for Human Nutrition of the College of Physicians and Surgeons of Columbia University, where she is now studying to become a physician. She has written for *Gourmet Magazine* as a specialist in natural foods. Ms. Katz is currently interested in health education for the community, and hosts a monthly radio program, *Salud*, on WBAI-FM.

THE COMPLETE BOOK OF HIGH-PROTEIN BAKING

Martha Ellen Katz

Illustrations by Marsha Richter

Eat bread and salt and speak
the truth . . .
—Russian proverb

BALLANTINE BOOKS • NEW YORK

The following recipes appeared in *Gourmet Magazine* in a similar form; in most cases one or two high-protein ingredients have been added:

Banana Bread
Brown Bread
Buttermilk Cracked Wheat Bread
Carrot Cake
Cranberry-Orange Anadama
Limpa Rye Bread (in *Gourmet* called "Swedish Rye")
Orange Muffins
Refrigerator Rise Dark Rye Bread
Rum-Raisin Bread
Sourdough Rye
Sponge Method Five-Grain Bread
Yogurt Pecan Coffee Cake

Library of Congress Catalog Card Number: 75-19055

ISBN 0-345-25747-2

Manufactured in the United States of America

First Edition: September 1975
Second Printing: November 1977

Contents

Protein

A Compendium of Ingredients

Everyone who has known me while this book grew has had a part in these pages. Thank you to the bakers, the tasters, the illustrator, the editors, the readers, and the reassurers for your encouragement, criticism, talents, and endurance.

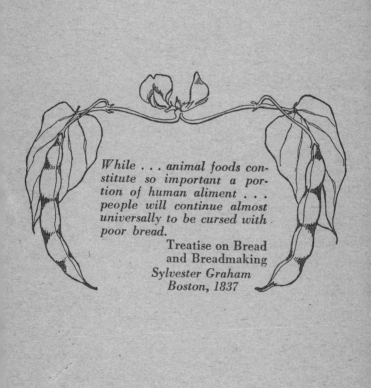

*While . . . animal foods con-
stitute so important a portion of human aliment . . .
people will continue almost
universally to be cursed with
poor bread.*

Treatise on Bread
and Breadmaking
*Sylvester Graham
Boston, 1837*

Introduction

I wrote this book for people like myself, who find pleasure in preparing their own food, want to know the principles of baking breads so they can invent their own bread recipes, and want high protein value from plant foods.

Bread suggests warmth and friendship. The word *companion*, in fact, literally means a person you share bread with—from *com*, meaning "together," and *panis*, meaning "bread." I would like to share these breads with you.

Baking bread is not a complicated process, although it does take experience to gain the confidence that makes it easy. Even for a beginner it is difficult to have an absolute bread-baking failure. Bread doughs are hardy, and the instructions explain each step carefully. As you become skillful you will be able to make perfect bread each time. After all, there was a time in this country when everyone knew how to bake bread, and often the baking was left to the children.

Each group of recipes begins with detailed instructions for the basic steps involved. The techniques are all fundamental; they are simply repeated with different ingredients. For instance, kneading is the same for bread loaves and coffee cake doughs; butter and flour are combined in the same manner for pie crusts and biscuits.

If possible, bake with a friend—either someone who

knows how to bake and can guide you, or someone who will read the instructions aloud while you are elbow deep in dough. It can be a good project for a Saturday afternoon.

People often ask if I made up all the recipes. Not really. I think of bread recipes as folk songs—passed from friend to friend, from book to book, then changed and adapted to suit a personal style, until you can call them your own. In the same way each of these recipes can be varied to suit your style or mood, or baked as written, which will always work well.

I have learned how to bake by baking at home, by baking with friends in their bakery, and by reading and experimenting with ideas from professional bakers' books. Most of what I have gathered together is scientific fact. Some is just my preference, so feel free to experiment.

Everyone needs protein to live. Unfortunately, finding land to supply protein foods is becoming harder, since there are more and more people to feed. Frances M. Lappé, in *Diet for a Small Planet,* explains how our meat-eating culture is at the heart of the waste of the earth's protein supply. Eating meat to fulfill our protein needs, she argues, is wasteful, uneconomical, and ultimately inadequate to nourish everyone.

Meat-eating is an inefficient way for human beings to satisfy their need for protein. To make one pound of beef protein, the steer is fed at least ten pounds of high-protein grain. We could eat the protein-rich grain and get almost ten pounds of protein value. In these days of high meat prices and forecasts of worldwide food shortages, we have good reason to make all our food count. Ms. Lappé recommends a way to eat that makes the most of the earth's protein-producing capacity. Less protein is wasted and good protein value is gained when we eat a variety of plant foods—grains, nuts, and dried beans. This principle is part of every recipe in this book.

Grains—wheat, corn, rye, millet, rice, barley, oats, and buckwheat—are the basic ingredients of bread. All breads, whether we call them crackers, pancakes, yeasted loaves, or pastry, begin simply with ground grain and water.

Grains are the sustaining foods for most people in the world. Yet, in the United States grain foods are not valued; they have been displaced in our diet by meat and sugar. In addition, the grains and breads that are available contain little more than starch, since most other nutrients are destroyed through processing long before these foods reach the table. "Enrichment" merely returns a few of the many burned-out vitamins and minerals.

But grains and bread can be more than empty calories. Grains and other plant foods grown and prepared with regard to good nutrition can make surprisingly satisfying meals, and, in particular, they can provide good protein. *A balanced diet of grains, dried beans, and nuts, supplemented with eggs and milk, contains proteins that are as valuable as those obtained from meat, fish, and poultry.*

I emphasize protein in this book to stress the vital role of protein in daily eating. Breads can supply this prime nutrient, as well as carbohydrates and fats. Those few vitamins and minerals that breads lack must come from vegetables and fruit. No single food can supply complete nutrition, and we cannot live by bread alone—but we can bake protein-rich, nutritious breads.

If you feel that eating meat, fish, or poultry has become too expensive for your pocketbook, too costly for the people of the earth, or if you avoid these foods for health or religious reasons, then the principles of variety and balance illustrated here can show you how to get more protein from the plant foods you eat. This book, however, is not only for vegetarians; it is for those of us who enjoy baking and sharing with friends a fresh warm loaf of bread.

Note: If you do not have some of the high-protein ingredients—milk powder and soy flour—or unusual flours—buckwheat or barley, for instance—you can substitute whole wheat or white wheat flour in any of the recipes in this book. Although there may be some sacrifice in protein, and slight differences in taste, there will be no sacrifice in texture.

Baking Basics

Preliminaries

Baked goods are more alike than they are different. Breads, cakes, cookies, and pancakes differ only in the *amount* of liquid added to flour, *how* air is incorporated, and the extras—eggs, sugar, oil, salt, and flavorings. A bread recipe is easy to vary once you know how the basic ingredients and proportions affect what comes out of the oven.

When friends ask me for a bread recipe that uses blackstrap molasses, or one that uses oil, not butter, I show them how molasses can be substituted for any sweetener, or oil for butter, with only a few minor adjustments. The section entitled "Interplay of Ingredients" describes how each ingredient works, so you will be able to alter recipes—for preference, lower cost, better taste, or higher nutritional value.

When I began baking, I liked to follow a specific recipe carefully to make sure the bread came out well; but soon I found myself substituting ingredients—whole wheat for white flour, molasses for sugar, yogurt for sour cream—in order to use foods that are fresher, less processed, and higher in protein.

In the following few pages you will find a guide to such experiments in baking: first, the necessary equipment; second, a note on measuring; third, basic proportions of ingredients for different kinds of breads, how these ingredients work together; fourth, h adapt recipes to use the ingredients you prefer; and, finally, suggestions for reusing leftovers and failures.

EQUIPMENT

To mix and bake breads a baker needs only a bowl, a board, a pan, and an oven—some bakers even manage without the bowl and pan and bake their breads on an open flame.

A baker does need sturdy, practical equipment. This does not mean expensive gear—a well-chosen makeshift substitute may turn out to be better suited to a recipe than the conventional pot or pan. As a rule, however, professional equipment is best. You can get new or secondhand pots, pans, mixers, bowls, knives, and gadgets at restaurant and bakery supply shops, or from friendly local bakers and restaurateurs.

Basic Tools

THE BOWL

A large mixing bowl is needed, preferably round-bottomed for easier mixing and steep-sided so that the rising dough can cling. A 3- or 4-quart bowl is about right for a two-loaf batch of bread.

Earthenware bowls are heavy and sturdy, and they

retain warmth best—important for rising yeast doughs. Glass bowls are nice to use because you can see the air bubbles as the dough rises.

THE BOARD

A sturdy table or counter top of about 2 feet by 2 feet with a smooth surface at a comfortable height to rest your hands provides a workspace to mix, knead, and shape breads. A wooden breadboard made from the reverse side of a cutting board or a heavy piece of wood used only for kneading breads and rolling doughs is a simple luxury. It must be kept clean and smooth. Place the board on a damp towel to keep it from slipping off the table.

THE PANS

Breads can be baked on flat sheets or in tins. Most modern pans are made of aluminum, but the best material for pans is heavy tinned steel which absorbs, retains, and conducts heat well. When the pans darken with age and frequent use, they help breads bake and brown evenly. I prefer heavy, old loaf pans with folded corners, because they are sturdy and bake breads thoroughly. Look for them in secondhand shops.

Flat baking sheets—sideless or with a low rim to allow the sides of the loaf to brown—should be at least two inches smaller than the inside of the oven to permit air circulation and even browning. A sheet metal shop will cut aluminum to a requested size. An upside-down pie or cake tin can also serve as a baking sheet.

Although most breads are baked in loaf pans, there are many other sizes and shapes. You can bake three loaves together in a large roasting pan if you butter the sides of the loaves where they touch each other, so that the breads will separate easily when they come out of the oven. Breads can be successfully baked in saucepans and frying pans that have ovenproof handles, or in casseroles, tin cans, flower pots, or sea shells.

There are square or rectangular shallow pans for cakes, bars, or brownies; round tins with straight sides for cakes; round tins with sloping sides for pies. Special pans are designed for brioches, kugelhopf, muffins, quiches, and tartlets. None is essential; they are simply pleasant to use.

When changing the size or shape or material of the baking pan from the one suggested in a recipe, you often need to make adjustments. For instance, earthenware (including flower pots), glass, or enameled pans absorb more heat than metal. To compensate, these pans must be used at a temperature 25–50 degrees lower than that for metal tins. If this adjustment is not made, the crust will bake faster and burn before the inside of the bread is ready. Particularly with glass pans, you must watch breads carefully so that they do not burn. If the crust has browned or burned before the insides are baked, make a tent out of aluminum foil and cover the bread. To convert a glass pan into a metal one, line the glass pan with aluminum foil. For fruit cakes which often burn because they must bake for a long time, leave about 3 inches of foil overhanging on each long edge. While the bread is baking, fold the foil flaps over the top when the crust begins to darken.

To substitute a different size pan for the pan suggested in a recipe, follow this chart which lists the approximate amount of dough or batter that will rise to the rim of each pan. Note the pan size suggested, and compare the volume in cups to the tin that you want to use. As pan sizes are not standardized measure your own pans across the inner rim of the top.

Pan		*Approximate cups, filled to allow for rising*
LOAF		
large	10 by 5¼ by 3¼	4
medium	8 by 4 by 3	2½
small	7½ by 3½ by 2¼	1½
1-POUND COFFEE CAN		2 for yeast bread, 2½ for quick bread
TWELVE-CUP MUFFIN TIN		2½
SQUARE {	9 by 9 by 2	4
	8 by 8 by 2	2½
ROUND	8 by 1½	2

When changing pan sizes or shapes, remember that the size and thickness of the loaf will change the baking time. A thick or large bread will take longer to bake than a small or thin one.

Clean all pans well after each use. After baking yeast breads, simply wipe the tin. If pans need scrubbing, use a stiff, non-wire brush and hot water without soap. Wipe the tins dry and oil them to prevent rusting.

As with heavy cast-iron frying pans, tinned steel pans should be seasoned or darkened when new so that they conduct heat well and do not rust. First wipe the pan, and place it in a 400° oven until the surface has a bluish tinge; then let it cool and wipe it, which will get rid of any mineral oil or other volatile chemicals on the surface of the pan. Oil the pan liberally, inside and out, and put it back in the oven for a few minutes until it begins to smoke; remove it, let it cool, and wipe off the excess oil. The treatment will fill in any pits and produce a smooth, dark surface. This seasoning method is also good for old, rusted, or pitted pans.

THE OVEN

Every oven is different. Baking consistently good breads requires sensitivity to the temperament of your oven. A good portable oven thermometer conveniently checks oven temperatures. If the thermometer and the oven dial disagree, either have the oven professionally calibrated, or adjust the dial so that the thermometer reads the temperature you want. Use the temperatures given in the recipes as a guide. If the oven is temperamental, do not hesitate to change the baking temperature so that the bread does not burn before it is baked through.

Often bad insulation or uneven heat flow makes breads bake unevenly. If the breads are not browning uniformly, rotate the loaves to a new position in the oven. If the oven does not heat well, bake only a few loaves at a time.

More Equipment

FOR MEASURING

Measuring cups in graduated sizes are convenient for measuring dry ingredients—such as 1 cup, ½ cup, ⅓ cup, and ¼ cup. Measure liquid ingredients in a cup with a lip for pouring—a 1-, 2- or 4-cup size. Measuring spoons are available in graduated sizes—1 tablespoon, 1 teaspoon, ½ teaspoon, ¼ teaspoon. Finally, a kitchen scale, to bake as the Europeans and profes-

sional bakers do, assures accuracy each time you bake because the quantity measured is not affected by how tightly the ingredients are packed in the cup.

FOR MIXING, BEATING, AND STIRRING

All mixing and stirring can be done by hand. You can then learn the feel of the ingredients and know the right consistency of the dough or batter by touch. You

may notice that people involved with food do not hesitate to hold it in their hands. The art is to use your hands in a manner that suits the mixing job. For instance, sometimes you need a warm palm to knead bread, and sometimes the light touch of cool fingertips to blend pastry.

For stirring, folding, mixing, or smearing, use a cupped hand, a wooden spoon, paddle, or stiff rubber spatula. A rubber spatula, like your finger, gets the last drop out of the bowl or cup.

For beating, use an implement that incorporates air —a fork, wire whisk, or rotary beater.

ELECTRIC EQUIPMENT

For home-size bakings, mixing and kneading doughs by hand works as well as or better than machine mixing and kneading. However, there are some things a machine does better than a hand; for instance, by hand it is hard to get as fine a puree as a blender can.

To substitute an electric appliance to save time, use the beaters of an electric mixer for blending and whipping, and a dough hook attachment to replace hand kneading. It is best not to use a mechanical gadget when a wooden spoon is suggested; for instance, overmixing pancakes and 'muffins will make them rubbery.

ODDS AND ENDS

A *bench scraper,* or pastry scraper, is a square of metal with a wooden or metal handle to keep the worktable free of sticky flour and to cut yeast doughs. A hardware-store paint scraper or a broad spatula works well too. A bench scraper is illustrated on page 52.

A *bread knife* with a long, thin serrated blade to cut bread easily without tearing it.

A *room thermometer* and a *candy thermometer.* Knowing the room temperature and the temperature of liquids takes the guesswork out of yeast baking. If you do not have a thermometer try to teach your hand to do the job; yeast grows well at wrist temperature.

A *wire rack* for cooling breads, cakes, and cookies; or *basket* of wicker or willow slats for cooling solid loaves and rolls.

A *sifter* is a mesh screen that separates dry flour with air. Sifting makes breads light, breaks up large particles of dry ingredients and makes sure that they are well mixed. Sifters come with a spring-action moving screen, a rotary arm (my preference), or simply a piece of wire mesh secured in a frame. Keep the sifter dry. It never needs washing; just bang it to clean.

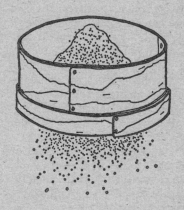

A *rolling pin* for making pie crusts and Danish pastries. A heavy large wooden rolling pin is best; a ball bearing pin is not necessary. You can improvise by using a wine bottle or a broom handle.

A brush or two, one for oily liquids and one for watery liquids, to coat tins and dough with butter or glazes. Fancy feather pastry brushes are available, but a sturdy natural bristle paintbrush is fine.

A *home flour mill,* which looks like a large meat grinder, grinds fresh flour from whole kernels. Many say that fresh hand-milled flour is like home-grown tomatoes—worth the effort. It takes a while to get fine flour because the grain must be ground several times. The advantages are that the flour is fresh (which means that it has better nutritive value and taste), you can adjust your own grind, and the uncracked grain kernels are inexpensive and keep indefinitely if properly stored. Electric mills are available for those who want the best of both worlds.

MEASURING

Measuring ingredients accurately insures consistent results from one bread to the next. This is necessary until you feel confident enough to judge a good dough or batter by sight, taste, and feel. When you begin to feel relaxed about baking, measure by the handful. It is also nice to know how many tablespoons half an egg shell will hold; the number of inches between thumb and little finger of an outstretched hand to gauge quickly the size of pans or rolled-out dough; or what a tablespoon of salt looks like when it is poured into your hand.

In the United States most measures are by *volume*, like a teaspoon, a pint, or a quart. A cup is a volume measure—it contains a specific quantity regardless of how much the contents of the cup weigh.

1 CUP	= 16 TABLESPOONS
1 TABLESPOON	= 3 TEASPOONS
1 CUP	= 8 FLUID OUNCES*

Comparing the quantities of each ingredient in a bread shows the proportions of one ingredient to another. Any set of volume measures can be used to prepare recipes as long as the measurements retain the proportions of ingredients. For instance, begin with a

---

* A fluid ounce is a volume measure and is *not* equal to an ounce of weight.

teacup or a mug as your standard cup. One-half cup in the recipe then means one-half of that particular teacup or mug.

Accuracy is less important in yeast breads than in pies and cakes.

To measure dry ingredients (like flour, for instance) for recipes in this book, take the appropriate-size measuring cup and spoon the flour out of the bin into the cup. Keep spooning until the cup overflows. Do not sift before measuring. Do not tap the cup, because dry ingredients, especially flour, tend to compress and distort the measure. Sweep off the excess with a knife so the flour is level with the rim of the cup. By this method, measure baking soda or baking powder very *carefully* in the appropriate-size measuring spoon.

To measure liquids, pour the liquid into a measuring cup, filling it to the line that indicates the amount you want—hold the cup at eye level to get an accurate measure. For honey, molasses, or any sticky liquid, first coat the inside of the measuring cup with oil—the sticky liquid will then easily slide out. Do not dip the measuring cup or spoon into the honey pot; extra honey will cling to the underside and will get into the recipe.

To measure solid fats (like butter) and brown sugar, pack them tightly into the measuring cup. One pound of butter, or four sticks, equals two cups. Another method for measuring butter is: if you are measuring half a cup, for example, fill a measuring cup with ½ cup water. Add butter until the water reaches the one-cup level. Drain off the water and you will have exactly half a cup of butter.

THE INTERPLAY OF INGREDIENTS

Bread-baking ingredients are not exotic. You can probably bake a fine loaf of bread with what is already in your kitchen.

The ingredients in breads are:

Flour for structure
Liquids to hold the bread together
Leavening to make the bread rise
Shortening for tenderness
Sweeteners for flavor and to feed the yeast
Salt for flavor and to control fermentation
Eggs for structure, liquid, shortening, leavening, and flavor
Flavorings for extra taste

After each section in this chapter, the basic proportions—the amount of each ingredient for each cup of flour—are shown. The proportions are not *rules;* they are guideposts to use until you feel confident enough to invent or alter recipes and judge the effect by the feel of the dough and the texture and taste of the finished bread.

At the end of the book in the Compendium of Ingredients, you will find more complete descriptions of each food group listed above.

Flour

GRINDING FLOURS

Flour begins with a kernel of grain, the meat of a nut, or a single bean which are then ground small to release the starchy interior. Each kernel of grain consists of a starchy *endosperm,* an oily *germ*—the embryo of a new plant—and a protective *bran* covering. Milling smashes the hard coating, pulverizes the starch, germ, and bran, and releases the kernel oils.

In *whole-grain flours,* all the components of the kernel have survived the milling process. In non-whole-grain flours, *sifting* or *bolting* the whole flour separates the starchy white flour from the flaky germ and coarse bran. Modern mills use steel rollers or hammers to crush the kernel; old-fashioned mills grind flour between granite stones

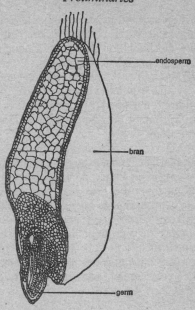

Stone-milling passes the kernels between two round stones—one rotating, the other stationary. The surface of each stone—the "land"—is chiseled with radiating "furrows" that cut and crush the grain and push the flour off the edge of the stone into a bin. The coarseness of the flour is regulated by the distance between the two grinding stones.

I prefer stone-milled flours to steel-milled flours, because the feel of the flours and the taste of the breads are better. Millstones do not get as hot as steel rollers or hammers do, so the flavor and nutrients are better preserved. The stones rub the germ oil evenly throughout the flour, which gives breads baked from stone-ground kernels a fresh, rich taste.

It is hard to list all the possible flours from grains, beans, and nuts and seeds, because mills and distributors name their products differently. With the help of the following descriptions, the Compendium of Ingredients, and the section "Using Flours," it should be easy to buy the flour you need (or a good substitute) from a store or a mail-order catalogue.

Whole-grain kernels (called *berries*) and nuts and seeds are available either *unhulled* (with the shell) or *hulled* (without the shell). The hulled variety is for cooking and grinding into flour; the unhulled variety is ideal for sprouting.

There are several varieties of ground kernels. *Grits* are kernels that are cut into angular pieces by the millstones so there is no floury powder—they are coarsely cracked. Sometimes the grits are steamed and toasted which, for instance, makes kasha from buckwheat grits or bulgur from wheat grits. *Meal* is made when the kernel is more finely ground; like cornmeal, it is gritty and granular when you rub it between your fingers. *Rolled, crinkled,* or *flaked* kernels are steamed and flattened, like commercial oatmeal—which is actually rolled oats.

GLUTEN: THE UNSEEN INGREDIENT

Gluten is a protein present in the endosperm of some grains. It makes breads cohesive and elastic rather than crumbly. The interaction of the two components of gluten—glutenin and gliadin—with water enables a dough to trap the leavening gas produced by growing yeast. The gluten is activated when flour is moistened, well stirred, and kneaded. Long, elastic strands of gluten interlock like a web or rubber sheet. The dough rises when the yeast produces gas, and the gas is trapped within the gluten balloon. The dough then stretches, ripens, and mellows. In the oven, the gluten sets and hardens, giving the bread its final shape and grain.

The baking quality of a flour depends on the quality and quantity of gluten. Wheat is the grain highest in gluten, therefore most American breads are made primarily with wheat. Non-wheat flours—rye, oats, corn, rice, barley, buckwheat, dried beans, and nuts—do not contain enough gliadin, the stretchy component of gluten, to hold a bread together without crumbling.

USING FLOURS

Flours vary considerably. Press some flour between your fingertips to feel the variety of textures. Different qualities of grains, different strains, and different milling make each flour unique. With mass-produced flour you can expect similar results from one day to the next and from one sack of flour to the next. But daily changes in humidity, particularly with whole-grain flours from small local mills, must be compensated for.

Flours differ primarily in the amount of liquid they will hold. A very powdery, high-gluten flour will need more liquid per cup of flour than will a coarse, low-gluten flour or meal. By feeling the flour, you can estimate how much to add to a recipe. The best way to add the right amount of flour is to stir it gradually into the batter or dough until it reaches the right consistency. Experienced breadmakers never bother to measure; they judge by the feel of the dough. It is a knack that is surprisingly easy to develop.

SUBSTITUTING FLOURS

Use any low-gluten flour to replace up to a third of the whole wheat or white wheat flour in a yeast bread recipe. A larger proportion of low-gluten flour can be used in quick breads, cakes, and cookies. More than three different kinds of flour in one bread makes the taste of each hard to distinguish.

Exchange 1 cup wheat flour for about:

> 1½ CUPS ROLLED OATS
> 1 CUP RYE FLOUR
> 1 CUP CORNMEAL
> ¾ CUP BUCKWHEAT FLOUR
> ¾ CUP RICE FLOUR
> ¾ CUP GLUTEN FLOUR
> ¾ CUP BARLEY FLOUR
> ½ CUP POTATO FLOUR
> ¼ CUP BEAN FLOUR

Wheat flour can always be used if other flours are not available.

When substituting flours that are darker, coarser, or lower in gluten for wheat flour, bake the breads in pans smaller than recommended in the recipe—the bread will be more compact and the loaves smaller.

In yeast doughs when using a mixture of high- and low-gluten flours, add the high-gluten flour for the first, second, and *last* cups to best develop the gluten network.

You can make your own flour and grits in small quantities in a blender from whole grains, rolled grains, or beans. Whirl for about fifteen seconds, stop to let the motor cool, and whirl again until the flour is powdery.

Meals or grits of any grain or bean, if soaked in boiling water, add a moist, substantial texture to breads without being gritty.

For a pleasant roasted taste toast the flour for a recipe. Put it in a shallow baking pan in a 300° oven, or in a frying pan on the top of the stove. Stir frequently to prevent burning and toast until brown.

STORING FLOURS

Whole grains store well because of their thick natural coverings. Flours, on the other hand, are open to the air, which invites bugs, molds, and odors. In addition, the oils in whole-grain, bean, and nut flours can become rancid from interacting with the oxygen in the air. Therefore, store flours in a dry, cool place in ventilated containers—paper bags, canisters, or 1-gallon pickle and mayonnaise jars with vents punctured into the lids. During the summer, and in warm climates, these flours should be refrigerated. Any flour freezes well in watertight and airtight packages.

USING WHOLE KERNELS

Any cooked grains or beans—leftover breakfast cereal, dinner grains such as rice, or a mush made of cooked beans, or porridge—added to dough will make a moist, dense, chewy bread. To avoid a bread that is too wet or too heavy, reduce the other liquids in the recipe by about ⅔ cup for each cup of cooked beans or grains used.

Whole kernels of grains and beans, soaked overnight and cooked until soft but still separate, taste crisp when sprinkled throughout a bread.

Rolled grains or beans, for instance rolled oats or rolled soybeans, if first soaked in boiling water make yeast breads cakey and cookies chewy.

Sprouts grown from grains, beans, or seeds when crushed in a meat grinder or finely chopped by hand make crunchy additions to yeast breads and a crisp garnish for sandwiches and salads. See page 319 for how to grow sprouts.

Liquids

Liquids dissolve the dry ingredients and make a bread hold together. Use water, eggs, syrupy sugars (honey, maple, molasses), milk (from cows, goats, sheep, soy beans, or coconuts), fruit and vegetable juices, vegetable cooking water, soup, pickle or olive juice, cider, thick wines and liqueurs, beer, or tea.

Different liquids bring different qualities to breads and cakes.

- Water brings out the wheaty taste and makes a hard, crunchy crust.
- Milk makes a soft, cakelike bread with a dark crust.
- Eggs make a rich, moist crumb.
- Syrupy sugars make a dark crust and moist grain.
- Potato water makes a smooth crumb and helps yeast grow.
- Cider, beer, and liqueurs make a smooth grain.

Too much liquid and the bread or cake will be soggy and sink in the middle; too little liquid and the bread or cake will be dense, dry, and bulge in the center.

AVERAGE PROPORTION OF LIQUID TO 1 CUP OF FLOUR

Yeast Bread	⅓ cup liquid (about 1 cup for each loaf)
Quick Breads and Muffins	½ cup liquid
Biscuits	⅓ cup liquid
Pancakes	¾ cup liquid
Pastry Crusts	¼ cup liquid
Cakes	⅔ cup liquid
Cookies	¼ cup liquid

Leavening

For me, the magic of baking breads is that they rise. In all forms of leavening, the batter or dough fills with air, pushes upward, and makes the bread or cake light and airy. A bread that does not fill with air will be solid, or flat. There are several ways of getting the essential bubbles into the batter or dough.

Steam. When the water in the dough turns to steam, it expands, forming large air pockets in the dough; this contributes to the lightness of all breads and cakes.

Trapped air. Air caught in the bubbles of beaten eggs and in the batters of cakes, quick breads, and pancakes expands when heated.

Biological leavening. Yeasts and sourdough produce carbon dioxide at a slow pace.

Chemical leavening. Baking soda and baking powder produce carbon dioxide quickly when an acid ingredient like lemon juice or yogurt combines with baking soda (a base) or when baking powder is mixed with water.

YEAST

Yeasts are one-celled living organisms that multiply by feeding on the starches and sugars in a dough. In warmth and moisture, yeast buds grow into long chains, converting their starch-sugar food into carbon dioxide and alcohol. The carbon dioxide gas gets trapped in the elastic gluten strands in the dough, and as the gases are released the dough stretches upward. In the oven, the heat kills the yeast, the alcohol evaporates, and the gas bubbles expand and raise the bread even more. The yeasts create the character of bread—the smell, the taste, and the porous texture.

Yeasts grow wild and live, unseen, in the air, particularly in warm kitchens. Baking yeasts, however, are captured and cultured and are available in dried granules or in moist, compressed cakes. Brewer's yeast cannot be used to raise breads.

YEAST EQUIVALENTS

1 tablespoon of dry yeast
one ¼-ounce foil package of dry yeast
one ⅔-ounce package of cake yeast
1 tablespoon of cake yeast

The amount of yeast needed depends on the strain of yeast, the growing time, the temperature and humidity of the kitchen, and the food supply in the dough. Most recipes use enough yeast so that in a warm kitchen the dough will take 1½ hours for the first rising in the bowl, 1 hour for the second, and 1 hour in the pans after the loaves are formed. If you are prepared to wait longer, or make the kitchen very warm, you can use less yeast. Quick-rising yeast breads, doughs that rise in the refrigerator, and doughs rich in butter, eggs, sweeteners, fruit, or nuts need more yeast than plain doughs—often two or three times the amount.

Too much yeast (and too much rising) gives a porous texture and a yeasty taste; too little yeast makes a dense loaf.

AVERAGE PROPORTION OF YEAST TO FLOUR

Plain bread   1 or 2 tablespoons of yeast to 8 cups flour
Sweet breads   2 tablespoons yeast to 6 cups of flour

SOURDOUGH

See the introduction to the chapter of sourdough recipes for a full description.

CHEMICAL LEAVENING—BAKING SODA AND BAKING POWDER

Baking soda (bicarbonate of soda) when combined

with an acid ingredient like sour milk, lemon juice, yogurt, honey, or vinegar produces carbon dioxide bubbles that raise breads and cakes.

Baking powder is a fine, white powder made of baking soda combined with an acid powder (usually tartaric acid). When mixed with a liquid, baking powder produces carbon dioxide bubbles.

Single-acting baking powder releases all its carbon dioxide immediately into the batter. (Baking soda and an acid ingredient act as a single-acting baking powder.)

Double-acting baking powder releases air bubbles twice; once in the cold batter, then again when the batter heats in the oven, giving a delayed, additional burst of rising power. Double-acting baking powder is used in all recipes in this book that call for baking powder.

I use double-acting baking powder or baking soda and yogurt to raise most quick breads or cakes. If you do not have baking powder at home, stir ½ tablespoon of lemon juice or vinegar into ½ cup of milk, then add ¼ teaspoon of baking soda. This has enough leavening power to raise 1 cup of flour. Subtract the milk from the total liquid in the recipe.

Too much baking soda or baking powder gives a

AVERAGE PROPORTION OF LEAVENING TO
1 CUP OF WHOLE GRAIN FLOUR

1 teaspoon baking powder
> *or*

¼ teaspoon baking soda and ½ cup sour milk
> *or*

⅛ teaspoon baking soda and 1 tablespoon vinegar or lemon juice
> *or*

½ teaspoon baking soda and ½ teaspoon baking powder

---

bitter taste, a coarse, uneven grain, and a crumbly, dry texture to quick breads or cakes; it may also overrise the batter and break the walls of the bubbles, causing the bread or cake to fall. Too little leavener will cause a heavy, coarse, or gummy texture.

Shortening

Oils and fats in breads give flavor and softness—they coat and "shorten" the gluten strands, which makes the bread tender. The lubricated gluten mesh can then expand smoothly and rise well.

Shortenings include butter* or margarine, oils, lard, solid vegetable shortenings, nut butters, and egg yolks. Shortenings can be used interchangeably in most recipes, but:

• Only butter tastes like butter.
• Pie crusts are best made with a solid shortening. Oil does not make a flaky crust texture.

Yeast breads without shortening are chewy and dry out quickly. Quick breads and cakes made with too little shortening will be coarse-grained and dry; too

---

AVERAGE PROPORTION OF SHORTENING TO 1 CUP OF FLOUR

Plain yeast bread	1 to 2 teaspoons shortening
Sweet yeast dough	1 to 2 tablespoons shortening
Quick breads	⅓ cup shortening
Muffins	¼ cup shortening
Biscuits	1 tablespoon shortening
Pancakes	1 tablespoon shortening
Pastry crusts	⅓ cup shortening
Cakes	¼ cup shortening
Cookies	¼ to ½ cup shortening

---

* The recipes in this book use unsalted butter; if you want to use salted butter, add less table salt to the recipe.

much shortening will make a greasy bread or cake with crisp edges and a crumbly texture.

I keep a small pan of melted butter on the stove to butter pans, bowls, and doughs. Use a brush to do this, or fingers if you prefer.

Sweeteners

Sugars in breads and cakes add flavor and crispness, aid browning, and are a quick-energy food for yeast. Crystalline sugars are made from beets and sugar cane, maple sap, sorghum, and malt; syrupy sweeteners include honey, molasses, maple and corn syrups; ripened fruit, fruit juices, jams, and jellies are also good sweeteners for breads.

Only a little sugar is necessary in a yeast bread; a drop encourages yeast to grow; too much overpowers it. It is possible, in fact, to make a yeast bread without sugar, like French, Italian, or traditional American breads. The yeast can feed on the starch in the flour, but the dough will rise more slowly.

Too much sugar gives quick breads and cakes a thick, porous crust, a sagging center, and a soggy texture. Not enough sugar will result in a small loaf or cake with a coarse interior.

Breads with a lot of sugar (especially molasses) burn easily. Therefore, if you add extra sweetening, lower the oven temperature by 25–50° from the baking temperature suggested. If you want to use a syrupy sweetener (such as honey) in a recipe that calls for a crystalline sweetener (such as white sugar), reduce the liquids by about ¼ cup for each cup of syrup added. Furthermore, since molasses and honey are acidic, add 1 teaspoon of baking soda, in addition to the baking soda already used, for each cup of sweetener to neutralize the bitter taste.

Quick breads and cakes made only with syrupy sweeteners will be dense and wet. I prefer to use half honey or molasses and half brown sugar to get the less processed sugar taste without sogginess.

AVERAGE PROPORTION OF SWEETENER TO 1 CUP OF FLOUR

Plain yeast bread	½ to 1 teaspoon sweetener
Sweet yeast dough	1 to 2 tablespoons sweetener
Quick breads	½ to ¾ cup sweetener
Muffins	¼ to ½ cup sweetener
Biscuits	2 teaspoons sweetener
Pancakes	1 to 2 teaspoons sweetener
Cakes	½ to ¾ cup sweetener
Cookies	⅓ cup sweetener

Salt

Salt brings out other flavors in all baked goods, and, in yeast breads, helps to slow the fermenting yeast to a pace at which the gluten can mature. Too much salt will retard or kill the multiplying yeast. Too little salt allows yeast to grow unchecked, which will cause the gluten to tear and the dough to sour.

AVERAGE PROPORTION OF SALT TO 1 CUP OF FLOUR

½ teaspoon salt	1 cup flour

Eggs

Eggs are considered the most usable protein we eat. In addition, they contribute the following to breads and cakes:

Structure. Egg white, especially when stiffly beaten, acts in much the same way as gluten, holding the cake or bread high as it bakes and hardens into shape.

Liquid. A whole egg is about ⅕ cup liquid. An egg white is about ⅛ cup liquid. An egg yolk is about ¹⁄₁₂ cup liquid.

Shortening. The yolk, almost a third fat, makes a tender and flaky crust and crumb.

Leavening. The rising power of eggs comes from the vaporized liquid of the egg, and the air trapped in beaten eggs. One egg provides the equivalent leavening of about ½ teaspoon of baking powder.

Flavor.

Appearance. Yolks give a bread or cake a yellowy

sheen and help the crust to brown. Egg brushed on the surface of breads makes a shiny glaze.

I find it convenient to keep a small container of egg whites in the freezer to be quickly defrosted and brushed on any bread or coffee cake as a glaze.

Proper proportions of eggs to flour depend on personal taste. The more eggs added to a bread, the richer in taste and protein it will be. When adding extra eggs to a recipe, reduce the other liquids by the amounts listed above. Do not combine eggs with hot ingredients; the heat will curdle and cook the eggs.

Flavorings

Beyond the simple taste of good bread, it is herbs, spices, nuts, seeds, and fruits that make each bread special.

Herbs are strong-flavored leaves of plants; spices are the roots, seeds, buds, blossoms, or bark of plants. For example, use caraway seeds in a rye bread; cinnamon in a coffee cake; a sprinkling of oregano or cumin in a plain yeast bread; a little spearmint in a chocolate cake.

Crack the seeds to release the flavor, sift ground spices with the flour, brew a tea of herbs or spices to use as a liquid, squeeze garlic or ginger root in a garlic press to extract the juice, or sprinkle whole seeds on the surface of unbaked breads.

AVERAGE PROPORTION OF DRIED HERBS OR
GROUND SPICES TO 1 CUP OF FLOUR
¼ teaspoon dried herbs or spices   1 cup flour

Thick fruit wines, liqueurs, and extracts like vanilla, lemon, orange, and mint concentrate a flavor essence in a liquid. The alcohol evaporates in the oven heat, leaving delicately scented breads. Add wines and liqueurs to the dough or batter as part of the liquid, or use as a marinade for any fruit that is added.

AVERAGE PROPORTION OF EXTRACTS
TO 1 CUP OF FLOUR

| ½ teaspoon | 1 cup flour |

Fruit—apples, pears, oranges, lemons, pineapples, bananas, raisins, apricots, prunes, persimmons, mangoes, figs, dates, peaches, guava, cherries, nectarines, melons, berries—are the best unprocessed sweeteners. They have the most flavor when overripe. Include fruit in breads as juice, puree (fresh or cooked), sun-dried, dehydrated, flaked, or simply fresh-cut and peeled. Fresh or glazed citrus rinds, as well as jams, jellies, and preserves, have concentrated fruit taste. Most fruit can be interchanged in a recipe. Remember to reduce the sugar or honey when substituting dried or presweetened fruit for fresh. Grated orange or lemon rind stores well in the freezer.

Nuts—whole, chopped, or ground into flour or butter—make a crunchy addition to any bread, cake, cookie, or pancake.

Use fruit and nuts generously. Expect a very dense, rich bread if the bread contains more than 1 cup of fruit or nuts for 2 cups of flour.

Cocoa and coffee are dark and bitter, carob is dark and sweet. Add cocoa and carob powder like flour, and add coffee as a liquid after it is brewed (leftover coffee is fine).

Adapting Recipes

Refer to each ingredient section in this chapter and to the Compendium of Ingredients if you want to replace, substitute, or leave out an ingredient. There

4 BAKING BASICS
should be no problem if you make the right adjustments. Be most careful about the liquid-to-flour ratio.

LOW PROTEIN TO HIGH PROTEIN

To adapt low-protein recipes from any cookbook to high-protein recipes, all you need to do is: replace white flour with whole wheat, then *complement* the wheat with soy or wheat germ, and *supplement* the wheat with milk or eggs. The new bread will not have exactly the same grain and taste as the original recipe, but it will be a more nutritious equivalent. A slice of average bread contains one to two grams of usable protein. The new bread will probably contain four to five grams of usable protein per slice. More detailed information on increasing protein value can be found in the chapter on protein.

HALF AND DOUBLE

To halve or double a batch of bread, simply divide or multiply all the ingredients by two, except for the yeast. Doubling the yeast for a triple-sized batch of bread is enough. Do not decrease or enlarge recipes by a factor of more than four without expecting changes in consistency and taste.

HIGH CALORIE TO LOWER CALORIE

Substitute skimmed milk, fruit or vegetable juices, or water for whole milk.

Use yogurt in place of sour cream, and drained yogurt cheese (see page 303) in place of cream cheese.

Use less sweetener and shortening.

LOWER COST SUBSTITUTES

Use sunflower seeds and peanuts in place of cashews or other expensive nuts.

Substitute margarine or oil for butter.

Purchase ingredients in wholesale quantities. Freeze to store, or share with friends.

HIGH SATURATED FAT AND CHOLESTEROL TO
LOWER SATURATED FAT AND CHOLESTEROL

Use less shortening and fewer eggs.

Replace butter with oil or margarine made from corn, safflower, soybeans, cottonseed, or sunflower seeds.

Use skimmed milk in place of whole milk.

Substitute egg whites for egg yolks.

Use a commercial egg substitute.

Recycling

Just remember that even if the texture is solid and the flavor is wrong, the loaf is still good, protein-rich food.

Dry bread is just dry, not stale. See page 65 for ways to freshen it.

Failures and leftover breads and cakes can be reused in many ways. A few suggestions:

- Grind into bread crumbs to use in puddings, as toppings for casseroles, in quick bread and cookie batters, or in pumpernickel bread. Dried bread and cake form the base of many commercial baked goods; ask your local bakery to tell you their tricks.

- Cut into cubes and oven-toast or pan-fry in butter (perhaps with garlic) to make croutons for salads and soups. Slice thin and toast or fry in salted butter—use as crackers for cheese or dips.

- Make bread pudding.

- Cover slices with tomato sauce and cheese and bake or broil for small pizzas.

- Make grilled cheese sandwiches or French toast.

Baking Instructions
and Recipes

Breads and Rolls

GENERAL INSTRUCTIONS

Nutritious bread need not be unappetizing, monotonous bread; the recipes in this section will produce loaves that range from delicate to compact in texture, from subtle to vigorous in flavor, from crisp to chewy, and from dry to very moist.

A plain yeast bread dough is versatile.

It is very easy to bake many different breads, as professional bakers do, from the same basic dough. First, vary the shape: make standard loaves, round loaves, cylindrical loaves, long or braided loaves, crescent, Parker House, or cloverleaf rolls, thin sheets of dough for crackers and bread sticks, or create elaborate bread sculpture. Next, vary the cooking method: instead of oven-baking, deep-fry rings of dough for doughnuts, boil and then bake rings of dough for bagels, fry circles of dough on a dry griddle for English muffins. Vary the filling: fruit or nuts rolled into the dough make coffee cakes or sweet rolls; tomato and cheese topping make pizza.

Most breads take 5 or 6 hours from start to finish, but the actual work time for a batch of dough is only about half an hour, with gaps of an hour or two between stages to let the dough rise. Some breads included here take as little as 2 hours from start to finish. Also, any dough can be refrigerated or frozen at any stage so that you can slow or stop the yeast action and adjust the bread preparation to your schedule.

PREPARATION

General Yeast Bread Recipe

FOR 2 LOAVES

2 cups liquid
  (water, milk, juice,
  yogurt, eggs)
¼ cup shortening
  (butter, margarine, oil,
  peanut butter)
⅓ cup sweetener

(honey, molasses,
  maple syrup)
1 tablespoon salt
1 tablespoon yeast
¼ cup warm water to
  dissolve the yeast
About 7 cups flour

- For plain bread: omit shortening and sweetener.
- For coffee cake: increase the shortening and sweetener and fill with fruit or nuts.
- For herb bread: add herbs.
- For raisin bread: add raisins.
- For a fancy bread: add nuts, sesame or sunflower seeds, or cheese.
- For rye bread: exchange ⅓ of the total amount of flour (about 2 cups) for rye flour; then add some caraway seeds.
- When using cracked wheat, cornmeal, or oatmeal, soak them first in the 2 cups of liquid.
- Add high-protein ingredients—wheat germ, powdered milk, and soy flour—in place of 1 or 2 cups of flour.

Basic Steps in Making a Yeast Bread

STRAIGHT-DOUGH METHOD	SPONGE METHOD
	Warm the liquid
Dissolve the shortening, sweetener, and salt in the liquid	Dissolve part of the sweetener in the liquid
	Dissolve the yeast
	Combine the dissolved yeast and liquid
Add ⅓ of the flour	Add ½ of the flour
Beat 100 strokes	Let rise
	Beat 50 strokes
	Add the remaining sweetener, shortening, and salt
Add the second ⅓ of the flour	Add and knead in the second ½ of the flour
Knead in last ⅓ of flour	
	Let rise
	Punch down
	Let rise
	Punch down
	Shape into loaves
	Let rise
	Bake
	Cool

Remember that no two baking days are exactly alike —weather and seasons change; ingredients differ from day to day. Be prepared to adjust to suit the environment since temperature and humidity are very important.

Warm the kitchen and close the windows to avoid fluctuations in temperature from drafts; if you cannot get rid of the drafts, get a small blanket or large terrycloth towel to wrap and cover the rising dough.

Have all ingredients at room temperature. If ingredients are too cold, the yeast will grow slowly and the dough will rise slowly.

MIXING

There are two main methods for combining the ingredients—the *straight-dough method,* in which all the ingredients are added before the first rising; and the *sponge method,* in which the flour, water, some sweetener, and yeast rise first, and then the remaining ingredients are stirred in.

A group of ingredients can be combined by either method. The straight-dough method takes less time from start to finish, since there is one less rising; the sponge method requires less beating of the batter, softens the bran of whole-grain flours while there is more liquid available, and gives the gluten more time to develop: this will make the bread less coarse.

Straight-Dough Method

Warm the liquid (usually milk) until bubbles form around the rim of the pan. The hot liquid helps to dissolve the sugar and shortening and it creates a warm environment for the yeast to grow in. For milk, this scalding process destroys proteins that would make the bread texture coarse and heavy. If the recipe calls for coarse flours such as cornmeal or cracked wheat, you may want to add them to the liquid now to soften them.

Dissolve the shortening, sugar, and salt in the liquid. If honey, molasses, or maple syrup is used, measure in a liquid measuring cup so that the cup can be used in the next step to dissolve the yeast. Transfer the liquid to a large bowl, and let it cool to a temperature that is comfortably warm when a drop is placed on your wrist. In the 10 or 15 minutes while it cools:

Prove the yeast. This process is necessary to make

sure the yeast is alive. Dissolve the yeast—either crumbled cake yeast or dry yeast granules—in a small amount of water that is comfortably warm. Do not use whole milk, because the butterfat in the milk will coat the yeast and inhibit dissolving; do not use fruit juices, because the acid will inhibit yeast growth. Add a pinch of sugar or a drop of honey or molasses or dissolve the yeast in the measuring cup in which the honey or molasses was measured. This gives the yeast a little simple sugar on which to grow. Many bakers swear that a pinch of ginger helps feed the growing yeast. Others add a pinch of powdered slippery-elm bark, which smooths the dough and speeds up kneading.

The yeast will multiply and show signs of life by bubbling in 5 to 10 minutes. If it does not bubble, start again with new yeast.

Add the foamy yeast to the cooled liquid. Never add ingredients hotter than your hand to a yeast batter or dough, because the heat will kill the yeast. Then *add* about a third of the flour. If you are using more than one kind of flour, use the flour with the highest gluten content.

Beat the dough with a wooden spoon or rubber spatula at least 100 strokes. Watch the dough begin to stretch as the gluten develops. The formless dough will begin to have long strands as you pull the spoon around the bowl. Watch it carefully. It will look cohesive and seem to jell.

Sponge Method

Warm the liquid and *dissolve* the yeast as in the straight-dough method. Then dissolve part of the sweetener in the liquid, transfer the mixture to a large bowl, and let it cool to wrist temperature.

Add the dissolved yeast to the liquid, and then add about half of the total amount of flour. Use the flour with the highest gluten content.

This yeasted batter, called a sponge, should be covered with a kitchen towel, cloth, or a plate and then set aside for at least half an hour or as long as overnight. If you let it stand overnight, store it in the refrigerator to prevent it from souring. Four or five hours at room temperature will not cause the dough to sour. When you mix the yeast, liquid, sugar, and flour into a soft batter, the yeast and gluten can begin working un-inhibited by salt, fat, or flours that are low in gluten and hard to raise. Gluten strands can then develop to support the remaining ingredients. While resting, the sponge will bubble, rise, and fall. After it has fallen, stir it well with a wooden spoon until all the air is forced out.

Stir in the remaining sweetener, shortening, and salt, trying to keep the dough in one large piece by stirring around the rim of the bowl.

Beat the dough with a wooden spoon or rubber spatula as in the straight-dough method—but only about fifty strokes are needed, since the gluten strands will have begun to form in the sponge.

For Both Straight-Dough Method and Sponge Method

Add dried fruit, nuts, cheese, sprouts, or other moist additions, if they are not too heavy. If the bread contains many of these extras, add them as instructed on page 51. Stir around the edge of the bowl to keep the dough in one piece.

For the straight-dough method, *add* the second third of the flour. This should be the low-gluten flour.

Then, *begin to add* the remaining third of the suggested amount of flour, adding the remaining low-gluten flour first.

For the sponge method, *gradually add* the second half of the flour.

The dough will become soft and dry and start to pull away from the sides of the bowl. Bakers call this the "clean up stage." It is time to take the dough in hand.

KNEADING

To knead is to mix and blend by hand a dough that is too stiff to mix with a spoon. Kneading brings warmth from your hands to the dough and works the gluten so that it absorbs moisture and begins to form the interlocking gluten web.

The trick in kneading is to handle the dough so that it does not stick to your hands and the table or board, yet not adding too much flour. The dough becomes less sticky as flour is added, but too much makes the bread

tough, dense, or dry: better too little flour than **too** much.

To knead the dough with a minimum of flour, keep a thin coating of flour on the outside of the dough. In this way the dough can be handled without sticking, even though the inside of the dough is still wet.

Coat the board with a small mound of flour and empty the bowl of dough onto it. *Scrape* the inside of the bowl clean by rubbing it with flour, and add all the dried scraps to the lump of dough. The dough is formless and loose. Dust the outer surface of the dough with flour.

To begin the kneading motion, lift the far side of the dough with cupped hands and *fold* it over itself toward you. *Turn* the dough one quarter turn, and take the far side of the dough in cupped hands and *fold* it over. Turn and repeat, gently doubling over the dough. The dough will begin to form a mound, no longer flowing onto the table. Now begin the rhythmic, rocking, knead-

ing motion. *Lift* the far side of the dough and fold it over itself. Gently *press* the heels of both hands onto the dough, rolling it slightly forward rather than press-

ing the heels of your hands into it. Use a firm, light, bouncy touch and try not to tear the surface of the dough.

Dust the board and the dough lightly with flour if the dough seems wet. Use a bench scraper or spatula to clean the table of any scraps that will cause the dough to stick. Rub your hands with flour to remove the sticky dough. Knead the scraps into the dough.

Lift, fold, push, turn. Lift, fold, push, turn. Kneading is like a rocking-chair rhythm; lean into the dough on each push. The more emphatic the rhythm, the finer will be the texture of the finished bread, or as the bakers say, the finer the crumb. You might sing as you knead—it helps keep the pace.

Feel the plump dough unfold itself as it begins to take life from your hands and the gluten strands knit into a microscopic web.

The moment when enough flour is added is often hard to determine. If you knead long enough, the dough will always become slightly sticky on the outside and seem to require more flour. Do not add more flour if creases caused by the folded-over dough remain after a few kneading strokes. Knead until the outside of the dough is smooth and springy, about 10 minutes. Often there are blisters under the surface. Experience will teach you how the dough should feel; some say it feels like an ear lobe.

Trust your hands more than the recipe. If the dough feels wet, add more flour; if it feels dry, knead well until all the dry flour is incorporated. On a humid or rainy day expect to add more flour to the dough than the recipe specifies because the ingredients will contain extra moisture.

It is hard, if not impossible, to overknead bread by hand, but it is possible to overknead with the bread hook attachment of an electric mixer. Use the next-to-lowest speed of the mixer so that the dough does not tear. Knead for 3 or 4 minutes, until the gluten is stretchy.

When using a dough hook it is important to learn to *see* the quality of a well-kneaded dough. A minute of hand-kneading after the hook is finished will help insure the proper consistency and texture.

RISING

Butter the mixing bowl.* The bowl does not have to be washed if all the dried dough is scraped out. Place the kneaded dough in the bowl and brush the surface of the dough with butter. The buttered surface will keep the dough from drying out, hardening, and cracking while it rises. Cover the bowl with a cloth and set the bowl to rise. The cloth will not stick to the dough if the dough has been well buttered.

---

* Oil can be used in place of butter to grease the dough, bowl, and pans.

The dough needs moisture and warmth to rise well. If the kitchen is cold, dry, or drafty, try one or several of these methods to help raise the dough.

- Set the bowl on a wooden surface, pillow, towel, quilt, or blanket. Metal, marble, and stone are too cold.
- Sprinkle warm water on the covering cloth.
- Yeast loves sunshine. On a windless summer day set the bowl outdoors.
- Heat rises. Set the bowl on a high shelf.
- Put the bowl in a sink or pan of warm water. Keep adding warm water as it cools.
- Place the bowl in an *unheated* oven to keep the rising dough away from drafts. Put a large pan of hot water on the shelf below to provide moisture.
- Take the dough to bed wrapped in quilts.

The exact time required for rising depends on temperature, altitude, the moisture in the room, and the type and weight of the ingredients. Dough rises most rapidly if the ingredients are light and glutenous and the environment is warm and high in humidity. Bread rises faster at a high altitude than at sea level.

Most recipes suggest that the dough rise until it is doubled in bulk. The best rise is slow, at about 80°, which provides time for the flour and gluten to ripen and mature, about 1½ to 2 hours for the recipes in this book.

Dark, coarse, and low-gluten flours take a longer time to rise than fine flours. These heavier breads may never double in bulk. Very sweet doughs will take a longer time to rise than plain doughs.

If you are concerned about estimating the size of the risen dough, when the dough is first put into the bowl mark the approximate doubled volume on the side of the bowl with a crayon.

To tell if the dough is risen, judge by eye and gentle touch. The surface should have a rounded dome shape.

A well-risen dough will be doubled in bulk and will look airy and tender; you can feel air pockets under the surface. With a glass bowl, you can see the air bubbles evenly distributed in the dough.

The standard test is to quickly poke a finger (up to the first joint) into the dough. If the indentation remains, the dough is sufficiently risen. If the hole fills again with rising dough, it is not yet ready. If the finger deflates the dome shape, the rising time is definitely over.

A dough has risen too much when the dough has stretched to its limit and yeast growth has been arrested by its own alcohol and carbon dioxide. The surface of the dough will look wrinkled and deflated, and the dough will smell fermented. Overrising will cause a yeasty-tasting, coarse, dry bread, because of the torn gluten and overfermentation by the yeast. The yeast taste will not be as obvious, however, if the bread is served warm. Underrising will make a coarse bread with a dense center.

Punch down the dough to break up the large air pockets. Plunge your fist into the center of the dough to release the yeast gases so fermentation can continue to distribute the yeast cells and their nutrients evenly, and to unite the gluten strands so that the dough will rise again. After punching down, knead the bread a few times in the bowl or on a lightly floured board to press out all the air. Return the dough to the bowl, brush the surface with melted butter. Let the dough rise again.

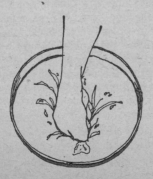

Dough can rise and be punched down repeatedly for almost a full day, or be refrigerated to slow down the rising until it is time to shape the bread. Many risings improve the texture and make a finer and lighter-grained loaf, but many risings also diminish the flavor slightly. Each subsequent rising period will take less time.

For a coarser loaf, you can omit the second rising in the bowl.

Punch down and *knead in* moist or heavy additions such as sprouts, cheese, nuts, and fruit if they were not added earlier. If the dough is too stiff for these additions let it rest, covered with a cloth or bowl, for about 10 minutes. This will relax the gluten in the dough and make it easier to incorporate these ingredients.

Dust the board with a little flour to prevent sticking. Use unbleached white wheat flour for a smooth crust or whole wheat flour for a grainy crust. Adding a lot of flour at this point will give the loaf dark streaks and a coarse texture because the gluten in the additional flour will not have had enough time to ripen. This unripened flour will make tough, tight spots in the finished bread.

On the board *knead* the dough briefly to press out all the air.

SHAPING

Cut the dough with a bench scraper, knife, or spatula into the number of loaves that you want to make. Make sharp cuts to break the gluten strands cleanly. Plan the size of the loaves so that they fill a pan half-full. Using a scale helps to divide the dough evenly—a medium-sized, light-grained loaf weighs about 1½ pounds.

Roll each lump of dough into a ball and let it rest on the board, covered with a towel, for about 10 minutes. This relaxes the gluten and permits a dry film to form on the surface, making loaf-shaping much easier.

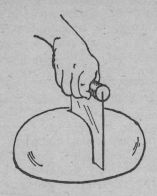

To Shape a Standard Loaf

Turn the ball of dough upside down so that the dry skin of dough is touching the table or board.

Press all the air out of the dough with flat hands, your knuckles, or a rolling pin.

Fold the dough into thirds—fold down the top third and press it into the dough with the heels of your hands, and then fold up the bottom third and press it into the dough.

Hold the ends of the roll of dough and gently *pull* the dough to lengthen it slightly. Try not to tear the dough as you pull.

Fold the roll into thirds—fold each end into the center, overlapping slightly at the middle. This puts

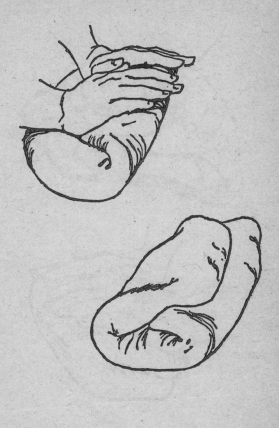

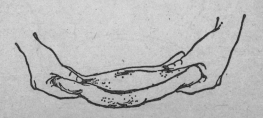

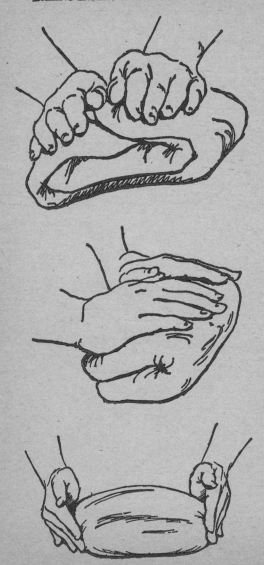

most of the dough into the center of the loaf so that the loaf is gracefully shaped with a swell in the middle.

Fold in half into a tight package and roll along the table so that the loaf is very compact and the seam is pressed into the dough.

With the side of your little fingers against the loaf and the table, *press* the ends of the loaf to seal the package.

Place each loaf into a buttered pan. With cupped hands and fingers pat the loaf so that it touches the sides of the pan and swells in the center.

If the shaping fails in any way, knead the dough lightly, let it rest for 10 minutes, and begin again. Dough is not fragile; feel free to shape and rework it.

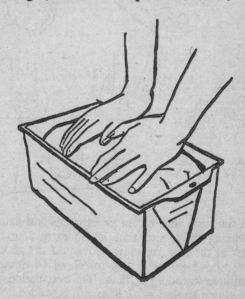

To Shape a Round Loaf

For a freestanding loaf, the dough must be stiff and formed so that the gluten tension supports the shape.

Press the air out of the resting dough. Shape the loaf by gently *kneading* the dough into a ball, leaving a smooth, rounded surface. Try not to tear the dough, which would leave a torn crust. Cup your hands and encircle the loaf. Shape the circumference of the loaf by *turning* the dough around and around between your hands. *Pinch* the dough underneath between your little fingers. To seal the underside, *drop* the loaf several times onto the table.

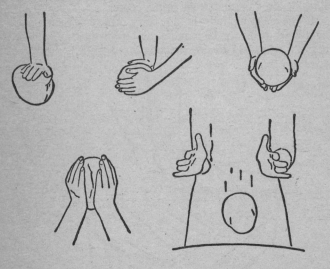

If you find that your baked loaf spreads and flattens on the baking sheet, next time knead extra flour into the dough at the first kneading. Cover the dough with an inverted bowl and let it rest for about 10 minutes. Then continue kneading in flour. The rest period will relax the gluten so that more flour can be added.

To Shape Rolls

A loaf-size ball of dough makes about a dozen rolls.
Some suggestions:

- Press three or four small balls of dough together.
- Roll a short rope of dough, about 6 inches long, and knot or coil it loosely.
- Braid three thin strands of dough. Pinch the ends to seal (see page 106).

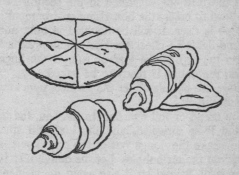

- Crescents: Roll a loaf-size ball of dough into a circle. Cut wedges and roll from the short side of the triangle.

- Flaky rolls: Roll a loaf-size ball of dough into a rectangle. Brush it with melted butter. Cut strips about 1½ inches wide and stack them. Cut cube-shaped slices and stand them in muffin tins.

FINAL RISING

Brush melted butter on the surface of the bread or rolls. Cover with a kitchen towel and set to rise. Use any of the methods suggested in the section on rising in the bowl to create the best rising environment. When the bread is risen, it will be doubled in bulk and look puffy and light. To check the rise, gently *press* a fingertip onto the top of the loaf or roll. If the fingerprint remains, the dough is ready to be baked.

If there are blisters under the surface, puncture them with a toothpick.

If the bread or roll overrises in the pan, the top will sink and look shriveled, and the loaf will smell fermented. Take the dough out of the pan, knead it, and squeeze out the air bubbles. Let the dough rest 10 minutes, reshape it, and let it rise again in the pans. The finished bread will only taste a bit yeasty. If the bread is served warm the yeast taste will be less noticeable.

After the bread is baked, check to see if the final rising was well-timed. Notice if the holes in a slice of the bread (the grain) are evenly spaced. A well-risen loaf will have evenly spaced holes on the inside and a tight compact texture near the crust. An uneven grain full of holes or a loaf that has sunk in the middle suggests that the bread rose too much; an uneven dense grain or a crust that has burst open suggests that the bread did not rise enough.

FOR BATTER BREADS

In a batter bread recipe there is less flour added so that the batter never becomes dry enough to knead. You will have added all the necessary flour before the batter turns to dough as described in the Kneading section on page 44. You will see the strands of dough form; it will be more cohesive and thicker than a cake batter. Brush with melted butter, cover with a towel or plate, and set this batter to rise in the mixing bowl for about an hour. Then mix it well until all the air is stirred out, and spoon it into buttered pans. Brush with melted butter, cover with a cloth, and let rise again. When the batter in the pans has risen about 1½ times the original volume, heat the oven and bake.

Batter breads made with whole-grain flours have a very porous texture and a less delicate crumb than kneaded breads.

DELAYED RISING

To slow the rising time and adjust the dough to the pace of your day, the dough can be refrigerated at any point. Place plastic wrap tightly on the bowl and put it in the refrigerator. Rising should take about two to three times longer than at room temperature. If you keep the surface of the dough well buttered and you punch down or stir the dough periodically, it can be refrigerated for two to three days. When ready to continue, let the dough warm to room temperature.

Shaped loaves can also be refrigerated to rise. Seal in a plastic bag, leaving enough room for the bread to double. Refrigerate. The length of rising time depends on the individual dough—probably between 2 and 6 hours. Unbaked loaves can be safely refrigerated for about a day and a half.

FREEZING UNBAKED DOUGH

Dough can be frozen for several weeks with varying results. Experiment; some doughs withstand freezing better than others. Simple ones which do not have much butter or many eggs seem to fare best.

To freeze dough at any stage of the mixing or kneading process, wrap the bowl tightly in plastic wrap and freeze; thaw it overnight in the refrigerator when you want to continue. The thawed dough may seem soggier than it should be, but do not add more flour.

To freeze shaped rolls or loaves, place the dough in buttered baking tins, let rise, and brush generously with oil or melted butter; then wrap the bread and tins in plastic bags. Freeze. When the dough is frozen solid, unwrap the tins and remove them to conserve space. Rewrap the frozen dough in well-sealed plastic bags.

To thaw the dough, remove it from the freezer and place the loaves or rolls in tins. At room temperature, rolls should thaw in about 2 hours and loaves in 6 hours. In the refrigerator the breads will thaw overnight. Refrigerator thawing is preferable because the temperature change between freezer and refrigerator is less dramatic than between freezer and kitchen; thus the breads will thaw more slowly and evenly. This slow thaw helps maintain a good texture.

CRUSTS, GLAZES, AND DECORATION

A Soft Crust

Do one or several of the following to get a soft crust:
- Bake the breads at 350°.
- Brush the top of the loaf with melted butter before and after baking.

- Make steam in the oven. Place a pan of water on the floor of the oven as it is heating and keep it in the oven during the baking period.
- Brush the surface of the loaf after baking with milk, cream, or undiluted evaporated milk.
- Cover baked breads with a kitchen towel as they cool.

A Crisp Crust

Do one or several of the following to get a crisp crust:

- Bake breads at 425° for the first 10 to 15 minutes and then reduce the temperature to 350°.
- Brush the top of the loaf with a glaze. The glaze can be brushed on before baking and during baking. Glazes store conveniently in a small container in the freezer.

    Egg glazes:
    1 egg beaten with 2 tablespoons milk or water
    or 1 egg yolk beaten with 1 tablespoon water
    or 1 egg white beaten with 1 tablespoon water
- Brush the surface of the loaf with salted water (1 teaspoon salt to ½ cup water). Brush on every 10 to 15 minutes as the bread bakes.
- Use a glass, darkened tin, or dull aluminum pan.
- Cool the bread in a drafty place to make a crackled crust.

Decoration

- Sprinkle a glazed loaf before baking with sesame seeds, flax seeds, poppy seeds, large crystal salt, or sauteed onions.
- Slash the top of risen loaves with a razor blade or a *sharp* knife. Diagonal, square, or crisscross patterns are most common, but you can use your imagination. Be careful not to cut more than ½

inch deep, or the loaf may fall. When baked, the bread will easily break at the slashes so a knife is not necessary.

BAKING

Heat the oven to the required temperature before you put the bread in. A hot oven will quickly convert the moisture in the dough to steam, which helps raise the bread. Some ovens take longer to heat than others, but 10 minutes is probably long enough. Most yeast breads should bake at 350°, or at 325° if there are fast-browning ingredients. A higher temperature will make a heavier crust.

Place the loaves on the middle rack of the oven with about 2 inches of space between the breads and between the pans and the oven walls. If there are too many loaves to fit on one oven shelf, stagger the pans on two or three shelves. Rotate the breads to a new position in the oven during the last 10 or 15 minutes of baking time to assure even browning.

Bake for the time specified—about 45 minutes for loaves, about 20 minutes for rolls; check the progress two-thirds of the way through—not sooner.

The baking time depends on several factors: oven temperature, the ingredients, the size and thickness of the bread, and the baking tin used. Dense, heavy breads with many fruit and nuts will take longer to bake than plain bread. Thick loaves need more baking time than thin ones. Breads baked in heavy, darkened metal pans will bake in less time than breads baked in shiny, light pans. Lower temperatures will, of course, mean longer baking times. If the bread is browning too quickly, cover the loaf with a tent of aluminum foil. Watch glass pans carefully; the bottom and sides of glass-baked loaves burn easily.

By now the whole house will smell of homemade bread.

Breads are *ready* when they are golden brown and starting to pull away from the sides of the pan. To make sure the bread is baked thoroughly, remove the loaf from the oven; it should feel lighter than when you put it in. Turn it out of the pan onto a cloth in your hand. Tap the bottom of the loaf and listen to the sound. If it sounds hollow, and the bottom crust is crisp, the insides are well baked and firm and the loaf is done. If the bottom of the loaf does not thud, feels soft, and is only light brown, the bread probably is not fully baked. Return it to the oven. Overdone bread is better than underdone bread. Unbaked, wet dough will be soft and taste yeasty or will leave a hollow space in the center of the loaf when the bread cools.

Cool the bread out of the pan so that air can circulate and the bread will not "sweat." Cool the loaf

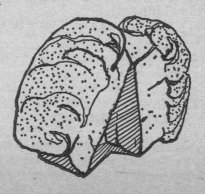

on a wire rack, across the top of the pan, in a basket, or tip two loaves on edge and balance them against each other. Encourage circulating air, but do not cool bread in a draft; this makes the bread shrink.

Eat fresh-baked bread when slightly cooled. Hot bread is gummy, too hot to taste, and has not yet baked through. Try to be patient and wait 20 minutes or half an hour for the bread to cool. Butter will still melt, the loaf will slice without tearing, and the flavor will be rich.

Once sliced, if the loaf is still doughy, replace the trial slice, and return the breads to the oven.

Always serve bread warm or at room temperature. Cold, refrigerated bread is often gritty and grainy.

A GOOD LOAF

If you bake with a critical eye, ask tasters for opinions, and see what is eaten and what is left, the next bread will always be better.

You may also want to look for:
- a smooth golden brown crust,
- an even shred or break along the sides just below the top crust,
- a fine, even texture (see if the holes in the grain are evenly distributed),
- a moist, springy texture that slices well and does not crumble,
- a mild yeasty aroma.

STORING AND FREEZING BAKED BREADS

Most breads degenerate quickly after baking. To keep breads fresh-tasting, you want to retain moisture without causing mold. In general, breads made with soured milks or potato water tend to remain moist longest.

Cool bread completely before wrapping, storing, or freezing. If the bread is not completely cooled, condensation will cause softening and molding. Slice bread as you need it so that the slices do not dry out.

Storing

Different weather conditions require different storing methods. When it is dry, store breads in a covered tin with a few small holes for ventilation. When it is damp, store breads in plastic bags. Refrigeration tends to dry out bread, but it does slow down molding.

To reheat breads and rekindle the fresh-baked taste, place bread or rolls in aluminum foil in a heated oven set at 250°–300° for about 15 minutes. Crusty loaves can be sprinkled with water and warmed at 400° for about 10 minutes without a foil covering.

Freezing

Although I prefer fresh-baked bread, by freezing bread you have homemade loaves available without baking every day. In general, freezing makes a baked loaf more tightly knit. For this reason I prefer to freeze unbaked loaves. (See page 60.)

If you want to freeze baked breads or rolls, bake them until light brown, about 5 minutes less than the total time recommended. This prevents the crust from separating from the loaf. Seal the cooled loaves or rolls in plastic bags and place them on a flat surface in the freezer until they are frozen solid. Rolls and breads can then be stacked and remain frozen for about three months. After three months, breads begin to lose moisture and flavor.

To return the fresh flavor to frozen breads, reheat them. If reheated directly from the freezer, the breads will take about twice as long as refrigerated breads to warm—about 25 minutes in a 250° oven. Toasting frozen bread slices also renews the flavor of a long-kept bread.

RECIPES

Basic High Protein Whole Wheat Bread

2 LOAVES EACH WITH ABOUT 54 GRAMS USABLE PROTEIN

This recipe began with a bread that Beth Arnold and Dick Margulis made famous in the Hudson Valley. It is the only appropriate recipe with which to begin this book because it is Beth and Dick who taught me the art of baking.

½ cup milk
¼ cup butter
¼ cup molasses
2 tablespoons honey
1 tablespoon salt
1 tablespoon yeast
1¾ cups warm water

About 5½ cups whole wheat flour (preferably hard wheat or bread flour)
¼ cup milk powder
¼ cup soy flour
1 cup wheat germ
Melted butter

1. Warm the milk in a saucepan until small bubbles form around the rim of the pan. Remove the pan from the heat and add the butter, molasses, honey, and salt. Stir until the butter melts and the molasses and honey dissolve. Transfer to a large bowl and let cool to wrist temperature.
2. In the cup in which the molasses was measured, dissolve the yeast in ¼ cup of the warm water. Let the yeast stand until bubbly, about 5 minutes.
3. When the milk mixture has cooled, add to it the dissolved yeast and the remaining 1½ cups warm water.
4. Add 2 cups of the whole wheat flour. Stir with a

wooden spoon or rubber spatula until the dough is well mixed. Beat the dough 100 strokes.

5. In a small bowl sift together the milk powder, soy flour, and 1 cup of the whole wheat flour. Add to the bowl any particles that did not go through the sifter. The sifting is to break up any lumps of milk powder and to distribute the soy flour evenly. Add these sifted ingredients to the dough in the large bowl.

6. Stir in the wheat germ. Then stir in just enough whole wheat flour to make a soft dough.

7. Scrape the dough out of the bowl onto a floured board and knead it until it is smooth, springy, and no longer sticky, about 10 minutes. Add more whole wheat flour if the dough feels wet. Try to avoid tearing the dough as you knead.

8. Place the dough in a large buttered bowl and brush the surface with melted butter. Cover the bowl with a cloth and let the dough rise in a warm, draft-free place until it is double in bulk, about 1½ hours.

9. Punch down the dough and knead it briefly in the bowl or on a lightly floured board to press out all the air. Return it to the bowl, brush the surface with melted butter, cover with a cloth, and let it rise again until double in bulk, about 1 hour.

10. Punch down the dough, knead it briefly on a lightly floured board, and divide it in half. Round each piece of dough into a smooth ball. Let the dough rest, covered with a cloth, for about 10 minutes.

11. Butter 2 medium-size loaf pans. Shape the dough into loaves, taking care not to tear the surface of the dough. Place the loaves in the pans. Brush the surface of the dough with melted butter, cover with a cloth, and let the breads rise until double in bulk, about 1 hour.

12. Heat the oven to 350°. Bake the breads until the crusts are brown, the bottoms sound hollow when tapped, and the breads have pulled away from the sides of the pans, about 50 minutes. Remove the loaves from the pans immediately and let the breads cool on a wire rack.

Whole Wheat Cinnamon Sunflower Raisin Bread

2 LOAVES EACH WITH ABOUT 68 GRAMS USABLE PROTEIN

This recipe can be followed to change any bread from plain to fancy. For this version prepare the basic dough through step 5.

1 cup sunflower seeds   1 tablespoon brown sugar
1 cup raisins   ½ teaspoon cinnamon

1. Add the sunflower seeds and the raisins to the dough after you have beaten it 100 strokes.

2. From this point follow the Basic High Protein Whole Wheat Bread recipe from Step 6 through Step 10—stir in just enough flour to make a soft dough; knead the dough; let it rise and punch it down twice; divide it in half and let it rest.

3. Sift together the sugar and cinnamon. Butter 2 medium-size loaf pans. Shape the dough into loaves, taking care not to tear the surface of the dough. As you shape the loaves sprinkle half of the cinnamon-sugar on each piece of dough after it is pressed into a rectangle and before the first folds of the loaf form. (See Shaping a Loaf on page 51, and illustrations.)

4. Place the dough in the pans. Brush the surface of the dough with melted butter, cover with a cloth, and let the breads rise until double in bulk, about 1 hour.

5. Heat the oven to 350°. Bake the breads until the crusts are brown, the bottoms sound hollow when tapped, and the breads have pulled away from the sides of the pans, about 50 minutes. Remove the loaves from the pans immediately and let the breads cool on a wire rack.

Cornell Bread

2 LOAVES EACH WITH ABOUT 52 GRAMS USABLE PROTEIN

The Cornell Triple Rich formula of bread enrichment was developed by Dr. Clive M. McCay and his colleagues to increase the protein, minerals, and vitamins in any bread recipe. Using the principles of complementary proteins, these Cornell nutritionists suggest as a general practice that you add a tablespoon each of soy flour, dried milk powder, and wheat germ to the bottom of every cup of flour that is measured. This has already been done for you in this recipe.

¾ cup milk
⅓ cup oil
⅓ cup honey
1 tablespoon salt
1 tablespoon yeast
2 cups warm water
3½ cups whole wheat flour

(preferably hard wheat
  or bread flour)
About 2 cups unbleached
  white wheat flour
⅜ cup soy flour
⅜ cup milk powder
⅜ cup wheat germ
Oil

1. Warm the milk in a saucepan until small bubbles form around the rim of the pan. Remove the pan from the heat and add the oil, honey, and salt. Stir until the honey dissolves. Transfer to a large bowl and let cool to wrist temperature.

2. In the cup in which the honey was measured, dissolve the yeast in ¼ cup of the warm water. Let the yeast stand until bubbly, about 5 minutes.

3. When the milk mixture has cooled, add to it the dissolved yeast and the remaining 1¾ cups of warm water.

4. Add 1 cup of the whole wheat flour and 1 cup of the white wheat flour. Stir with a wooden spoon or rubber spatula until the dough is well mixed. Beat the dough 100 strokes.

5. In a small bowl sift together 1 cup of the whole wheat flour, the soy flour, and the milk powder. Add to the bowl any particles that did not go through the sifter. The sifting is to break up any lumps of milk powder and to distribute the soy flour evenly. Add these sifted ingredients to the dough in the large bowl.

6. Stir in the wheat germ and the remaining 1½ cups of the whole wheat flour. Then stir in just enough white wheat flour to make a soft dough.

7. Scrape the dough out of the bowl onto a floured board. From this point follow the BASIC HIGH PROTEIN WHOLE WHEAT BREAD recipe from step 7—knead the dough; let it rise and punch it down twice; divide it in half and let it rest; shape the dough into loaves; let them rise; heat the oven to 350°, and bake the breads for about 50 minutes. Use white wheat flour when additional flour is necessary and use oil to grease the dough, bowl, and pans.

French Bread

2 LOAVES EACH WITH ABOUT 23 GRAMS USABLE PROTEIN.

This is a standard French bread recipe with wheat germ added. The bread alone (flour, yeast, water, salt, and wheat germ) is not very high in protein; therefore I suggest that you eat the bread with cheese. If each loaf is eaten with ¼ pound of cheese, the protein value is doubled. A ripe, creamy brie is my favorite.

1 tablespoon yeast	1½ teaspoons salt
A drop of honey	¾ cup wheat germ
1¼ cups warm water	Oil
About 3 cups unbleached white wheat flour	

1. In a large bowl dissolve the yeast and a drop of honey in ¼ cup of the warm water. Let the yeast stand until bubbly, about 5 minutes.

2. Add the remaining 1 cup of warm water, salt, and 1 cup of the flour to the dissolved yeast. Stir with a wooden spoon or rubber spatula until the dough is well mixed. Beat the dough 100 strokes.

3. Stir in the wheat germ. Then stir in just enough flour to make a soft dough.

4. Scrape the dough out of the bowl onto a floured board and knead it until it is smooth, springy, and no longer sticky, about 10 minutes. The dough will be soft. Add more flour if the dough feels wet. Try to avoid tearing the dough as you knead.

5. Place the dough in a large oiled bowl and brush the surface with oil. Cover the bowl with a cloth and let the dough rise in a warm, draft-free place until it has tripled in bulk, about 3 hours.

6. Punch down the dough and knead it briefly in the bowl or on a lightly floured board to press out all the air. Add a sprinkling of flour if the dough feels wet. Return the dough to the bowl, brush the surface with oil, cover with a cloth and let the dough rise again until it has tripled in bulk, about 2 hours.

7. Punch down the dough, knead it briefly on a lightly floured board, and divide it in half. Round each piece of dough into a smooth ball. Let the dough rest, covered with a cloth, for about 10 minutes.

8. Rub 2 cotton or linen towels with flour. Shape the dough into 2 loaves, taking care not to tear the surface of the dough. For long loaves, pat the dough into a rectangle about 16 inches long, and roll it tightly, starting at the wide edge. Pinch the ends and the seam to seal the loaf.

9. Place the loaves seam-side-up on the towels. If you are adventurous, lift the four corners of the towel and tack this sling to a bulletin board or wall; if not, cover the loaves with a cloth. Let the breads rise until double in bulk, about 2 hours.

10. Heat the oven to 450° and put a shallow pan of water on the oven floor. Oil a baking sheet. Gently roll the loaves off the towel onto the baking

sheet so that the seam side is down. Leave ample room for the breads to double in size. Slash each loaf with a sharp knife or razor blade, being careful not to deflate the dough. (See illustration, page 62.)

11. Brush the surface of the loaves with water and place them in the oven. Brush the crusts with water about every 5 minutes. Bake the breads until the crusts are brown and the bottoms sound hollow when tapped, about 25 minutes. Remove the loaves from the baking sheet immediately and let them cool on a wire rack.

Linderstrom-Lang One Hour Bread

3 SMALL LOAVES EACH WITH ABOUT 36 GRAMS
USABLE PROTEIN

It is said that Linderstrom-Lang, the Danish scientist, developed a recipe similar to this one during World War II to provide high protein, conserve fat, and to shorten rising time. This bread is ready for the table in just about one hour.

3 tablespoons yeast
A drop of honey
½ cup warm water
2 cups skimmed milk
1 tablespoon honey
½ cup milk powder

About 3½ cups unbleached
    white wheat flour
1 teaspoon salt
1 cup wheat germ
2 cups whole wheat flour
    (preferably hard wheat
    or bread flour)
Oil

1. Warm a large bowl in the oven or in a sink of hot water. In the bowl dissolve the yeast and the drop of honey in the warm water. Let the yeast stand until bubbly, about 5 minutes.

2. Warm the milk in a saucepan until small bubbles form around the rim of the pan. Remove the pan from the heat and add the honey and milk powder. Stir until the honey dissolves and no lumps of milk powder re-

main. Let the milk mixture cool to wrist temperature, and then add it to the dissolved yeast in the large bowl.

3. Add 2 cups of the white wheat flour to the milk-yeast mixture. Stir with a wooden spoon or a rubber spatula until the dough is well mixed. Beat the dough 100 strokes.

4. Add the salt, wheat germ, and whole wheat flour to the dough and mix well. For a lighter bread, cover the bowl with a cloth and let the dough rest for an hour. The bread will then have a finer grain, but it will take twice as long to prepare.

5. Stir in just enough white wheat flour to make a soft dough.

6. Scrape the dough out of the bowl onto a floured board and knead it until it is smooth, springy, and no longer sticky, about 10 minutes. Add more white wheat flour if the dough feels wet. Try to avoid tearing the dough as you knead.

7. Oil 3 small-size loaf pans. Divide the dough into thirds. Shape the dough into loaves and place them in the pans. Brush the tops of the dough with oil and slash each loaf down the center with a sharp knife or razor blade.

8. Put the loaves into a cold oven. Turn the oven to 150° for 15 minutes. The breads should almost double. Turn the oven temperature up to 350° and bake the breads until the crusts are brown, the bottoms sound hollow when tapped, and the breads have pulled away from the sides of the pans, about 45 minutes longer. This bread will not bake thoroughly if it has not risen enough. Before taking it out of the oven, make sure that the loaf is baked in the center by pressing the underside to feel for soft spots, which would indicate unbaked dough. Remove the loaves from the pans immediately and let them cool on a wire rack.

Refrigerator Rise Dark Rye

2 LOAVES EACH WITH ABOUT 40 GRAMS USABLE PROTEIN

This is a remarkably hearty bread that freezes well before it is baked.

2 tablespoons yeast
A drop of honey
2 cups warm water
2 tablespoons oil
¼ cup molasses
2 tablespoons honey
1 tablespoon salt

1 tablespoon unsweetened
  cocoa or carob powder
1 tablespoon caraway seeds
About 4 cups unbleached
  white wheat flour
3 cups whole rye flour
¾ cup wheat germ
Oil

1. In a large bowl dissolve the yeast and the drop of honey in ½ cup of the warm water. Let the mixture stand until bubbly, about 5 minutes.

2. Add the remaining 1½ cups warm water, oil, molasses, honey, salt, cocoa or carob, caraway seeds, and 3 cups of the white wheat flour to the dissolved yeast. Stir with a wooden spoon or rubber spatula until the dough is well mixed. Beat the dough 100 strokes.

3. Stir in the rye flour and the wheat germ. Then stir in just enough white wheat flour to make a soft dough.

4. Scrape the dough out of the bowl onto a floured board and knead it until it is smooth, springy, and no longer sticky, about 10 minutes. Add more white wheat flour if the dough feels wet or soft. This should be a firm dough. Try to avoid tearing the dough as you knead.

5. Place the dough on a sheet of oiled plastic wrap or waxed paper, brush the surface with oil, and cover it with plastic wrap and then a kitchen towel. Let the dough rest for 20 minutes.

6. Oil 2 baking sheets. The reverse side of a pie or cake tin is good to use. Punch down the dough, knead it briefly on a lightly floured board to press out

all the air, and divide it in half. Shape each half into a smooth round loaf, taking care not to tear the surface of the dough.

7. Place the loaves on the baking sheets, leaving ample room for the breads to double in size. Brush the surface of the breads with oil, and place each bread and baking sheet in a loose plastic bag. Seal the bags.

8. Refrigerate the loaves for at least 3 hours and not more than 36 hours. For freezing, first let the dough rise in the refrigerator for a few hours, then transfer the loaf to the freezer. When the bread has frozen, remove the tin (to conserve space) and reseal the plastic bag. To defrost, return the loaf to the refrigerator on the baking sheet and let remain overnight. Then proceed as if the bread had never been frozen.

9. Remove the loaves from the refrigerator and unwrap them. Slash the surface of each loaf with a sharp knife or razor blade. Let the bread warm to room temperature for about 45 minutes.

10. Heat the oven to 400°. Bake the breads until the crusts are dark brown and the bottoms sound hollow when tapped, about 50 minutes. Remove the breads from the baking sheets immediately and let them cool on a wire rack.

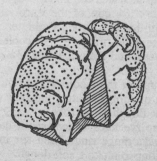

Limpa Rye Bread

2 LOAVES EACH WITH ABOUT 59 GRAMS USABLE PROTEIN

This is a sweet, light Swedish rye that gets its charac-ter from anise seeds, caraway seeds, and orange rind.

1½ cups milk
3 tablespoons butter
½ cup honey
2 tablespoons molasses
1 tablespoon salt
1 tablespoon yeast
1½ cups warm water
About 5 cups whole wheat

flour (preferably hard
   wheat or bread flour)
2 cups whole rye flour
1½ cups wheat germ
1 tablespoon caraway seeds
1 tablespoon anise seeds
1 tablespoon grated orange
   rind
Melted butter

1. Warm the milk in a saucepan until small bubbles form around the rim of the pan. Remove the pan from the heat and add the butter, honey, molasses, and salt. Stir until the butter melts and the molasses and honey dissolve. Transfer to a large bowl and let cool to wrist temperature.

2. In the cup in which the honey was measured, dissolve the yeast in ¼ cup of the warm water. Let the yeast stand until bubbly, about 5 minutes.

3. When the milk mixture has cooled, add to it the dissolved yeast and the remaining 1¼ cups of warm water.

4. Add 2 cups of the whole wheat flour. Stir with a wooden spoon or rubber spatula until the dough is well mixed. Beat the dough 100 strokes.

5. Stir in the rye flour, wheat germ, caraway seeds, anise seeds, and orange rind. Then stir in just enough whole wheat flour to make a soft dough.

6. Scrape the dough out of the bowl onto a floured board and knead it until it is smooth, springy, and no longer sticky, about 10 minutes. Add more whole wheat

flour if the dough feels wet. Try to avoid tearing the dough as you knead.

7. Place the dough in a large buttered bowl and brush the surface with melted butter. Cover the bowl with a cloth and let the dough rise in a warm, draft-free place until it is double in bulk, about 1½ hours.

8. Punch down the dough and knead it briefly in the bowl or on a lightly floured board to press out all the air. Return it to the bowl, brush the surface with melted butter, cover with a cloth, and let it rise again until double in bulk, about 1 hour.

9. Punch down the dough, knead it briefly on a lightly floured board, and divide it in half. Round each piece of dough into a smooth ball. Let the dough rest, covered with a cloth, for about 10 minutes.

10. Butter 2 baking sheets. Shape the dough into smooth round loaves, taking care not to tear the surface of the dough. Place the loaves on the baking sheets, leaving ample room for the bread to double in size. Brush the surface of the loaves with melted butter, cover them with a cloth, and let them rise until they are double in bulk, about 1 hour.

11. Heat the oven to 350°. Bake the breads until the crusts are brown and the bottoms sound hollow when tapped, about 50 minutes. Remove the breads from the baking sheets immediately and let them cool on a wire rack.

Steel-Cut Oat Bread

2 LOAVES EACH WITH ABOUT 58 GRAMS USABLE PROTEIN

This is a dark, compact loaf. Any coarse ground grain, for example buckwheat, barley, or millet grits, would make a good substitute for the oats.

1½ cups milk
1 cup steel-cut oats
3 tablespoons butter
3 tablespoons molasses
1 tablespoon salt
1 tablespoon yeast
A drop of molasses

1¾ cups warm water
About 4 cups whole wheat
   flour (preferably hard
   wheat or bread flour)
1½ cups wheat germ
Melted butter

1. Warm the milk in a saucepan until small bubbles form around the rim of the pan. Stir in the oats and cook over low heat until the oats are soft, about 15 minutes. Remove the pan from the heat and add the butter, molasses, and salt. Stir until the butter melts and the molasses dissolves. Transfer to a large bowl and let cool to wrist temperature.

2. In a cup dissolve the yeast and a drop of molasses in ¼ cup of the warm water. Let the yeast stand until bubbly, about 5 minutes.

3. When the oat-milk mixture has cooled, add to it the dissolved yeast and the remaining 1½ cups of warm water.

4. Add 2 cups of the flour. Stir with a wooden spoon or rubber spatula until the dough is well mixed. Beat the dough 100 strokes.

5. Stir in the wheat germ. Then stir in just enough flour to make a soft dough.

6. Scrape the dough out of the bowl onto a floured board. From this point follow the BASIC HIGH PROTEIN WHOLE WHEAT BREAD recipe from step 7—knead the dough; let it rise and punch it down twice; divide it in half and let it rest; shape the dough into loaves; let them rise; *heat the oven to 400° and bake the breads for about 40 minutes.*

Buttermilk Cracked Wheat Bread

2 LOAVES EACH WITH ABOUT 49 GRAMS USABLE PROTEIN

The buttermilk in this recipe makes the bread rise quickly and gives it a fine, light grain. Any coarse ground grain makes a good substitute for the cracked wheat.

1¼ cups cracked wheat	2 cups whole wheat flour
¼ cup butter	(preferably hard wheat
1¼ cups boiling water	or bread flour)
1 tablespoon yeast	1 cup wheat germ
A drop of honey	Melted butter
¼ cup warm water	2 tablespoons soy nuts
1 cup buttermilk	(roasted soybeans)
⅓ cup honey	1 egg white
1 tablespoon salt	1 tablespoon water
About 2 cups unbleached	
white wheat flour	

1. Put the cracked wheat and butter in a large bowl, add the boiling water. Stir until the butter melts and the cracked wheat is moistened. Let stand until the cracked wheat is soft and has cooled to wrist temperature, about 20 minutes.

2. In a cup dissolve the yeast and a drop of honey in the warm water. Let the yeast stand until bubbly, about 5 minutes.

3. Add the buttermilk, honey, and salt to the cracked wheat mush. Mix this well to break up any lumps of cracked wheat. Add the dissolved yeast.

4. Add 1 cup of the white wheat flour and 1 cup of the whole wheat flour. Stir with a wooden spoon or rubber spatula until the dough is well mixed. Beat the dough 100 strokes.

5. Stir in the wheat germ and the remaining 1 cup of whole wheat flour. Then stir in just enough white wheat flour to make a soft dough.

6. Scrape the dough out of the bowl onto a floured board and knead it until it is smooth, springy, and no longer sticky, about 10 minutes. Add more white wheat flour if the dough feels wet. Try to avoid tearing the dough as you knead.

7. Place the dough in a large buttered bowl and brush the surface with melted butter. Cover the bowl

with a cloth and let the dough rise in a warm, draft-free place until it is double in bulk, about 1 hour.

8. Punch down the dough and knead it briefly on a lightly floured board to press out all the air. Divide the dough in half and round each piece of dough into a smooth ball. Let the dough rest, covered with a cloth, for about 10 minutes.

9. Butter 2 medium-size loaf pans. Shape the dough into loaves, taking care not to tear the surface of the dough. Place the dough in the pans. Brush the surface of the dough with melted butter, cover with a cloth, and let the breads rise until double in bulk, about 45 minutes.

10. Heat the oven to 350°. Chop the soy nuts coarse. In a cup mix the egg white with the 1 tablespoon of water. Brush the loaves with this egg wash and sprinkle the soy nuts on top.

11. Bake the breads until the crusts are golden brown, the bottoms sound hollow when tapped, and the loaves have pulled away from the sides of the pans, about 45 minutes. Take the loaves from the pans immediately, and let them cool on a wire rack.

Oatmeal Refrigerator Rise Bread

2 LOAVES EACH WITH ABOUT 63 GRAMS USABLE PROTEIN

This bread is moist, light, and cakelike. You can use any rolled grain such as rye or wheat in place of the rolled oats.

1¾ cups milk	About 3 cups unbleached white wheat flour
¼ cup oil	1 cup wheat germ
⅓ cup maple syrup	1¼ cups rolled oats
1 tablespoon salt	2½ cups whole wheat flour (preferably hard wheat or bread flour)
½ cup milk powder	
2 tablespoons yeast	
½ cup warm water	Oil

1. Warm the milk in a saucepan until small bubbles form around the rim of the pan. Remove the pan from the heat and add the oil, maple syrup, salt, and milk powder. Stir until the maple syrup dissolves and no lumps of milk powder remain. Transfer to a large bowl and let cool to wrist temperature.

2. In the cup in which the maple syrup was measured, dissolve the yeast in the warm water. Let the yeast stand until bubbly, about 5 minutes.

3. When the milk mixture has cooled, add to it the dissolved yeast.

4. Add 2 cups of the white wheat flour. Stir with a wooden spoon or rubber spatula until the dough is well mixed. Beat the dough 100 strokes.

5. Stir in the wheat germ, rolled oats, and whole wheat flour. Then stir in just enough white wheat flour to make a soft dough.

6. Scrape the dough out of the bowl onto a floured board and knead it until it is smooth and springy, about 10 minutes. Add more white wheat flour if the dough feels wet. However, do expect this to be a slightly sticky dough. Try to avoid tearing the dough as you knead.

7. Place the dough on a sheet of oiled plastic wrap or waxed paper, brush the surface with oil, and cover it with plastic wrap and then a kitchen towel. Let the dough rest for 20 minutes.

8. Punch down the dough, knead it briefly on a lightly floured board to press out all the air, and divide it in half. Round each piece of dough into a smooth ball. Let the dough rest, covered with a cloth, for about 10 minutes.

9. Oil 2 medium-size loaf pans. Shape the dough into loaves, taking care not to tear the surface. Place the dough in the pans. Brush the surface with oil, and place each loaf and pan in a loose-fitting plastic bag. Seal the bags.

10. Refrigerate the loaves for at least 2 hours and not more than 24 hours.

11. Remove the loaves from the refrigerator and unwrap them. Let the dough warm to room temperature for about 25 minutes. Meanwhile, heat the oven to 350°.

12. Bake the breads until the crusts are brown, the bottoms sound hollow when tapped, and the breads have pulled away from the sides of the pans, about 50 minutes. Remove the loaves from the pans immediately, and let them cool on a wire rack.

Three-Grain Bread

2 LOAVES EACH WITH ABOUT 50 GRAMS USABLE PROTEIN

This is a fine-grained and light-textured bread. Any low-gluten flour can be substituted for the corn and buckwheat.

1 cup milk
¼ cup butter
⅓ cup maple syrup
1 tablespoon salt
1 tablespoon yeast
1 cup warm water
About 2 cups unbleached
  white wheat flour
⅓ cup milk powder
⅓ cup soy flour
2 cups whole wheat flour
  (preferably hard wheat
  or bread flour)
⅔ cup cornmeal
⅔ cup buckwheat flour
¾ cup wheat germ
Melted butter

1. Warm the milk in a saucepan until bubbles form around the rim of the pan. Remove the pan from the heat and add the butter, maple syrup, and salt. Stir until the butter melts and the maple syrup dissolves. Transfer to a large bowl and let cool to wrist temperature.

2. In the cup in which the maple syrup was mea-

sured, dissolve the yeast in ¼ cup of the warm water. Let the yeast stand until bubbly, about 5 minutes.

3. When the milk has cooled, add to it the dissolved yeast and the remaining ¾ cup of warm water.

4. Add 2 cups of the white wheat flour. Stir with a wooden spoon or rubber spatula until the dough is well mixed. Beat the dough 100 strokes.

5. In a small bowl sift together the milk powder, the soy flour, and 1 cup of the whole wheat flour. Add to the bowl any particles that did not go through the sifter. This is to break up any lumps of milk powder and to distribute the soy flour evenly. Add these sifted ingredients to the dough in the large bowl.

6. Stir in the corn flour, buckwheat flour, and wheat germ. Then stir in the remaining 1 cup of whole wheat flour and just enough white wheat flour to make a soft dough.

7. Scrape the dough out of the bowl onto a floured board. From this point follow the BASIC HIGH PROTEIN WHOLE WHEAT recipe from step 7—knead the dough; let it rise and punch it down twice; divide it in half and let it rest; shape the dough into loaves; let them rise; heat the oven to 350° and bake the breads for about 50 minutes. Use white wheat flour when additional flour is necessary.

Sponge Method Five-Grain Bread

2 LOAVES EACH WITH ABOUT 46 GRAMS USABLE PROTEIN

This is a dense, moist bread that is easy to experiment with. Hard cider, fruit juice, or water from boiled vegetables would make a good liquid. Try keeping the same amount of wheat flours in the recipe and substituting other grains for the corn, buckwheat, rye, and oats. Use this recipe as a model to make a yeast bread by the sponge method.

2¾ cups vegetable broth, cider, beer, fruit juice, or water
½ cup cornmeal
⅓ cup molasses
2 tablespoons honey
1 tablespoon yeast
¼ cup warm water
1½ cups whole wheat flour (preferably hard wheat or bread flour)

3 tablespoons oil
1 tablespoon salt
½ cup milk powder
2 tablespoons brewer's yeast
½ cup buckwheat flour
1 cup whole rye flour
½ cup rolled oats
½ cup wheat germ
About 1½ cups unbleached white wheat flour
Oil

1. Warm the vegetable broth or whatever liquid you are using in a saucepan until small bubbles form around the rim of the pan. Gradually add the cornmeal, stirring with a fork or wire whisk. Reduce the heat and cook, stirring constantly until it is thick, about 2 minutes. Break up any lumps of cornmeal. Remove the pan from the heat and add the molasses and honey. Stir until the molasses and honey dissolve. Transfer to a large bowl and let cool to wrist temperature.

2. In the cup in which the molasses was measured, dissolve the yeast in the warm water. Let the yeast stand until bubbly, about 5 minutes.

3. When the cornmeal mixture has cooled, add the dissolved yeast and the whole wheat flour. Stir with a wooden spoon or rubber spatula until the dough is well mixed. Cover the bowl with a plate and let this sponge rise for at least 1 hour and not more than overnight.

4. With a wooden spoon or rubber spatula beat the dough 50 strokes. Stir in the oil and salt.

5. In a small bowl sift together the milk powder, the brewer's yeast, and the buckwheat flour. Add to the bowl any particles that did not go through the sifter. The sifting is to break up any lumps of milk powder and to distribute the brewer's yeast evenly. Add these sifted ingredients to the dough in the large bowl.

6. Stir in the rye flour, rolled oats, and wheat germ.

Then stir in just enough white wheat flour to make a soft dough.

7. Scrape the dough out of the bowl onto a floured board. From this point follow the BASIC HIGH PROTEIN WHOLE WHEAT BREAD recipe from step 7—knead the dough; let it rise and punch it down twice; divide it in half and let it rest; shape the dough into loaves; let them rise; heat the oven to 350° and bake the breads for about 50 minutes. Use white wheat flour when additional flour is necessary and oil to grease the dough, the bowl, and pans.

Greens and Cashew Bread

2 LOAVES EACH WITH ABOUT 52 GRAMS USABLE PROTEIN

This is a crunchy, compact bread for which you make your own cashew flour. For a different taste and texture simply chop the nuts coarse.

1 cup sour milk or
    buttermilk
¼ cup oil
3 tablespoons honey
2 tablespoons molasses
1 tablespoon salt
1 tablespoon yeast
A drop of molasses
1 cup warm water
About 3 cups unbleached
    white wheat flour

2 cups whole wheat flour
    (preferably hard wheat
    or bread flour)
1½ cups cashews
¼ cup fresh or
    2 tablespoons dry
    chopped parsley
¼ cup chopped celery
½ cup wheat germ
Oil

1. Warm the sour milk or buttermilk in a saucepan until small bubbles form around the rim of the pan. Remove the pan from the heat and add the oil, honey, molasses, and salt. Stir until the honey and molasses dissolve. Transfer to a large bowl and let cool to wrist temperature.

2. In a cup dissolve the yeast and the drop of

molasses in ¼ cup of the warm water. Let the yeast stand until bubbly, about 5 minutes.

3. When the milk mixture has cooled, add to it the dissolved yeast and the remaining ¾ cup of warm water.

4. Add 2 cups of the white wheat flour. Stir with a wooden spoon or rubber spatula until the dough is well mixed. Beat the dough 100 strokes. Stir in the whole wheat flour.

5. Grind the nuts to a coarse powder in a blender. Without a blender either chop the nuts fine with a knife, or place the nuts in a plastic bag or between two sheets of waxed paper and roll into a powder with a rolling pin. Chop the celery and parsley fine.

6. Stir in the chopped cashews, the wheat germ, parsley, and celery into the dough in the large bowl. Then stir in just enough white wheat flour to make a soft dough.

7. Scrape the dough out of the bowl onto a floured board. From this point follow the BASIC HIGH PROTEIN WHOLE WHEAT BREAD recipe from step 7—knead the dough; let it rise and punch it down twice; divide it in half and let it rest; shape the dough into loaves; let them rise; heat the oven to 350°, and bake the breads for about 50 minutes. Use oil to grease the dough, bowl, and pans; and use white wheat flour when additional flour is necessary.

Cranberry-Orange Anadama

2 LOAVES EACH WITH ABOUT 42 GRAMS USABLE PROTEIN

This moist, dark corn-and-wheat bread is a variation of the bread that originated in New England. The bread got its name from a fisherman's wife, Anna, who would cook only cornmeal mush. Out of boredom with his wife's meals, the fisherman decided to make his own dinner and concocted a bread recipe from Anna's mush. As he kneaded the bread, it is said, he cursed his wife —"Anna, damn her. Anna, damn her"—thus creating and naming Anadama bread.

1 cup whole raw cranberries
1 tablespoon grated
   orange rind
1⅔ cups orange juice
¼ cup honey
½ cup cornmeal
2 tablespoons oil
⅓ cup molasses
2 teaspoons salt

1 tablespoon yeast
¼ cup warm water
About 2 cups unbleached
   white wheat flour
2 cups whole wheat flour
   (preferably hard wheat
   or bread flour)
1½ cups wheat germ
Oil

1. Put the cranberries, orange rind, ⅓ cup of the orange juice, and honey in a blender and blend until the cranberries are chopped coarse. Without a blender, chop the cranberries and stir in the orange rind, orange juice, and honey.

2. Warm the remaining 1⅓ cups orange juice until small bubbles form around the rim of the pan. Gradually add the cornmeal, stirring with a fork or wire whisk. Reduce the heat to a small flame, and cook and stir the mixture until it is thick, about 2 minutes. Break up any lumps of cornmeal. Remove the pan from the heat and add the oil, molasses, and salt. Stir until the molasses dissolves. Transfer to a large bowl and let cool to wrist temperature.

3. In the cup in which the molasses was measured, dissolve the yeast in the warm water. Let the yeast stand until bubbly, about 5 minutes.

4. When the cornmeal mixture has cooled, add to it the dissolved yeast, 1 cup of the white wheat flour and 1 cup of the whole wheat flour. Stir with a wooden spoon or rubber spatula until the dough is well mixed. Beat the dough 100 strokes.

5. Stir in the cranberry mixture, the wheat germ, and the remaining 1 cup of whole wheat flour. Then stir in just enough white wheat flour to make a soft dough.

6. Scrape the dough out of the bowl onto a floured board. From this point follow the BASIC HIGH PROTEIN WHOLE WHEAT BREAD recipe from step 7—knead the dough; let it rise and punch it down twice; divide it in

half and let it rest; shape the dough into loaves; let them rise; heat the oven to 350° and bake the breads for about 50 minutes. Use white wheat flour when additional flour is necessary and oil to grease the bowl, dough, and pans.

Wheat Berry Refrigerator Bread

2 LOAVES EACH WITH ABOUT 37 GRAMS USABLE PROTEIN

This bread is moist and sweet. Substitute any cooked whole grain, for instance leftover brown rice, for the wheat berries.

½ cup wheat berries and
  1½ cups water or 1 cup
  cooked wheat berries
1¾ cups apple cider
  or juice
3 tablespoons butter
3 tablespoons honey
1 tablespoon molasses
1 tablespoon salt
2 tablespoons yeast
A drop of honey

½ cup warm water
About 3 cups unbleached
  white wheat flour
½ cup milk powder
½ cup soy flour
¼ teaspoon ground cloves
2 cups whole wheat flour
  (preferably hard wheat
  or bread flour)
Melted butter

1. In a covered saucepan over low heat cook the wheat berries in the water until they are soft, about 40 minutes. Add water if necessary to keep the berries from burning. Cooking time can be reduced by half if the berries are first soaked overnight. Omit this step if cooked wheat berries or other cooked whole grains are used. Drain the berries and set aside.

2. Warm the cider or juice in a saucepan until small bubbles form around the rim of the pan. Remove the pan from the heat and add the butter, honey, molasses, and salt. Stir until the butter melts and the honey and

molasses dissolve. Transfer to a large bowl and let cool to wrist temperature.

3. In a cup dissolve the yeast and a drop of honey in the warm water. Let the yeast stand until bubbly, about 5 minutes.

4. When the cider mixture has cooled, add to it the dissolved yeast.

5. Add 2 cups of the white wheat flour. Stir with a wooden spoon or rubber spatula until the dough is well mixed. Beat the dough 100 strokes.

6. In a small bowl sift together the milk powder, soy flour, cloves, and 1 cup of the whole wheat flour. Add to the bowl any particles that did not go through the sifter. The sifting is to break up any lumps of milk powder and to distribute the soy flour and cloves evenly. Add these sifted ingredients to the dough in the large bowl.

7. Stir in the wheat berries and the remaining 1 cup of whole wheat flour. Then stir in just enough white wheat flour to make a soft dough.

8. Scrape the dough out of the bowl onto a floured board and knead it until it is smooth, springy, and no longer sticky, about 10 minutes. The dough will be soft. Add more white wheat flour if the dough feels wet. Try to avoid tearing the dough as you knead.

9. Place the dough on a sheet of buttered plastic wrap or waxed paper, brush the surface with melted butter, and cover it with plastic wrap and then a kitchen towel. Let the dough rest for 20 minutes.

10. Punch down the dough and knead it briefly on a lightly floured board to press out all the air. Divide the dough in half and round each piece of dough into a smooth ball. Let the dough rest, covered with a cloth, for about 10 minutes.

11. Butter 2 medium-size loaf pans. Shape the dough into loaves, taking care not to tear the surface. Place the dough in the pans. Brush the surface with melted butter and place each loaf and pan in a loose-fitting plastic bag. Seal the bags.

12. Refrigerate the loaves for at least 2 hours and not more than 24 hours.

13. Remove the loaves from the refrigerator and unwrap them. Let the dough warm to room temperature for about 25 minutes. Meanwhile, heat the oven to 350°.

14. Bake the loaves until the crusts are brown, the bottoms sound hollow when tapped, and the breads have pulled away from the sides of the pans, about 50 minutes. Remove the breads from the pans immediately and let them cool on a wire rack.

Sprouted Bread

2 LOAVES EACH WITH ABOUT 49 GRAMS USABLE PROTEIN

This bread is moist and compact and similar to the commercial loaf.

¾ cup milk
⅓ cup butter
¼ cup honey
2 tablespoons molasses
1 tablespoon salt
1 tablespoon yeast
1 teaspoon ground ginger
1½ cups warm water
About 3 cups unbleached white wheat flour

1½ cups sprouts (for instance rye, wheat, or bean)
1 cup wheat germ
3½ cups whole wheat flour (preferably hard wheat or bread flour)
Melted butter

1. Warm the milk in a saucepan until small bubbles form around the rim of the pan. Remove the pan from the heat and add the butter, honey, molasses, and salt. Stir until the butter melts and the molasses and honey dissolve. Transfer to a large bowl and let cool to wrist temperature.

2. In the cup in which the honey was measured, dis-

solve the yeast and ground ginger in ¼ cup of the warm water. Let the yeast stand until bubbly, about 5 minutes.

3. When the milk mixture has cooled, add to it the dissolved yeast and the remaining 1¼ cups of warm water.

4. Add 2 cups of the white wheat flour. Stir with a wooden spoon or rubber spatula until the dough is well mixed. Beat the dough 100 strokes.

5. Chop the sprouts coarse or grind them with the coarse blade of a meat grinder. Add the sprouts to the dough in the large bowl.

6. Stir in the wheat germ and the whole wheat flour. Then stir in just enough white wheat flour to make a soft dough.

7. Scrape the dough out of the bowl onto a floured board. From this point follow the BASIC HIGH PROTEIN WHOLE WHEAT BREAD recipe from step 7—knead the dough; let it rise and punch it down twice; divide it in half and let it rest; shape the dough into loaves; let them rise; heat the oven to 350° and bake the breads for about 50 minutes. Use white wheat flour when additional flour is necessary.

Rum Raisin Bread

2 LOAVES EACH WITH ABOUT 48 GRAMS USABLE PROTEIN

Named for the famous ice cream, this bread has a similar taste and a very light texture.

2 tablespoons rum
¾ cup white raisins
1 cup milk
3 tablespoons butter
¼ cup honey
2 teaspoons salt
⅓ cup milk powder
1 tablespoon yeast
¼ cup warm water

2 eggs
About 2 cups unbleached white wheat flour
2 cups whole wheat flour (preferably hard wheat or bread flour)
1 cup wheat germ
Melted butter

1. In a small bowl combine the rum and the raisins. If the raisins are very moist, first dry them in a 200° oven for 15 minutes so that they will absorb more of the rum. Set the raisins aside.

2. Warm the milk in a saucepan until small bubbles form around the rim of the pan. Remove the pan from the heat and add the butter, honey, salt, and milk powder. Stir until the butter melts, the honey dissolves, and no lumps of milk powder remain. Transfer to a large bowl and let cool to wrist temperature.

3. In the cup in which the honey was measured, dissolve the yeast in ¼ cup of the warm water. Let the yeast stand until bubbly, about 5 minutes.

4. When the milk mixture has cooled, add to it the dissolved yeast and the eggs.

5. Add 1 cup of the white wheat flour and 1 cup of the whole wheat flour. Stir with a wooden spoon or rubber spatula until the dough is well mixed. Beat the dough 100 strokes.

6. Stir in the rum raisin mixture, the wheat germ, and the remaining 1 cup whole wheat flour. Then stir in just enough white wheat flour to make a soft dough.

7. Turn the dough out of the bowl onto a floured board. From this point, follow the BASIC HIGH PROTEIN WHOLE WHEAT BREAD recipe from step 7—knead the dough; let it rise and punch it down twice; divide it in half and let it rest; shape the dough into loaves; let them rise; heat the oven to 350°, and bake the breads for about 50 minutes. Use white wheat flour when additional flour is necessary.

Peanut Butter Bread

2 LOAVES EACH WITH ABOUT 54 GRAMS USABLE PROTEIN

Peanut butter and egg yolks are the shortening for this bread so that dairy butter is not needed to give the bread a rich taste.

1¾ cups milk
½ cup peanut butter
⅓ cup honey
2 teaspoons salt
1 tablespoon yeast
¼ cup warm water
2 eggs

About 3 cups unbleached
  white wheat flour
3 cups whole wheat flour
  (preferably hard wheat
  or bread flour)
Oil

1. Warm the milk in a saucepan until small bubbles form around the rim of the pan. Remove the pan from the heat and add the peanut butter, honey, and salt. Stir until the honey and peanut butter dissolve. Transfer to a large bowl and let cool to wrist temperature.

2. In the cup in which the honey was measured, dissolve the yeast in the warm water. Let the yeast stand until bubbly, about 5 minutes.

3. When the milk mixture has cooled, add to it the dissolved yeast, the eggs, and 2 cups of the white wheat flour. Stir with a wooden spoon or rubber spatula until the dough is well mixed. Beat the dough 100 strokes. Stir in the whole wheat flour.

4. Stir in just enough white wheat flour to make a soft dough.

5. Scrape the dough out of the bowl onto a floured board. From this point on, follow the BASIC HIGH PROTEIN WHOLE WHEAT BREAD recipe from step 7—knead the dough; let it rise and punch it down twice; divide it in half and let it rest; shape the dough into loaves; let them rise; heat the oven to 350°, and bake the breads for about 50 minutes. Use oil to grease the dough, bowl, and pans; and use white wheat flour when additional flour is necessary.

Cottage Cheese Batter Bread

2 LOAVES EACH WITH ABOUT 70 GRAMS USABLE PROTEIN

This bread is moist, porous, and easy to prepare.

2 tablespoons yeast
A drop of honey
½ cup warm water
3 tablespoons oil
¼ cup honey
2 eggs
2 cups cottage cheese
½ cup milk powder

½ teaspoon baking soda
2 teaspoons salt
4 cups whole wheat flour
  (preferably hard wheat
  or bread flour)
2 tablespoons sesame seeds
Oil

1. Warm all ingredients to room temperature.
2. In a large bowl dissolve the yeast and a drop of honey in the warm water. Let the yeast stand until bubbly, about 5 minutes.
3. With a wooden spoon or rubber spatula, stir in the oil, honey, eggs, and cottage cheese.
4. In a small bowl sift together the milk powder, baking soda, salt, and 2 cups of the flour. Add to the bowl any particles that did not go through the sifter. The sifting is to break up any lumps of milk powder and to distribute the baking soda and salt evenly. Add these sifted ingredients to the cottage cheese mixture in the large bowl. Stir with a wooden spoon or rubber spatula until the dough is well mixed. Beat the dough 100 strokes.
5. Add the remaining 2 cups of flour and mix well. Round the dough into a smooth piece, brush with oil, and cover the bowl with a cloth. Let the batter rise in a warm, draft-free place until it is double in bulk, about 1½ hours.
6. Stir the batter well, brush oil on the surface, cover with a cloth, and let it rise again until it is double in bulk, about 1 hour.

7. Oil 2 medium-size loaf pans. Stir the batter well and divide it in half. The batter is thicker than a cake batter and may have to be cut. Place each piece of dough in a pan. Pat the dough to smooth the surface.

8. Brush the surface of the loaves with oil, sprinkle a tablespoon of sesame seeds on each loaf, cover the pans with a cloth, and let the breads rise until the dough reaches the rims of the pans, about 45 minutes. They should *not* double in bulk this time.

9. Heat the oven to 350°. Bake the loaves until the crusts are brown and the bottoms sound hollow when tapped, about 40 minutes. Remove the loaves from the tins immediately, and let them cool on a wire rack.

Marni's Soy Grits Batter Bread

2 LOAVES EACH WITH ABOUT 56 GRAMS USABLE PROTEIN

This batter bread is easy to prepare and has a moist, fine texture because it is made with white wheat flour.

1 cup soy grits	2 tablespoons yeast
1 tablespoon oil	½ cup warm water
⅓ cup honey	5 cups unbleached
2 teaspoons salt	white wheat flour
2 cups boiling water	Oil

1. Put the soy grits, oil, honey, and salt in a large bowl and add the boiling water. Stir until the honey dissolves and the soy grits are moistened. Let stand until the soy grits are soft and have cooled to wrist temperature, about 15 minutes.

2. In the cup in which the honey was measured dissolve the yeast in the warm water. Let the yeast stand until bubbly, about 5 minutes.

3. When the soy grits mixture has cooled, add to it the dissolved yeast and 3 cups of the flour. Stir with a wooden spoon or rubber spatula until the dough is well mixed. Beat the dough 100 strokes.

4. Add the remaining 2 cups of flour and mix well. Round the dough into a smooth piece, brush with oil, and cover the bowl with a cloth. Let the batter rise in a warm, draft-free place until it is double in bulk, about 1 hour.

5. Stir the batter well, brush oil on the surface, cover with a cloth, and let it rise again until it is double in bulk, about 1 hour.

6. Oil 2 medium-size loaf pans. Stir the batter well and divide it in half. The batter is thicker than a cake batter and may have to be cut. Place each piece of dough in a pan. Pat the dough to smooth the surface.

7. Brush the surface of the loaves with oil, cover the pans with a cloth, and let the breads rise until double in bulk, about 45 minutes.

8. Heat the oven to 350°. Bake the loaves until the crusts are brown and the bottoms sound hollow when tapped, about 50 minutes. Remove the loaves from the pans immediately, and let them cool on a wire rack.

Peasant Bread

2 LOAVES EACH WITH ABOUT 53 GRAMS USABLE PROTEIN

This bread is made with bread crumbs. If you use the end slices and crust of the loaf to make bread crumbs to add to the next batch of peasant bread, each new loaf will become darker and darker.

1 cup coffee and
  1 cup water
¼ cup oil
3 tablespoons molasses
1 tablespoon salt
1 tablespoon yeast
¼ teaspoon ground ginger
A drop of molasses
¼ cup warm water

About 2 cups whole wheat
  flour (preferably hard
  wheat or bread flour)
2½ cups whole rye flour
1 cup coarse bread crumbs
1½ cups wheat germ
Oil
Cornmeal

1. Warm the coffee and water in a saucepan until small bubbles form around the rim of the pan. Remove the pan from the heat and add the oil, molasses, and salt. Stir until the molasses dissolves. Transfer to a large bowl and let cool to wrist temperature.

2. In a cup dissolve the yeast, ginger, and a drop of molasses in the ¼ cup warm water. Let the yeast stand until bubbly, about 5 minutes.

3. When the coffee has cooled add to it the dissolved yeast.

4. Add 1 cup of the whole wheat flour and 1 cup of the rye flour. Stir with a wooden spoon or rubber spatula until the dough is well mixed. Beat the dough 100 strokes.

5. Toast the bread crumbs and the wheat germ in a frying pan over low heat until brown, about 5 minutes. Stir frequently to prevent burning.

6. Stir the bread crumb-wheat germ mixture and the remaining 1½ cups of rye flour into the dough in the large bowl. Then stir in just enough whole wheat flour to make a soft dough.

7. Scrape the dough out of the bowl onto a floured board and knead it thoroughly for several minutes, working in as much whole wheat flour as is necessary to prevent sticking. Try to avoid tearing the dough as you knead. Turn the bowl upside down over the ball of dough and let the dough rest for about 10 minutes. Knead again, using more whole wheat flour if necessary, to make a very stiff dough.

8. Place the dough in a large oiled bowl and brush the surface with oil. Cover the bowl with a cloth, and let the dough rise in a warm, draft-free place until it is double in bulk, about 1½ hours.

9. Punch down the dough, knead it briefly in the bowl or on a lightly floured board to press out all the air, and return the dough to the bowl. Brush the surface of the dough with oil, cover with a cloth, and let it rise again until double in bulk, about 1 hour.

10. Punch down the dough, knead it briefly on a

lightly floured board, and divide it in half. Round each piece of dough into a smooth ball. Let the dough rest, covered with a cloth, for about 10 minutes.

11. Oil 2 baking sheets and sprinkle them with cornmeal. Shape the dough into smooth round loaves, taking care not to tear the surface of the dough, and place them on the baking sheets, leaving ample room for the breads to double in size. Brush the surface of the loaves with oil, cover them with a cloth, and let them rise until double in bulk, about 1 hour.

12. Heat the oven to 350°. Bake the breads until the crusts are dark brown and the bottoms sound hollow when tapped, about 1 hour. Remove the loaves from the baking sheets immediately, and let them cool on a wire rack.

Mrs. Sorenson's Pumpernickel

2 LOAVES EACH WITH ABOUT 44 GRAMS USABLE PROTEIN

This recipe makes heavy, unsweetened, coarse loaves that are good for open-faced sandwiches when thinly sliced. Add more molasses for a sweeter bread.

1 tablespoon yeast	About 2 cups unbleached
½ teaspoon molasses	white wheat flour
2½ cups warm water	1 tablespoon salt
4 cups rye meal	1 cup wheat germ
	Oil

1. In a large bowl dissolve the yeast and molasses in ¼ cup of the warm water. Let the yeast stand until bubbly, about 5 minutes.

2. Add the remaining 2¼ cups warm water (potato water is particularly good), rye meal, and 1 cup of the white wheat flour to the dissolved yeast. Stir with a wooden spoon or rubber spatula until the dough is well mixed. Cover the bowl with a plate and let the dough rise for at least 4 hours and not more than overnight.

3. With a wooden spoon or rubber spatula beat the dough 50 strokes. Stir in the salt and wheat germ. Then stir in just enough white wheat flour to make a soft dough.

4. Turn the dough out of the bowl onto a floured board and knead it until it is smooth, about 10 minutes. The dough will be sticky, so add white wheat flour to make it manageable. Try to keep a thin layer of flour on the dough surface to make the bread dry enough to handle.

5. Place the dough in a large oiled bowl. From this point follow the BASIC HIGH PROTEIN WHOLE WHEAT BREAD recipe from step 8—let the dough rise and punch it down twice; divide it in half and let it rest; shape the dough into loaves; let them rise; *heat the oven to 400° and bake the breads for about 45 minutes*. Use white wheat flour when additional flour is necessary and oil to grease the dough, bowl, and pans.

Cheese Bread

2 LOAVES EACH WITH ABOUT 62 GRAMS USABLE PROTEIN

This bread is as strong-flavored as the cheese that you add. Cheddar and Cheshire are particularly good.

½ cup milk	2¼ cups grated hard
¼ cup honey	cheese, about ½ pound
2 teaspoons salt	About 5½ cups whole
½ teaspoon dry mustard or	wheat flour (preferably
1 teaspoon prepared	hard wheat or
mustard	bread flour)
1 tablespoon yeast	½ cup wheat germ
1½ cups warm water	Oil

1. Warm the milk in a saucepan until small bubbles form around the rim of the pan. Remove the pan from the heat and add the honey, salt, and mustard. Stir

until the honey dissolves. Transfer to a large bowl and let cool to wrist temperature.

2. In the cup in which the honey was measured, dissolve the yeast in ¼ cup of the warm water. Let the yeast stand until bubbly, about 5 minutes.

3. When the milk mixture has cooled, add to it the

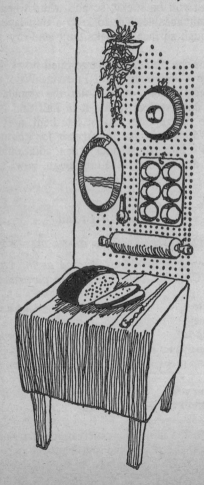

dissolved yeast, the remaining 1¼ cups of warm water and 2 cups of the flour. Stir with a wooden spoon or a rubber spatula until the dough is well mixed. Beat the dough 100 strokes.

4. Stir in the cheese and the wheat germ. Then stir in just enough flour to make a soft dough.

5. Turn the dough out of the bowl onto a floured board. From this point, follow the BASIC HIGH PROTEIN WHOLE WHEAT BREAD recipe from step 7—knead the dough; let it rise and punch it down twice; divide it in half and let it rest; shape the dough into loaves; let them rise; *heat the oven to 375°, and bake the breads for about 40 minutes.* Use oil to grease the dough, bowl, and pans.

Herb-Egg Bread

2 LOAVES EACH WITH ABOUT 65 GRAMS USABLE PROTEIN

This bread is rich-tasting and compact, taking its special flavor from the blend of herbs used. Prepare one of the following combinations of herbs or make up your own.

½ teaspoon dried
  marjoram
½ teaspoon dried
  oregano   OR
½ teaspoon dried
  thyme

½ teaspoon crushed
  fresh garlic
1 teaspoon chopped
  fresh dill
  or ½ teaspoon dried
  dill weed

2 cups milk
3 tablespoons butter
3 tablespoons honey
1 tablespoon salt
1 cup soy grits
1 tablespoon yeast
A drop of honey

¼ cup warm water
3 eggs
About 4 cups whole wheat
  flour (preferably hard
  wheat or bread flour)
Melted butter

1. Combine the herbs and set the mixture aside.

2. Warm the milk in a saucepan until small bubbles form around the rim of the pan. Remove the pan from the heat and add the butter, honey, salt, and soy grits. Stir until the butter melts and the honey dissolves. Transfer to a large bowl and let cool to wrist temperature.

3. In a cup dissolve the yeast and a drop of honey in the warm water. Let the yeast stand until bubbly, about 5 minutes.

4. When the milk mixture has cooled, add to it the dissolved yeast, the eggs, and 1½ cups of the flour. Stir with a woden spoon or rubber spatula until the dough is well mixed. Beat the dough 100 strokes.

5. Stir in the herb mixture. Then stir in just enough flour to make a soft dough.

6. Scrape the dough out of the bowl onto a floured board. From this point on follow the BASIC HIGH PROTEIN WHOLE WHEAT BREAD recipe from step 7—knead the dough; let it rise and punch it down twice; divide it in half and let it rest; shape the dough into loaves; let them rise; heat the oven to 350° and bake the breads for about 50 minutes.

Dill Soy Rye Bread

2 LOAVES EACH WITH ABOUT 58 GRAMS USABLE PROTEIN

This bread is dark brown, light textured, and strong flavored.

1 cup uncooked soybeans and 2 cups water or 2 cups cooked soybeans
1 tablespoon yeast
A drop of molasses
1¼ cups warm water
3 tablespoons oil
⅓ cup molasses

1 tablespoon salt
1½ tablespoons dill weed
1½ tablespoons dill seed
About 3 cups unbleached white wheat flour
1½ cups whole rye flour
¾ cup wheat germ
Oil

1. In a covered saucepan over low heat cook the beans in the water until the beans are soft, about 3 hours. Cooking time can be reduced by about half if the beans are first soaked overnight. Omit this step if cooked soybeans are used.

2. Drain the soybeans and save the liquid. Grind into a paste in a blender. If the blender blades become stuck add some of the cooking liquid. Without a blender press the beans through a sieve or mash well with a fork. Set the beans aside.

3. In a large bowl dissolve the yeast and a drop of molasses in ¼ cup of the warm water. Let the yeast stand until bubbly, about 5 minutes.

4. Add the remaining 1 cup of warm water (use the cooking liquid from the beans and add water to make 1 cup), the oil, molasses, salt, dill weed, dill seed, and 2 cups of the white wheat flour. Stir with a wooden spoon or rubber spatula until the dough is well mixed. Beat the dough 100 strokes.

5. Stir in the soybeans, rye flour, and wheat germ. Then stir in just enough white wheat flour to make a soft dough.

6. Scrape the dough out of the bowl onto a floured board and knead the dough until it is smooth, springy, and no longer sticky, about 10 minutes. Add more white wheat flour if the dough feels wet. Try to avoid tearing the dough as you knead. Turn the bowl upside down over the dough and let it rest for about 10 minutes.

7. Knead again, using more white wheat flour if necessary, to make a stiff dough. Place the dough in a large oiled bowl, brush the surface of the dough with oil, and let the dough rise, covered with a cloth, in a warm, draft-free place until it is double in bulk, about 1½ hours.

8. Punch down the dough and knead it briefly in the bowl or on a lightly floured board to press out all the air. Return the dough to the bowl, brush the surface with oil, cover with a cloth, and let the dough rise

again until double in bulk, about 1 hour. Punch down the dough and knead it briefly on a lightly floured board.

9. Divide the dough in half, round each piece of dough into a smooth ball, and let it rest covered with a cloth for about 10 minutes.

10. Oil 2 baking sheets. Shape the dough into smooth round loaves, taking care not to tear the surface of the dough. Put the loaves on the baking sheets, leaving ample room for the breads to double in size. Brush the loaves with oil, cover with a cloth, and let them rise until they are double in bulk, about 1 hour.

11. Heat the oven to 350°. Bake the breads until the crusts are brown and the bottoms sound hollow when tapped, about 50 minutes. Remove the loaves from the baking sheets immediately and let them cool on a wire rack.

Saffron Challah

2 LOAVES EACH WITH ABOUT 44 GRAMS USABLE PROTEIN

The braided challah symbolizes the ladder to heaven. You do not have to slice challah since the braid easily breaks into small pieces.

1 cup warm water	A drop of honey
⅓ cup oil	4 eggs
2 tablespoons honey	About 4 cups unbleached
2 teaspoons salt	white wheat flour
A pinch of saffron (for	1 cup wheat germ
color)	Oil
1 tablespoon yeast	1 tablespoon water

1. Warm ¾ cup of the water, the oil, honey, salt, and saffron in the top of a double boiler, or use a 4-cup measuring cup and stand it in a pan of simmering water.

2. In a cup dissolve the yeast and a drop of honey in the remaining ¼ cup of warm water. Let the yeast stand until bubbly, about 5 minutes.

3. In a small bowl beat the eggs well. Set aside 3 tablespoons.

4. Add the remaining eggs to the mixture in the double boiler. Heat and stir until it is of custard consistency, about 5 minutes. Be careful not to overcook the custard, as this will cause the eggs to curdle. Remove the pan from the heat, transfer the mixture to a large bowl and let cool to wrist temperature.

5. When the custard mixture has cooled, add to it the dissolved yeast and 2 cups of the flour. Stir with a wooden spoon or rubber spatula until the dough is well mixed. Beat the dough 100 strokes.

6. Stir in the wheat germ. Then stir in just enough flour to make a soft dough.

7. Scrape the dough out of the bowl onto a floured board and knead it until it is smooth, springy, and no longer sticky, about 10 minutes. Add more flour if the dough feels wet. Try to avoid tearing the dough as you knead.

8. Place the dough in a large oiled bowl and brush the surface with oil. Cover the bowl with a cloth and let the dough rise in a warm, draft-free place until it is double in bulk, about 1½ hours.

9. Punch down the dough and knead it briefly in the bowl or on a lightly floured board to press out all the air. Return it to the bowl, brush the surface with oil, cover with a cloth, and let it rise again until double in bulk, about 1 hour.

10. Punch down the dough, knead it briefly on a lightly floured board, and divide it in half. Round each piece of dough into a smooth ball. Let the dough rest, covered with a cloth, for about 10 minutes.

11. Oil 2 baking sheets. Take one piece of dough and divide it into thirds. Roll these into three long strands and braid them, beginning in the center and working

toward each end. Pinch the ends to secure the braid. Divide and braid the second loaf as the first.

For a double braided loaf, divide each half of the dough into 4 equal parts. Roll three of them into long strands, then braid them. Divide the fourth into thirds, roll into strands, and braid them, too. Lay the smaller braid on top of the larger one and pinch the ends securely.

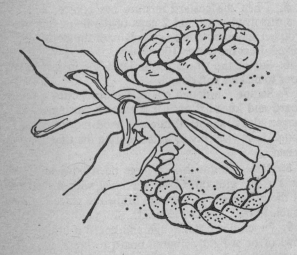

12. Place each loaf on a baking sheet leaving ample room for the bread to double in size and brush the surface with oil. Cover the loaves with a cloth and let the breads rise until they are double in bulk, about 1 hour.

13. Heat the oven to 400°. Mix 1 tablespoon of water with the 3 tablespoons of beaten egg that were set aside. Brush this glaze on the loaves. Bake the breads until the crusts are golden brown and the bot-

toms sound hollow when tapped, about 35 minutes. Remove the loaves from the baking sheets immediately and let them cool on wire racks.

Egg Bagels

ABOUT A DOZEN BAGELS EACH WITH ABOUT 6 GRAMS USABLE PROTEIN

These whole wheat bagels taste surprisingly like their white flour cousins.

1 tablespoon yeast	flour (preferably hard
A drop of honey	wheat or bread flour)
1¼ cups warm water	½ cup wheat germ
2 eggs	Oil
2 tablespoons honey	2 tablespoons water
1 tablespoon salt	A kettle of salted water
About 4 cups whole wheat	(1 tablespoon of salt in
	2 quarts of water)

1. In a large bowl dissolve the yeast and a drop of honey in ¼ cup of the warm water. Let the yeast stand until bubbly, about 5 minutes.

2. Separate one of the eggs and set aside one tablespoon of egg white in a cup.

3. Recombine the separated egg and add the eggs, the remaining 1 cup of water, honey, salt, and 2 cups of the flour to the dissolved yeast in the large bowl. Stir with a wooden spoon or rubber spatula until the dough is well mixed. Beat the dough 100 strokes.

4. Stir in the wheat germ. Then stir in just enough flour to make a soft dough.

5. Scrape the dough out of the bowl onto a floured board, and knead it until it is smooth, springy, and no longer sticky, about 10 minutes. Add more flour if the dough feels wet. Try to avoid tearing the dough as you knead.

6. Place the dough in a large oiled bowl and brush the surface with oil. Cover the bowl with a cloth and let the dough rise in a warm draft-free place until it is double in bulk, about 1½ hours.

7. Punch down the dough and knead it briefly on a lightly floured board to press out all the air. Divide the dough into 12 pieces. Round each piece of dough into a smooth ball. Let them rest, covered with a cloth, for about 10 minutes.

8. Heat a 2- or 3-quart kettle of salted water until it boils.

9. Shape the bagels by rolling a piece of dough into a rope about 7 inches long. Wrap the rope around your fingers to form a ring. Moisten the ends and squeeze to seal. Make sure that the ends are well joined. Let the bagels rest on the board for 15 minutes.

10. Oil 2 baking sheets. Heat the oven to 425°.

11. Drop the bagels into the boiling water, and boil for 2 or 3 minutes on each side. Boil as many bagels at one time as will fit in the kettle side by side without crowding. Scoop the bagels out of the boiling water with a slotted spoon or fork. Place the boiled bagels carefully on the baking sheets; they will be slippery.

12. Mix the reserved egg white with the 2 tablespoons of water and brush this glaze on the surface of the bagels. Bake the bagels until the crusts are golden brown, about 25 minutes. Remove the bagels from the

baking sheets immediately. Let them cool briefly on wire racks. Serve the bagels warm.

Soft Pretzels

ABOUT 16 PRETZELS EACH WITH ABOUT 4 GRAMS
USABLE PROTEIN

This is a soft, twisted, salted German-style pretzel sold in New York City subway stations, in parks, on street corners, and at ball games.

1 tablespoon yeast	½ cup wheat germ
A drop of honey	Oil
1¼ cups warm water	1 tablespoon lye or
2 tablespoons oil	baking soda
¼ cup honey	1 quart cold water
1 teaspoon salt	1 egg yolk
1 egg	2 tablespoons water
About 4 cups unbleached	Coarse salt (sold as kosher
white wheat flour	salt)

1. In a large bowl dissolve the yeast and a drop of honey, salt, egg, and 1 cup of the flour. Stir with a wooden spoon until bubbly, about 5 minutes.
2. Add the remaining 1 cup of warm water, the oil, honey, salt, eggs, and 1 cup of the flour. Stir with a wooden spoon or rubber spatula until the dough is well mixed. Beat the dough 100 strokes.
3. Stir in the wheat germ. Then stir in just enough white wheat flour to make a soft dough.
4. Scrape the dough out of the bowl onto a floured board and knead it until it is smooth, springy, and no longer sticky, about 10 minutes. Add more flour if the dough feels wet. Try to avoid tearing the dough as you knead.
5. Place the dough in a large oiled bowl and brush

the surface with oil. Cover the bowl with a cloth and let the dough rise in a warm, draft-free place until it is double in bulk, about 1½ hours.

6. Punch down the dough and knead it briefly on a lightly floured board to press out all the air. Divide it into 16 equal pieces and round them into balls. Cover the dough with a cloth and let it rest for about 10 minutes.

7. In a 2- or 3-quart kettle (do not use aluminum) dissolve the lye in the cold water. The lye is not harmful in this dilute solution: still, handle the lye carefully. Read the precautions on the package. Lye gives the pretzels their characteristic flavor; however, if you prefer, substitute baking soda, which gives a similar taste. Heat the lye or baking soda solution until it steams but does not boil.

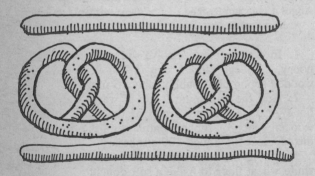

8. Oil 2 baking sheets and cover them with waxed paper. Brush oil on the waxed paper.

9. Roll each ball of dough into a rope about 20 inches long. Dip the dough into the lye or baking soda solution and then form the rope into a pretzel. Seal the knot well. Place the pretzels on the baking sheets and cover with a cloth. Let the pretzels rise until just less than double, about 25 minutes.

10. Heat the oven to 400°.

11. Combine the egg yolk and water. Brush the pretzels with this egg wash and sprinkle them with coarse salt. Bake the pretzels until they are golden brown, about 15 minutes. Remove the pretzels from the baking sheets immediately. Let them cool briefly on wire racks. Serve the pretzels warm.

Quizza

2 QUIZZAS EACH WITH ABOUT 62 GRAMS USABLE PROTEIN

Half-quiche, half-pizza. It makes a good meal for six people or a snack for a dozen.

¾ cup milk
2 tablespoons oil
2 teaspoons salt
1 tablespoon yeast
1 teaspoon honey
¼ cup warm water

1 egg
About 4 cups whole wheat
flour (preferably hard
wheat or bread flour)
Oil

1. Warm the milk in a saucepan until small bubbles form around the rim of the pan. Remove the pan from the heat and add the oil and salt. Transfer to a large bowl and let cool to wrist temperature.

2. In a cup dissolve the yeast and honey in the warm water. Let the yeast stand until bubbly, about 5 minutes.

3. When the milk mixture has cooled, add to it the dissolved yeast, the egg, and 2 cups of the flour. Stir with a wooden spoon or rubber spatula until the dough is well mixed. Beat the dough 100 strokes.

4. Stir in just enough flour to make a soft dough.

5. Scrape the dough out of the bowl onto a floured board and knead it until it is smooth, springy, and no longer sticky, about 10 minutes. Add more flour if the dough feels wet. Try to avoid tearing the dough as you knead.

6. Place the dough in a large oiled bowl and brush the surface with oil. Cover the bowl with a cloth and let the dough rise in a warm, draft-free place until it is double in bulk, about 1½ hours.

7. Punch down the dough and knead it briefly in the bowl or on a lightly floured board to press out all the air. Return it to the bowl, brush the surface with oil, cover with a cloth, and let it rise again until double in bulk, about 1 hour. Prepare the filling during this rising period.

8. Punch down the dough, knead it briefly on a lightly floured board, and divide it in half. Round each piece of dough into a smooth ball. Let the dough rest, covered with a cloth, for 10 minutes.

9. Heat the oven to 375°. Oil 2 baking sheets.

10. On a lightly floured board, roll out each piece of dough into a ¼-inch-thick rectangle, about the size of your baking sheet. Arrange the dough on each baking sheet. Make a thick rim around the edges to prevent the filling from running off.

11. Spread one half of the filling over each sheet of shaped dough. Bake the quizzas until the crust is brown and the filling is firm, about 30 minutes. Serve the quizzas hot.

FILLING

2 onions	5 eggs
1 tablespoon oil	1½ cups yogurt
2 tablespoons butter	2 tablespoons fennel seeds
2½ cups grated cheese, about ½ pound (for instance, Swiss)	½ teaspoon salt
	A pinch of pepper

1. Slice the onions thin. In a large frying pan stir together the onions, oil, and butter. Cook over low heat until the onions are soft and translucent. Set them aside to cool.

2. In a large bowl beat the eggs well. Add to them the cooked onions, cheese, yogurt, fennel seeds, salt, and pepper.

Pita and Humus

ABOUT 16 PITA-HUMUS SANDWICHES EACH WITH ABOUT 10 GRAMS USABLE PROTEIN

Pita are small round Middle Eastern flat breads that bake into little envelopes. They can be used for sandwiches, or they can be torn apart and used to scoop up dips. Pita can be filled with shredded cheese, boiled egg, grains, vegetables, nuts, beans, relishes—to make a complete meal from what might appear to be unusable leftovers. Humus is a traditional Middle Eastern chick-pea dish that is easy to make and often served with pita. If you start with dried chick-peas, it is best to begin soaking them the night before. For chewier pita substitute some whole wheat flour in place of white.

PITA

1 tablespoon yeast	About 6 cups unbleached
A drop of honey	white wheat flour
2¾ cups warm water	1 cup wheat germ
2 tablespoons honey	Oil
1 tablespoon salt	

1. In a large bowl dissolve the yeast and a drop of honey in ¼ cup of the warm water. Let the yeast stand until bubbly, about 5 minutes.

2. Add to the dissolved yeast the remaining 2½ cups of warm water, the honey, salt, and 2 cups of the flour. Stir with a wooden spoon or rubber spatula until the dough is well mixed. Beat the dough 100 strokes.

3. Stir in the wheat germ. Then stir in just enough flour to make a soft dough.

4. Scrape the dough out of the bowl onto a floured board and knead it until it is smooth, springy, and no longer sticky, about 10 minutes. Add more flour if the dough feels wet. Try to avoid tearing the dough as you knead.

5. Place the dough in a large oiled bowl and brush the surface with oil. Cover the bowl with a cloth and let the dough rise in a warm, draft-free place until it is double in bulk, about 1½ hours.

6. Punch down the dough and knead it briefly in the bowl or on a lightly floured board to press out all the air. Return it to the bowl, brush the surface with oil, cover with a cloth, and let it rise again until double in bulk, about 1 hour.

7. Punch down the dough, knead it briefly on a lightly floured board, and divide it into 16 parts. Round each piece of dough into a smooth ball. Let the dough rest, covered with a cloth, for about 10 minutes.

8. Heat the oven to 450°.

9. Roll or pat each ball into a ¼-inch-thick circle and place on ungreased baking sheets. Bake them until brown and puffy, about 10 minutes. Wrap the loaves in

a towel to cool them. This will soften and deflate the bread, leaving a hollow pouch inside.

HUMUS

2 cups dried chick-peas and about 6 cups water or two 20-ounce cans of prepared chick-peas	4 cloves garlic
	¼ cup olive oil
	A pinch of pepper
	1 cup tahini
2 lemons	Fresh parsley

1. In a covered saucepan over low heat cook the chick-peas in the water until the peas are soft, about 3 hours. Add water if necessary to keep the peas from burning. Cooking time can be reduced by about half if the peas are first soaked overnight. Omit this step if canned or cooked chick-peas are used.
2. Drain the chick-peas and save the liquid. Squeeze the lemons. In a blender combine the peas, lemon juice, garlic, olive oil, and pepper and blend into a smooth paste. Add some of the chick-pea liquid if the blades become stuck. Without a blender crush the garlic and mash the chick-peas with a fork; then mix well with the lemon juice, oil, and pepper.
3. Stir the tahini into the chick-pea mixture.
4. To serve, open the pita by cutting off part of the edge. Fill the pocket with humus and lots of fresh chopped parsley. Or, in a bowl garnish the humus with parsley; tear off pieces of pita to scoop up the humus.

Whole Wheat Poppy Rolls

ABOUT A DOZEN ROLLS EACH WITH ABOUT 5 GRAMS USABLE PROTEIN

These are light, easy to prepare rolls. The unbaked dough freezes well so that a supply of fresh rolls can be on hand.

¾ cup warm water   flour (preferably hard
5 tablespoons oil   wheat or bread flour)
¼ cup honey   1 tablespoon yeast
1 teaspoon salt   ½ cup wheat germ
1 egg   ⅓ cup poppy seeds
About 3 cups whole wheat   Oil

1. In a large bowl combine ½ cup of the warm water, the oil, honey, salt, egg, and 1 cup of the flour.

2. In the cup in which the honey was measured, dissolve the yeast in the remaining ¼ cup of warm water. Let the yeast stand until bubbly, about 5 minutes.

3. Add the dissolved yeast to the mixture in the large bowl, and stir with a wooden spoon or rubber spatula until the dough is well mixed. Beat the dough 100 strokes.

4. Stir in the wheat germ. Then stir in enough flour to make a soft dough.

5. Scrape the dough out of the bowl onto a floured board and knead it until it is smooth, springy, and no longer sticky, about 10 minutes. Add more flour if the dough feels wet. Try to avoid tearing the dough as you knead.

6. Place the dough in a large oiled bowl and brush the surface with oil. Cover the bowl with a cloth, and let the dough rise in a warm, draft-free place until it is double in bulk, about 1½ hours.

7. Punch down the dough and knead it briefly on a lightly floured board to press out all the air. Divide the dough into 12 equal portions. Round each piece of dough into a smooth ball and let them rest, covered with a cloth, for about 10 minutes.

8. Oil a baking sheet or a 12-cup muffin tin. Shape each portion of dough into a roll and coat it with poppy seeds. Some possible ways to shape the dough are:

• Cut each ball of dough into thirds or quarters. Make three small balls and coat each with poppy seeds. Press the balls together to form a roll.

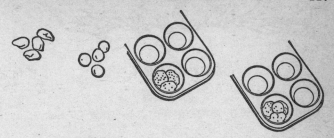

- Roll the ball of dough in your hands to form a rope about 6 inches long. Coat the surface with poppy seeds and tie the dough rope into a loose knot.

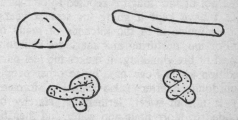

- See other suggestions for roll shapes on page 57.

9. Place the rolls in the muffin tin, or on the baking sheet. If using a baking sheet leave ample room for the rolls to double in size. Brush the surface with oil, cover with a cloth, and let rise until double in bulk, about 1 hour.

10. Heat the oven to 400°. Bake the rolls until the crust is brown, about 15 minutes. Serve the rolls hot.

Sourdough

GENERAL INSTRUCTIONS

My old pot of sourdough is reputed to be half a century old. I have kept it going for several years and some of its flavor is in the kitchens of many of my friends. For me, nurturing and sharing a sourdough is a vital part of breadmaking: it makes me feel part of a long tradition which I can pass on to other people.

A sourdough starter (also called a ferment, or sponge) is a sour-sweet, fermenting, starchy batter. When added to more flour and water and then baked, it makes a moist, tart bread. In the making of sourdough breads, as in the fermenting of beer and wine, a small portion of each batch is set aside as the "starter" for the next batch so that the essential microorganisms will be passed from bread to bread.

Sourdough makes breads rise by trapping yeast and bacteria in the batter. As the bacteria are fed simple sugars, they produce acids that impart a sour taste to the dough. The yeast thrives in this acid environment, and ferments the starches in the flour to produce carbon dioxide, which leavens the bread.

Each sourdough culture has a unique taste and pace of fermenting, so, in time, you will get to know your starter intimately—learn to control the sourness and figure out how long it will take to rise.

If you like the flavor, you may want to add sourdough to all baked goods—breads, sweet rolls, quick breads, pancakes, biscuits, cakes, or cookies. Sourdough biscuits and pancakes were favorites of the nineteenth-century Alaskan outdoorsmen, and they are still enjoyed today by hikers and campers.

The longer a sourdough ferments the richer the flavor, so the best way to begin a sourdough pot is to take some of a starter that has been fermenting for a while. A tablespoon is enough to begin building a respectable starter, because all that is needed is a few of the mature bacteria and yeast to begin multiplying. About a cup, however, is a convenient amount to keep on hand. To enlarge a small amount of starter, add to it gradually. Start by stirring in 2 tablespoons each of flour and milk and 1½ teaspoons of sweetener. Let this stand, uncovered. A day or two later, stir in ¼ cup each of flour and milk and 1 tablespoon of sweetener. Let this stand until the smell is pungent—a few days more. When the aroma is strong and the batter bubbly, the starter is ready to use.

You can begin your own sourdough pot by following the recipe on page 121—or you can buy a dehydrated commercial starter.

A sourdough starter will last forever if the tiny organisms that multiply and sour are kept well fed. To pamper a starter, it should be refrigerated in a clean glass jar or crock (do not use metal) twice the size of the sourdough to be stored. It should be stirred each day; however, my starter has survived the indignity of being ignored for weeks and weeks. If alcohol forms on the top, just stir it in. Do clean the jar occasionally. If the starter has not been used for a few weeks, or if you want to make more sourdough, add

1 CUP FLOUR
1 CUP MILK
¼ CUP SWEETENER

Most people add only flour and water to their sourdough pot, but I believe my starter has a special taste because it has always been replenished with milk.

The microbes that make the dough sour grow most enthusiastically at room temperature, or more slowly in the refrigerator. Sourdough can also be frozen. To coax it out of dormancy, let it warm to room temperature and feed it.

To convert any recipe to a sourdough recipe, prepare a sponge of 1 cup sourdough, 1 cup flour, 1 cup milk, and ¼ cup sweetener. Take off 1 cup and refrigerate it. This is the new sourdough starter. Let the remaining mixture stand to sour. Then add the other ingredients in the recipe to the sponge *except* 1 cup of the liquid and about 1 cup of the flour. *Include* the baking powder, baking soda, or yeast. Watch the consistency of the batter carefully; expect the consistency to vary each time a recipe is made.

To use the sourdough starter to bake a yeast bread, enlarge your stock of sourdough with the liquid in the recipe and part of the flour and sweetener, but not the oil or salt. Take off one cup and refrigerate it. This is the new sourdough starter for the next batch of bread. Let the remaining sponge mixture sour for a few hours to a few days. To prepare the bread dough add the other ingredients to the sponge—the shortening, salt, eggs, flavorings, remaining sweetener, and flour—and finish the steps in the instructions. The longer the sponge has soured the more soupy it becomes, so more flour may have to be added. Rising time depends on the individual starter, the temperature, the humidity, and the other ingredients. If you are in a rush for the bread to rise, add some dissolved yeast.

Some people add ground ginger to sourdough recipes to help fermentation and to bring out the sour taste; others use a small amount of baking soda to control the sourness and help the rising. Nowadays, yeast is usually added to sourdough bread recipes as a leavener, so the sourdough primarily contributes taste.

The recipes in this chapter assume that you have 1 cup of sourdough starter on hand. Each recipe then increases this amount so that there is some sourdough for the bread and 1 cup to return to the refrigerator for the next time that you want to use it.

Sourdough Starter

1 tablespoon yeast	2 cups warm water
A drop of sweetener (honey, molasses, sugar)	¼ cup sweetener
	3 cups flour, any kind

1. In a ceramic bowl or large crock dissolve the yeast and the drop of sweetener in the ¼ cup warm water. Let the yeast stand until bubbly, about 5 minutes.
2. Beat the sweetener, 2 cups of the flour, and the remaining 1¾ cups of warm water into the dissolved yeast. Let this mixture ferment, uncovered, for 4 days. Stir the mixture daily.
3. On the fourth day, stir in the last cup of flour and let the mixture ferment for a day more. The starter should be bubbly and smell fresh and pungent.
4. If this first attempt is unsuccessful, try again, using skimmed milk this time instead of water.

RECIPES

Sourdough Rye

2 LOAVES EACH WITH ABOUT 43 GRAMS USABLE PROTEIN

This is a substantial yet fine-grained bread with a thick crust.

1 cup sourdough starter	¼ cup warm water
1¼ cups skimmed milk	2 tablespoons oil
3 tablespoons honey	1 tablespoon salt
2 cups whole rye flour	1 cup wheat germ
About 3 cups unbleached white wheat flour	1 tablespoon caraway seeds Oil
1 tablespoon yeast	Salted water (1 teaspoon
A drop of honey	salt in 1 cup of water)

1. In a ceramic bowl or large crock mix together the sourdough starter, milk, honey, 1 cup of the rye flour and 1 cup of the white wheat flour. Stir until the dough is well mixed. Remove 1 cup of this mixture and refrigerate. This is the new sourdough starter for the next batch of bread. Cover the bowl with a plate and let the remaining sponge mixture stand to sour for at least 3 hours, or as long as overnight. The longer the sponge stands, the more sour the bread will be.

2. In a cup dissolve the yeast and a drop of honey in the warm water. Let the yeast stand until bubbly, about 5 minutes.

3. Stir the sponge, transfer it to a large bowl if necessary, and add to it the dissolved yeast, oil, and salt. Stir with a wooden spoon or rubber spatula until the dough is well mixed. Beat the dough 100 strokes.

4. Stir in the wheat germ, caraway seeds, and the remaining cup of rye flour. Then stir in just enough white wheat flour to make a soft dough. The longer the sponge has soured, the more flour will be needed.

5. Scrape the dough out of the bowl onto a floured board and knead the dough until it is smooth, springy, and no longer sticky, about 10 minutes. Add more white wheat flour if the dough feels wet. Try to avoid tearing the dough as you knead.

6. Turn the bowl upside down over the dough and let it rest for about 10 minutes.

7. Knead again, using more white wheat flour if necessary to make a stiff dough.

8. Place the dough in a large oiled bowl, brush the surface of the dough with oil, and let the dough rise, covered with a cloth, in a warm, draft-free place until it is double in bulk, about 1½ hours.

9. Punch down the dough, and knead it briefly in the bowl or on a lightly floured board to press out all the air. Return the dough to the bowl, brush the surface with oil, cover with a cloth and let the dough rise again until double in bulk, about 1 hour.

10. Punch down the dough and knead it briefly on a lightly floured board. If the dough is sticky, knead in a *small amount* of white wheat flour. Divide the dough in half. Round each piece of dough into a smooth ball. Let the dough rest, covered with a cloth, for about 10 minutes.

11. Oil 2 baking sheets. Shape the dough into smooth round loaves, taking care not to tear the surface of the dough. Put the loaves on the baking sheets, leaving ample room for the breads to double in size.

12. Brush the loaves with oil, cover with a cloth, and let them rise until they are double in bulk, about 45 minutes.

13. Heat the oven to 450°, and put a shallow pan of water on the oven floor.

14. With a sharp knife or razor blade, slash the surface of each loaf, being careful not to deflate the dough as you cut. Brush the bread with salted water.

15. Bake the loaves, brushing with salted water every 15 minutes, until the crusts are brown and the bottoms sound hollow when tapped, about 50 minutes. Remove the loaves from the baking sheets immediately and let them cool on a wire rack.

Sourdough English Muffins

ABOUT A DOZEN MUFFINS EACH WITH ABOUT 8 GRAMS
USABLE PROTEIN

*Any bread dough can be fried into English muffins
by following steps 9 through 11 of this recipe. However,
this dough is special because of its slightly tart taste.
The muffins are shaped like the store-bought variety,
but they are darker and heavier.*

1 cup sourdough starter	3 tablespoons oil
1 cup skimmed milk	1 egg
⅜ cup maple syrup	1 teaspoon salt
About 2½ cups unbleached white wheat flour	¼ cup milk powder
	¼ cup soy flour
1 tablespoon yeast	½ cup cornmeal
A drop of maple syrup	½ cup wheat germ
¼ teaspoon ground ginger	Oil
¼ cup warm water	Cornmeal

1. In a ceramic bowl or a large crock, mix together
the sourdough starter, milk, maple syrup, and 1 cup of
the white wheat flour. Stir until the dough is well mixed.
Remove 1 cup of this mixture and refrigerate. This is
the new sourdough starter for the next batch of muffins.
Cover the bowl with a plate and let the remaining
sponge mixture stand to sour for at least 3 hours, or as
long as overnight. The longer the sponge stands, the
more sour the bread will be.

2. In a cup dissolve the yeast, a drop of maple syrup,
and the ginger in the warm water. Let the yeast stand
until bubbly, about 5 minutes.

3. Stir the sponge, transfer it to a large bowl if necessary, and add to it the dissolved yeast, the oil, egg,
and salt. Add 1 cup of the white wheat flour. Stir with
a wooden spoon or rubber spatula until the dough is
well mixed. Beat the dough 100 strokes.

4. In a small bowl sift together the milk powder and

soy flour. Add to the bowl any particles that did not go through the sifter. This sifting is to break up any lumps of milk powder and to distribute the soy flour evenly. Add these sifted ingredients and the ½ cup cornmeal to the dough in the large bowl.

5. Stir in the wheat germ. Then stir in just enough white wheat flour to make a soft dough.

6. Scrape the dough out of the bowl onto a floured board and knead it until it is smooth, springy, and no longer sticky, about 10 minutes. Add more white wheat flour if the dough feels wet. Try to avoid tearing the dough as you knead.

7. Place the dough in a large oiled bowl and brush the surface with oil. Cover the bowl with a cloth and let the dough rise in a warm, draft-free place until it is double in bulk, about 1½ hours.

8. Punch the dough down and knead it briefly on a lightly floured board to press out all the air. Let the dough rest, covered with a cloth, for about 10 minutes.

9. On a lightly floured board, pat or roll the dough to ½-inch thickness and cut it into 4-inch rounds with a muffin cutter or a glass dipped in flour. When all the cuts have been made, gather the scraps of dough, knead them briefly, and let them rest, covered with a cloth, for about 10 minutes. Pat and then cut the remaining muffins.

10. Let the muffins rise, covered with a cloth, until they are just less than double, about 30 minutes. Heat an ungreased heavy frying pan and sprinkle it with cornmeal.

11. Fry the muffins on both sides until the crusts are firm, about 5 minutes on each side. Regulate the heat to prevent burning the outside before the inside is cooked. Split the muffins with a fork or knife and toast. Serve hot.

Sourdough Lentil Bread

2 LOAVES EACH WITH ABOUT 41 GRAMS USABLE PROTEIN

This bread is good company for a thick soup and a crisp salad.

1 cup sourdough starter	1 tablespoon yeast
1½ cups skimmed milk	A drop of honey
¼ cup molasses	¼ cup warm water
About 4½ cups whole wheat flour (preferably hard wheat or bread flour)	3 tablespoons oil
	2 tablespoons honey
	1 tablespoon salt
	½ teaspoon curry powder
½ cup uncooked lentils and 1½ cups water or 1½ cups cooked lentils	Oil

1. In a ceramic bowl or large crock, mix together the sourdough starter, milk, molasses, and 1½ cups of the flour. Stir until the dough is well mixed. Remove 1 cup of this mixture and refrigerate. This is the new sourdough starter for the next batch of bread. Cover the bowl with a plate and let the remaining sponge mixture stand to sour for at least 3 hours, or as long as overnight. The longer the sponge stands, the more sour the bread will be.

2. In a covered saucepan over low heat cook the lentils in the water until they are soft but not mushy, about 40 minutes. Add water if necessary to keep the beans from burning. Drain the lentils (save the liquid for soup stock or bread dough) and let it cool to wrist temperature. Omit this step if cooked lentils are used.

3. In a cup dissolve the yeast and a drop of honey in the warm water. Let the yeast stand until bubbly, about 5 minutes.

4. Stir the sponge, transfer it to a large bowl if necessary, and add to it the dissolved yeast, the oil, honey, salt, curry powder, and 1 cup of the flour. Stir with a

wooden spoon or rubber spatula until the dough is well mixed. Beat the dough 100 strokes.

5. Stir in the cooked lentils and just enough flour to make a soft dough.

6. Scrape the dough out of the bowl onto a floured board. From this point follow the BASIC HIGH PROTEIN WHOLE WHEAT BREAD recipe from step 7—knead the dough; let it rise and punch it down twice; divide it in half and let it rest; shape the dough into loaves; let them rise; heat the oven to 350° and bake the breads for about 50 minutes. Use oil to grease the dough, bowl, and pans.

Sourdough Bread Sticks or Crackers with Onion Spread

ABOUT 2 DOZEN BREAD STICKS OR 5 DOZEN CRACKERS WITH ONION SPREAD, ABOUT 103 GRAMS USABLE PROTEIN

Most commercial crackers and all bread sticks are made from yeast doughs. Follow steps 8 through 11 to shape bread sticks and crackers from any yeast bread recipe. For onion spread that is tart and higher in protein, substitute drained yogurt for the cream cheese. (See page 303 for how to drain yogurt.)

1 cup sourdough starter
1 cup skimmed milk
¼ cup honey
About 1½ cups whole wheat flour (preferably hard wheat or bread flour)
1 tablespoon yeast
A drop of honey
¼ cup warm water

1 tablespoon oil
2 teaspoons salt
1 cup rye flour
Oil
1 egg white
2 tablespoons water
¼ cup flax seeds
2 tablespoons coarse salt (sold as kosher salt)

1. In a ceramic bowl or a large crock, mix together the sourdough starter, milk, honey, and 1 cup of the whole wheat flour. Stir until the dough is well mixed. Remove 1 cup of this mixture and refrigerate. This is the new sourdough starter for the next batch of bread. Cover the bowl with a plate and let the remaining sponge mixture stand to sour for at least 3 hours, or as long as overnight. The longer the sponge stands, the more sour the bread will be.

2. In a cup dissolve the yeast and a drop of honey in the warm water. Let the yeast stand until bubbly, about 5 minutes.

3. Stir the sponge, transfer it to a large bowl if necessary, and add to it the dissolved yeast, the oil, salt, and rye flour. Stir with a wooden spoon or rubber spatula until the dough is well mixed. Beat the dough 100 strokes.

4. Stir in just enough whole wheat flour to make a soft dough.

5. Scrape the dough out of the bowl onto a floured board and knead it until the dough is smooth, springy, and no longer sticky, about 10 minutes. Add more whole wheat flour if the dough feels wet. Try to avoid tearing the dough as you knead.

6. Place the dough in a large oiled bowl and brush the surface with oil. Cover the bowl with a cloth, and let the dough rise in a warm, draft-free place until it is double in bulk, about 1½ hours.

7. Punch down the dough and knead it briefly on a lightly floured board until the air is pressed out. Round the dough into a smooth ball. Let the dough rest, covered with a cloth, for about 10 minutes.

FOR BREAD STICKS

8. Oil 2 baking sheets. Heat the oven to 425°. On a lightly floured board, roll or pat the dough into a ½-inch-thick square. Cut the dough into about 24 long strips, each about ½ inch wide. Roll each strip into a

rope on the table or between your hands, and place it on a baking sheet. Leave ample room for the bread sticks to double in size.

9. Cover the dough strips with a cloth and let them rise until they are almost double in bulk, about 30 minutes.

10. In a cup, mix the egg white with the 2 tablespoons water and brush this glaze on the bread sticks. Sprinkle them with flax seeds and coarse salt.

11. Bake the bread sticks until the crusts are brown, about 20 minutes. Remove the bread sticks from the baking sheets immediately and let them cool on wire racks. Serve warm or at room temperature, with onion spread.

FOR CRACKERS

8. Oil 2 baking sheets. Heat the oven to 400°. Divide the dough in half. On a lightly floured board, roll each piece of dough ⅛ inch thick in the appropriate shape to fit your baking sheet.

9. Place the dough on the oiled pans. Cut the dough into 2-inch squares, but do not separate them. Prick the surface of the dough with a fork.

10. Mix the egg white with the water and brush this glaze on the crackers. Sprinkle them with flax seeds and coarse salt.

11. Bake the crackers until they are crisp and brown, about 15 minutes. Remove the crackers from the baking sheet immediately, separate them and let cool on wire racks. Serve warm or at room temperature with onion spread.

ONION SPREAD

8 ounces cream cheese	6 sprigs fresh parsley
2 whole scallions	2 cups ricotta cheese
2 cloves garlic	Salt and pepper
2 tablespoons chives	

Warm the cream cheese to room temperature. Chop the scallions, garlic, chives, and parsley fine and combine with the ricotta and cream cheese in a small bowl. Salt and pepper to taste.

Sourdough Blueberry Pancakes

ABOUT A DOZEN PANCAKES EACH WITH ABOUT 3 GRAMS USABLE PROTEIN

These are thick but light pancakes. Try them with other berries or bananas. See Pancake chapter for more pancake-making suggestions.

1 cup sourdough starter	2 eggs
1 cup whole wheat flour (preferably soft wheat or pastry flour)	1 tablespoon honey
	1 teaspoon salt
	1 teaspoon baking soda
1 cup skimmed milk	1 tablespoon oil
¼ cup honey	1 pint fresh blueberries

1. In a ceramic bowl or large crock mix together the sourdough starter, flour, milk, and honey. Stir until the dough is well mixed. Remove 1 cup of this mixture and refrigerate. This is the new sourdough starter for the next batch of pancakes. Cover the bowl with a plate and let the remaining sponge mixture stand to sour for at least 3 hours, or as long as overnight. The longer the sponge stands, the more sour the pancakes will be.

2. Stir the sponge, transfer it to a large bowl if necessary, and add to it the eggs, the 1 tablespoon honey, salt, baking soda, and oil. Mix well, making sure that no lumps of baking soda remain. Stir in the blueberries.

3. On a hot, ungreased frying pan or griddle, fry about ¼ cup batter until bubbles form on the surface and the edges are dry, about 2 minutes. Turn once and fry until brown, about ½ minute. Continue with the remaining batter. Keep the pancakes hot by stacking,

wrapping in a kitchen towel, and placing them in a 200° oven. If the pancakes are too thick, or when the batter thickens as you reach the bottom of the bowl, add milk and stir. Serve hot.

Eggplant Quiche in Sourdough Pastry

1 QUICHE WITH ABOUT 72 GRAMS USABLE PROTEIN

Sourdough makes a flaky tart crust which is well suited to the quiche custard and cheese. See Pies and Crusted Pastries chapter for crust-making directions.

1 cup sourdough starter	½ teaspoon salt
¼ cup skimmed milk	⅛ teaspoon baking soda
¼ cup flour, any kind	¼ cup wheat germ
1 tablespoon honey	⅓ cup butter
¾ cup unbleached white wheat flour	1 egg white

1. In a ceramic bowl or large crock mix together the sourdough starter, milk, flour, and honey. Stir until the dough is well mixed. Remove 1 cup of this mixture and refrigerate. This is the new sourdough starter for the next pastry. You will have about ¼ cup left in the bowl, all you will need for this recipe. Cover the bowl with a plate and let the remaining sponge mixture stand to sour for at least 1 hour, or as long as overnight. The longer the sponge stands, the more sour the crust will be.

2. In a small bowl sift together the white wheat flour, salt, and baking soda. Stir in the wheat germ.

3. Cut the butter into the sifted ingredients with a pastry blender or two knives, or crumble the butter with the flour mixture by rubbing it quickly with your fingertips. The mixture should resemble coarse cornmeal. Tossing the flour lightly with a fork, gradually add enough sourdough to make a soft dough. Add less sour-

dough than you think is needed, since the dry particles will be easily gathered in when you take the ball of dough and press it gently in your hands. If time permits wrap the dough in waxed paper and refrigerate until chilled, about 2 hours.

4. Roll the dough into a 10-inch circle. Place the dough into an 8-inch quiche pan or pie tin. For a quiche

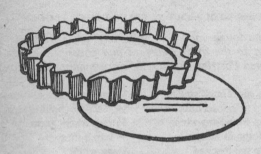

pan trim the dough so that it is flush with the vertical sides of the pan by rolling the rolling pin across the top of the pan. For a pie tin trim the overhanging dough, and pinch the edges with your fingertips or a fork in order to attach the crust to the rim of the pan. If time permits, place the crust in the refrigerator until chilled, about 1 hour.

5. Heat the oven to 425°. Prick the bottom of the pastry with a fork, place a piece of buttered aluminum foil over the crust, butter side towards the crust, and cover the aluminum foil with clean pebbles or dried beans.

6. Bake the crust for 10 minutes. Then remove the foil and beans or pebbles, and repair any damaged portions of the crust. If the sides of the crust have slipped into the pan, press them back with a blunt knife. Brush the crust with the egg white and return it to the oven. Bake until light brown, about 5 minutes longer. The crust is now ready for filling.

EGGPLANT QUICHE FILLING

4 or 5 ¼″ slices of fresh eggplant	3 eggs
	1½ cups milk
Salt	½ teaspoon salt
2 tablespoons butter	A pinch of pepper
1½ cups grated cheese, about 5 ounces (for instance Gruyere, Swiss, or Jarlsberg)	A pinch of nutmeg

7. Slice and peel enough eggplant to cover the bottom of an 8-inch pie tin or quiche pan. Salt the slices and let them drain on a paper towel for about 15 minutes. Pat them dry.

Lightly fry the eggplant slices on both sides in the butter until tender, then arrange them on the bottom of the pastry shell. Sprinkle the cheese over the eggplant.

8. Heat the oven to 375°.

9. In a bowl beat together the eggs, milk, and seasonings. Pour over the eggplant and cheese.

10. Bake the quiche until the cheese and custard are firm, puffy, and brown, about 30 minutes. If the crust begins to brown too much, lower the baking temperature to 350° and cover the rim of the pastry with a strip of aluminum foil. Serve hot or warm.

Sourdough Coconut Cookies

ABOUT 2 DOZEN COOKIES WITH ABOUT 89 GRAMS USABLE PROTEIN

These cookies have a sweet-tart taste and a crunchy, chewy texture. See Cookies and Crackers chapter for baking suggestions.

1 cup sourdough starter	½ cup brown sugar
⅓ cup skimmed milk	1 cup wheat germ
⅓ cup flour, any kind	2 cups unsweetened dried grated coconut
1 tablespoon brown sugar	
⅔ cup almonds	A pinch of salt
½ cup honey	4 egg whites

1. In a ceramic bowl or large crock mix together the sourdough starter, milk, flour, and sugar. Stir until the dough is well mixed. Remove a cup of this mixture and refrigerate. This is the new starter for the next batch of cookies. You will have about ½ cup left in the bowl, all you will need for this recipe. Cover the bowl with a plate and let the remaining sponge mixture stand to sour for at least 1 hour, or as long as overnight. The longer the sponge stands, the more sour the cookies will be.

2. Heat the oven to 325°. Butter and flour a large baking sheet.

3. Chop the almonds coarse. Stir the sponge, transfer it to a large bowl if necessary, and add to it the almonds, honey, sugar, wheat germ, coconut, and salt. Mix well.

4. In another large bowl beat the egg whites with a wire whisk or rotary beater until stiff. With a large spoon or rubber spatula gently fold the egg whites into the coconut mixture.

5. Drop the batter by the teaspoonful onto the baking sheet, about an inch apart. Bake the cookies until the center of each cookie is firm and the crust is brown, about 20 minutes. Cool the cookies on a wire rack.

Yeasted Pastries

GENERAL INSTRUCTIONS

Follow the directions given in the chapter on Breads and Rolls since yeasted pastries are simply sweeter and richer breads. In fact, any yeast-bread dough makes a fine sweet pastry if it is rolled with a filling like marmalade, nuts, fruit, or cheese. For a 9-inch ring, use about 1½ cups of filling; for an individual sweet roll use about 2 tablespoons of filling.

Often yeast doughs are layered with butter to make the pastry flaky. The layering method described in the recipe for Danish pastries on page 142 can be used with any sweet yeast dough.

SHAPING

Coffee Cakes

Coffee cakes should be shaped and cut so that the filling will show and the cake will rise without tearing.

With a rolling pin roll a loaf-size ball of dough into a ¼-inch-thick rectangle. Spread the filling evenly over the dough. Roll like a jelly roll, beginning at the long edge of the rectangle. Pinch the seam to seal, moistening the dough with water if necessary.

Form the roll into a circle or crescent. Place it on a buttered baking sheet. Cut slices halfway through the dough with scissors or a knife.

For another example of how to shape a coffee cake, see the recipe "Refrigerator Sweet Dough With Orange-Fig Filling" page 146.

Sweet Rolls or Buns

Two simple methods for shaping sweet rolls are:

1. Form and fill the dough as for coffee cake. Cut the rolled dough into 2-inch-thick slices. Arrange the buns cut-side-up in a shallow baking dish or cake tin so that they are almost touching. Or:

2. Roll the dough into a ¼-inch-thick rectangle. Cut it into squares or triangles. Put some filling onto each piece. Bring the corners of the dough together to cover the filling and pinch to seal. Place on a buttered baking sheet.

For Both Coffee Cakes and Sweet Rolls

Brush the surface of the pastry with melted butter and cover with a cloth. Let the coffee cake or sweet rolls rise until almost double, about 1 hour. Brush with any of the glazes on page 61. Bake, cool on a wire rack, and serve warm.

RECIPES

Basic Whole Wheat Sweet Dough

ABOUT 69 GRAMS USABLE PROTEIN

The uses for this dough are limitless. You can use it with or without layering with butter. Butter layers make the pastry flaky, like Danish; without butter layers the pastry will simply be rich and sweet, like sticky buns. This is enough dough for 2 coffee cakes or 16 buns or Danish.

½ cup milk
¼ cup butter
⅓ cup honey
1½ teaspoons salt
2 tablespoons yeast
½ cup warm water
2 eggs
1½ teaspoons lemon extract

½ teaspoon orange extract
½ teaspoon ground cardamom
About 2½ cups whole wheat flour (preferably hard wheat or bread flour)
¾ cup wheat germ
Melted butter

1. Warm the milk in a saucepan until small bubbles form around the rim of the pan. Remove the pan from the heat and add the butter, honey, and salt. Stir until the butter melts and the honey dissolves. Transfer to a large bowl and let cool to wrist temperature.

2. In the cup in which the honey was measured, dissolve the yeast in the water. Let the yeast stand until bubbly, about 5 minutes.

3. When the milk mixture has cooled, add to it the dissolved yeast, the eggs, extracts, and cardamom.

4. Add 1 cup of the flour. Stir with a wooden spoon or rubber spatula until the dough is well mixed. Beat the dough 100 strokes.

5. Stir in the wheat germ. Then stir in just enough flour to make a soft dough.

6. Scrape the dough out of the bowl onto a floured board and knead it until it is soft, springy, and no longer sticky, about 10 minutes. Add more flour if the dough feels wet. Try to avoid tearing the dough as you knead.

7. Place the dough in a large buttered bowl and brush the surface with melted butter. Cover the bowl with a cloth and let the dough rise in a warm draft-free place until it is double in bulk, about 1½ hours.

8. Punch down the dough and knead it briefly in the bowl or on a lightly floured board to press out all the air. Return it to the bowl, brush the surface with melted butter, cover with a cloth, and let it rise again until double in bulk, about 1 hour.

9. Punch down the dough, knead it briefly on a lightly floured board, and divide it in half. Round each piece of dough into a ball, cover with a cloth, and let them rest for about 10 minutes. Now follow the recipe for YOGURT-PECAN-FILLED COFFEE CAKE, STICKY BUNS, or WHOLE WHEAT CHEESE DANISH.

Yogurt-Pecan-Filled Coffee Cake

2 COFFEE CAKES EACH WITH ABOUT 43 GRAMS
USABLE PROTEIN

This is a whole wheat version of a traditional breakfast or dessert coffee cake. The yogurt often takes an hour to prepare, so plan accordingly.

¼ cup butter
1 cup drained yogurt
½ cup honey
1 tablespoon grated
  lemon rind

1 cup pecans
1 recipe Basic Whole Wheat
  Sweet Dough

1. Melt the butter and set it aside to cool.

2. Drain the yogurt in a funnel or sieve lined with a paper towel or filter paper. Set the funnel in a glass or the sieve in a bowl to catch the water (whey) that drains out. (Save the whey for yeast bread baking.) Let the yogurt drain until it is of thick pudding consistency, about 1 hour. The amount of yogurt needed initially to make 1 cup drained yogurt and the amount of time it takes to drain depend upon the original thickness of the yogurt. When it is ready, combine it with the butter, honey, and lemon rind in a small bowl. Mix well and set it aside. Chop the pecans coarse. Use half the yogurt filling and half the pecans for each cake.

3. Butter 2 baking sheets. On a lightly floured board roll out half the basic sweet dough recipe (1 ball of dough) into a rectangle about ¼ inch thick.

4. Spread a thin layer of yogurt filling on two-thirds of the rectangle. Fold the uncoated third over the center third and then fold the doubled portion over the remaining third. The dough is now in three layers. Pinch the edges to seal in the yogurt and rotate the rectangle one quarter-turn.

5. Roll out the dough again to about ¼-inch thickness, flouring the board as needed. Spread the yogurt filling as before and fold in thirds, pinch the dough around the edges, and turn.

6. Roll out the dough again to about ¼-inch thickness, again spread yogurt filling over two-thirds of the rectangle, and sprinkle half of the pecans over the filling. Fold in thirds as before, pinch the edges, and roll the dough out again to about ⅜-inch thickness.

If at any time the dough becomes too stiff to roll out, cover it with a cloth and let it rest for about

10 minutes. Since this relaxes the gluten, the rolling should be easier.

7. Roll the dough like a jelly roll, beginning at the long edge of the rectangle. Pinch to seal the seam, moistening the dough with water if necessary. Form the roll into a circle or crescent. Place seam-side-down on a baking sheet. Cut slices about 2 inches apart halfway through the dough with scissors or a knife. (See illustration page 136.)

8. Repeat step 3 through step 7 for the second half of the basic sweet dough.

9. Brush the surface of the cakes with melted butter, cover with a cloth, and let them rise until they are almost double in bulk, about 40 minutes.

10. Heat the oven to 350°. Bake the cakes until the crusts are brown and the dough is firm to the touch, about 30 minutes. Remove the coffee cakes from the baking sheets immediately and let them cool on wire racks. Serve warm.

Sticky Buns

ABOUT 16 STICKY BUNS EACH WITH ABOUT 6 GRAMS
USABLE PROTEIN

These buns are substantial and not too sweet.

1 cup brown sugar
1 tablespoon ground
   cinnamon
1 teaspoon ground allspice
1 teaspoon ground nutmeg

½ cup butter
1 cup walnuts
1 recipe Basic Whole Wheat
   Sweet Dough
1 cup raisins

1. In a small bowl sift together the sugar and spices. Melt the butter. Chop the nuts coarse. Butter two 1-quart shallow baking dishes or tins.

2. On a lightly floured board, roll out half the basic sweet dough recipe (1 ball of dough) into a rectangle about ¼ inch thick. Brush the dough with melted but-

ter and sprinkle about 3 tablespoons of the sugar-spice mixture on two-thirds of the rectangle. Fold the uncoated third over the center third, and then fold the doubled portion over the remaining third. The dough is now in three layers. Pinch the edges to seal and rotate the rectangle one quarter-turn.

3. Roll out the dough again to about ¼-inch thickness, flouring the board as needed. Brush with butter and sprinkle about 3 tablespoons of the sugar-spice mixture and ½ cup of the raisins over two-thirds of the rectangle. Fold in thirds, pinch the dough around the edges, and turn.

4. Roll the dough out to about ⅜-inch thickness, brush with butter, sprinkle about 3 tablespoons of the sugar-spice mixture and ½ cup of the chopped nuts over two-thirds of the rectangle. Fold in thirds as before, pinch the edges, and roll the dough out again to about ⅜-inch thickness.

If at any time the dough becomes too stiff to roll out, cover it with a cloth and let it rest for about 10 minutes. Since this relaxes the gluten the rolling should be easier.

5. Roll the dough like a jelly roll beginning at the long edge of the rectangle. Pinch to seal the seam, moistening the dough with water if necessary.

6. Cut into 2-inch thick slices. Arrange the slices cut-side-up in the baking dish so that they are almost touching. (See illustration page 136.)

7. Repeat the layering and shaping—step 2 through step 7—for the second half of the basic sweet dough.

8. Brush the surface of the buns with melted butter, cover with a cloth, and let them rise until almost double in bulk, about 40 minutes.

9. Heat the oven to 350°. Bake the buns until the crusts are brown and the dough is firm to the touch, about a half hour. Remove the buns from the pans and let them cool briefly on wire racks. Separate the buns and serve warm.

Whole Wheat Cheese Danish

**ABOUT 16 PASTRIES EACH WITH ABOUT 9 GRAMS
USABLE PROTEIN**

Follow this method for layering the dough with butter to make a flaky pastry out of any yeast bread recipe.

**1 recipe Basic Whole Wheat   ½ cup butter
  Sweet Dough**

LAYERING THE DOUGH WITH BUTTER

1. Melt the butter and set it aside.

2. On a lightly floured board roll out half the basic sweet dough recipe (1 ball of dough) into a rectangle about ¼ inch thick. Brush two-thirds of the rectangle with melted butter. Fold the uncoated third over the center third and then fold the doubled portion over the remaining third. The dough is now in three layers. Rotate the rectangle a quarter-turn.

3. Roll out the dough again to about ¼-inch thickness, flouring the board as needed. Brush with butter as before, fold in thirds, and turn.

4. Repeat the rolling, buttering, and folding process 2 or 3 more times. This layers the butter between thin sheets of dough, which gives the characteristic flakiness of Danish pastry.

If at any time the dough becomes too stiff to roll out, let it rest covered with a cloth for about 10 minutes, and then continue layering. Since this rest relaxes the gluten, the rolling should be easier.

If the dough becomes too soft, wrap it in waxed paper and refrigerate it for about 30 minutes to chill and harden the butter.

5. Repeat the layering—step 1 through step 3—for the second half of the basic sweet dough.

6. Wrap the folded, buttered dough in waxed paper and refrigerate it while preparing the filling.

TO SHAPE, FILL, AND GLAZE THE PASTRIES

1 egg	2 tablespoons water

7. Butter 2 baking sheets.

8. On a lightly floured board roll a chilled rectangle of dough into a 10- by 20-inch rectangle. Cut into 8 squares. Place about 3 tablespoons of filling on each square of dough. Bring the corners together and pinch closed or leave a small center opening. (See illustration page 5.) Place the pastries on a baking sheet. Repeat this step—the rolling, shaping, and filling—for the second rectangle of dough.

9. Brush the surface of the pastries with melted butter, cover with a cloth, and let rise until almost double in bulk, about 30 minutes.

10. Heat the oven to 350°. In a cup beat the egg with the water. Brush this glaze on the pastries. Bake until the crusts are brown and the dough is firm to the touch, about 25 minutes. Remove the pastries from the baking sheets immediately and let them cool on wire racks. Serve warm.

CHEESE FILLING

2½ cups drained cottage cheese	1 cup brown sugar
3 eggs	1½ tablespoons grated lemon rind
6 tablespoons butter	

1. Drain the cottage cheese in a funnel or sieve lined with a paper towel or filter paper or hang the cottage cheese in a cheesecloth bag. Set the funnel in a glass or the sieve in a bowl to catch the water (whey) that drains out. (Save the whey for yeast bread-baking.) Let the cottage cheese drain until it is dry and cakey, about 1 hour. The amount of cottage cheese needed

initially to make 2½ cups drained cottage cheese and the amount of time it takes to drain depend upon the original wetness of the cottage cheese.

2. Separate the eggs. In a small bowl beat the butter with a fork or rotary beater until it is creamy. Stir in the egg yolks, the drained cottage cheese, sugar, and lemon rind.

3. In a large bowl beat the egg whites with a wire whisk or rotary beater until they are stiff. With a large spoon or rubber spatula fold the egg whites gently into the cottage cheese mixture.

Nut-Filled Yogurt Coffee Cake

2 COFFEE CAKES EACH WITH ABOUT 85 GRAMS
USABLE PROTEIN

This is a rich, nutty cake that does not use eggs. Wheat germ is used in the filling to complement the protein of the flour and the nuts.

1 cup yogurt
½ cup butter
½ cup honey
1¼ teaspoons salt
2 tablespoons yeast

½ cup warm water
About 4 cups whole wheat
    flour (preferably hard
    wheat or bread flour)
Melted butter

1. Warm the yogurt in a saucepan until small bubbles form around the rim of the pan. Remove the pan from the heat and add the butter, honey, and salt. Stir until the butter melts and the honey dissolves. Transfer to a large bowl and let cool to wrist temperature.

2. In the cup in which the honey was measured, dissolve the yeast in the water. Let the yeast stand until bubbly, about 5 minutes.

3. When the yogurt mixture has cooled, add to it the dissolved yeast and add 1 cup of the flour. Stir with a wooden spoon or rubber spatula until the dough is well mixed. Beat the dough 100 strokes.

4. Stir in just enough flour to make a soft dough. Scrape the dough out of the bowl onto a floured board and knead it until it is smooth, springy, and no longer sticky, about 10 minutes. Add more flour if the dough feels wet. Try to avoid tearing the dough as you knead.

5. Place the dough in a large buttered bowl and brush the surface with melted butter. Cover the bowl with a cloth and let the dough rise in a warm, draft-free place until it is double in bulk, about 1½ hours.

6. Punch down the dough and knead it briefly in the bowl or on a lightly floured board to press out all the air. Return it to the bowl, brush the surface with melted butter, cover with a cloth and let it rise again until double in bulk, about 1 hour.

7. Prepare the filling.

8. Punch down the dough, knead it briefly on a lightly floured board, and divide it in half. Round each piece of dough into a ball, cover with a cloth, and let them rest for about 10 minutes.

9. Butter 2 baking sheets.

10. On a lightly floured board, roll out one ball of dough into a rectangle about ½ inch thick. Spread a little less than half of the filling over the dough and roll like a jelly roll, beginning at the long edge of the rectangle. Pinch to seal the seam, moistening the dough with water if necessary. Form the roll into a circle or crescent. Place seam-side-down on the baking sheet. Repeat this step—the rolling and shaping—with the second ball of dough. Save a sprinkling of the filling for the tops of the coffee cakes.

11. Brush the surface of the cakes with melted butter. Spread the remaining filling on the tops of the cakes and slash the dough with a sharp knife or razor blade in a long straight line about ½ inch deep along the top of each coffee cake.

12. Cover the cakes with a cloth and let them rise until almost double in bulk, about 45 minutes.

13. Heat the oven to 350°. Bake the cakes until the

crusts are brown and the dough is firm to the touch, about 45 minutes. Remove the cakes from the baking sheets immediately, and let them cool on wire racks. Serve warm.

NUT FILLING

3 cups nuts	1/3 cup butter
2 cups wheat germ	1 cup maple syrup

Chop the nuts fine. Toast the nuts and the wheat germ in a frying pan over low heat until brown, about 5 minutes. Stir frequently to prevent burning. Melt the butter. In a small bowl, combine the wheat germ and nuts with the butter and maple syrup. Mix well to blend.

Refrigerator Sweet Dough with Orange Fig Filling

2 COFFEE CAKES EACH WITH ABOUT 65 GRAMS USABLE PROTEIN

This coffee cake can be prepared quickly in the evening, refrigerated, and baked in the morning for breakfast. Some may find the fig filling too strong tasting; any chopped dried fruit can be substituted.

2/3 cup orange juice	About 2 cups unbleached white wheat flour
1/2 cup butter	
1/4 cup molasses	2 cups whole wheat flour (preferably hard wheat or bread flour)
1/4 cup honey	
1 1/2 teaspoons salt	
1 teaspoon lemon extract	1/2 cup milk powder
2 tablespoons yeast	1/2 cup soy flour
1/2 cup warm water	1/2 cup wheat germ
2 eggs	Melted butter
2 tablespoons grated orange rind	

1. Warm the orange juice in a saucepan until small bubbles form around the rim of the pan. Remove the pan from the heat and add the butter, molasses, honey, salt, and lemon extract. Stir until the butter melts and the molasses and honey dissolve. Transfer to a large bowl and let cool to wrist temperature.

2. In the cup in which the honey or molasses was measured, dissolve the yeast in the water. Let the yeast stand until bubbly, about 5 minutes.

3. When the juice mixture has cooled, add to it the dissolved yeast, eggs, and orange rind.

4. Add 1 cup of the white wheat flour and 1 cup of the whole wheat flour. Stir with a wooden spoon or rubber spatula until the dough is well mixed. Beat the dough 100 strokes.

5. In a small bowl sift together the milk powder, soy flour, and the remaining 1 cup of whole wheat flour. Add to the bowl any particles that did not go through the sifter. This sifting is to break up any lumps of milk powder and to distribute the soy flour evenly. Add these sifted ingredients to the dough in the large bowl.

6. Stir in the wheat germ. Then stir in just enough white wheat flour to make a soft dough.

7. Scrape the dough out of the bowl onto a floured board and knead it until it is smooth and springy, about 10 minutes. Add more white wheat flour if the dough feels wet. Try to avoid tearing the dough as you knead. The dough will be soft and slightly sticky.

8. Place the dough on a sheet of buttered plastic wrap or waxed paper. Brush the surface of the dough with melted butter and cover the dough with plastic wrap and then a kitchen towel. Let the dough rest for about 20 minutes. Prepare the filling.

9. Punch the dough down and knead it briefly on a lightly floured board to press out all the air. Divide the dough in half and roll each piece into a ball. Let the dough rest, covered with a cloth, for about 10 minutes.

10. Butter 2 baking sheets.

11. On a lightly floured board, roll out one ball of dough into a rectangle about ½ inch thick.

12. Spread about 1 cup of the filling on the center third of the rectangle. Fold the right-hand third over the filling. Then spread about 1 cup of the filling on the top of the third that was just folded over. Cover with the left-hand third. There should be three layers of dough and two layers of filling. Place the dough on the baking sheets.

13. Cut about 7 slices in the dough as if you were cutting the teeth of a comb. Slice through all the dough thicknesses, but do not cut across the entire piece of dough. Twist each cut piece so that it overlaps the next.

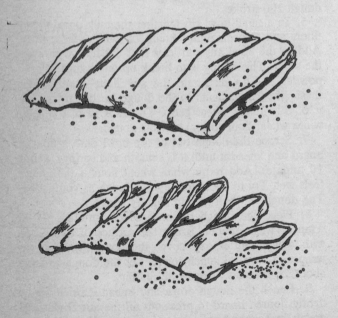

14. Repeat the rolling, shaping, and filling—step 11 through step 14—with the second ball of dough.

15. Brush the surface of the cakes with melted butter, then wrap each cake and baking sheet loosely in plastic wrap.

16. Refrigerate the cakes for at least 3 hours and not more than 24 hours.

17. Take the cakes out of the refrigerator, unwrap them from the plastic, and let the dough warm to room temperature for about 25 minutes. Meanwhile, heat the oven to 350°.

18. Bake the cakes until the crusts are brown and the dough is firm to the touch, about 30 minutes. Remove the cakes from the baking sheets immediately, and cool on wire racks. Serve warm.

FILLING

3 cups dried figs	2 tablespoons grated
1 cup almonds	orange rind
½ cup honey	

Chop the figs coarse. If they are very dry, soak them in water until they are plump. Chop the almonds fine. Combine the figs and nuts with the honey and orange rind in a small bowl. Mix well.

Cheese Brioche

2 BRIOCHES EACH WITH ABOUT 61 GRAMS USABLE PROTEIN

This is a light, eggy bread resembling a French brioche. It will look like one if it is baked in a tall fluted pan and a ball of dough is placed on top. Or it can be baked in a small saucepan.

Because the loaf stales quickly, it should be eaten or frozen soon after it is baked. Slightly stale brioche toasts well and is good with jam.

Any domestic or imported Swiss-type cheese can be used. My preference is Appenzeller.

¼ cup milk
⅓ cup butter
¼ cup honey
¾ teaspoon salt
1 tablespoon yeast
¼ cup warm water
5 eggs

About 4 cups unbleached
   white wheat flour
1 cup wheat germ
2 cups grated cheese, about
   6 ounces
Melted butter
1 egg yolk
1 tablespoon water

1. Warm the milk in a saucepan until small bubbles form around the rim of the pan. Remove the pan from the heat and add the butter, honey, and salt. Stir until the butter melts and the honey dissolves. Transfer to a large bowl and let cool to wrist temperature.

2. In the cup in which the honey was measured, dissolve the yeast in the water. Let the yeast stand until bubbly, about 5 minutes.

3. When the milk mixture has cooled, add to it the dissolved yeast, the eggs, and 2 cups of the flour. Stir with a wooden spoon or rubber spatula until the dough is well mixed. Beat the dough 100 strokes.

4. Stir in the wheat germ. Then stir in just enough flour to make a soft dough.

5. Scrape the dough out of the bowl onto a floured board and knead it until it is smooth and springy, about 10 minutes. Add more flour if the dough feels wet. Try to avoid tearing the dough as you knead. This is a soft, sticky dough.

6. Place the dough in a large buttered bowl and brush the surface with melted butter. Cover the bowl with a cloth and let the dough rise in a warm, draft-free place until it is double in bulk, about 1½ hours.

7. Punch down the dough and knead it briefly in the bowl or on a lightly floured board to press out all the air. Return the dough to the bowl, brush it with melted butter, cover with a cloth and let it rise again until double in bulk, about 1 hour.

8. Punch down the dough on a lightly floured board. Knead in the cheese. If the dough is too stiff to in-

corporate the cheese, let it rest, covered with a cloth or bowl, for about 10 minutes. This will relax the gluten in the dough and make it easier for you to incorporate the cheese. Try to prevent tearing the dough as you knead. Chill the dough in a bowl in the refrigerator, if necessary, to make the dough firm enough to handle.

9. Divide the dough in half and round it into two balls. Let the dough rest, covered with a cloth, for about 10 minutes.

10. Butter two 6-cup fluted brioche tins or saucepans with ovenproof handles.

11. To shape the brioche, cut off about ⅙ of one portion of dough and round it into a ball. Form the remainder into a round loaf and place it in the buttered tin. Roll the small ball of dough into a cone shape. Cut a small, deep "X" in the loaf with a knife or scissors, and place the pointed end of the cone in the hole.

To make small, individual brioches, divide the dough into 20 portions. Shape them as for the large brioche, and place in buttered half-cup fluted brioche tins, muffin tins, or custard cups. Repeat this step with the second portion of the dough.

12. Brush the surface of the dough with melted butter, cover with a cloth, and let rise until double in bulk, about 1 hour.

13. Heat the oven to 375°.

14. In a cup beat together the egg yolk and 1 tablespoon water. Brush the surface of the dough with this glaze.

15. Bake the brioches until the crusts are brown and the bottoms sound hollow when tapped, about 35 minutes for the large brioches, and about 15 minutes for the small brioches. Remove the breads from the tins immediately, and let them cool on wire racks. Serve warm.

Fruited Sweet Bread

2 LOAVES EACH WITH ABOUT 74 GRAMS USABLE PROTEIN

This is a half whole wheat half white wheat version of traditional fruited Christmas breads such as German stollen *or Italian* panettone. *Fill with any variety of fruits and nuts.*

½ cup milk
½ cup butter
⅔ cup honey
1 teaspoon salt
1 teaspoon almond extract
2 tablespoons rum
2 tablespoons yeast
½ cup warm water
5 eggs
About 2 cups unbleached white wheat flour

2 cups whole wheat flour (preferably hard wheat or bread flour)
2 cups wheat germ
¾ cup chopped candied ginger
½ cup diced citron
1 cup raisins
2 cups sliced almonds
Melted butter

1. Warm the milk in a saucepan until small bubbles form around the rim of the pan. Remove the pan from the heat and add the butter, honey, salt, almond extract, and rum. Stir until the butter melts and the honey dissolves. Transfer to a large bowl and let cool to wrist temperature.

2. In the cup in which the honey was measured, dissolve the yeast in the water. Let the yeast stand until bubbly, about 5 minutes.

3. When the milk mixture has cooled, add to it the dissolved yeast, eggs, 1 cup of the white wheat, and 1 cup of the whole wheat flours. Stir with a wooden spoon or rubber spatula until the dough is well mixed. Beat the dough 100 strokes.

4. Toast the wheat germ in a frying pan over low heat until brown, about 5 minutes. Stir frequently to prevent burning.

5. Stir in the remaining 1 cup of whole wheat flour and the toasted wheat germ and then stir in just enough white wheat flour to make a soft dough.

6. Scrape the dough out of the bowl onto a floured board and knead it until it is smooth, springy, and no longer sticky, about 10 minutes. Add more flour if the dough feels wet. Try to avoid tearing the dough as you knead. This is a firm, pliable dough.

7. Place the dough in a large buttered bowl and brush the surface with melted butter. Cover the bowl with a cloth and let the dough rise in a warm, draft-free place until it is double in bulk, about 1½ hours.

8. Punch down the dough and knead it in the bowl or on a lightly floured board to press out all the air. Return the dough to the bowl, brush the surface with melted butter, cover with a cloth, and let it rise again until double in bulk, about 1 hour.

9. In a small bowl, mix together the fruit with the 1½ cups of the sliced almonds. Punch down the dough and knead in the fruit and nuts on a lightly floured board. If the dough is too stiff to incorporate the fruit and nuts, let it rest, covered with a cloth or bowl, for about 10 minutes. This will relax the gluten in the dough and make it easier for you to incorporate them. It may take several kneading and resting periods to incorporate and distribute all the fruit and nuts evenly.

10. Divide the dough in half and round each piece of dough into a smooth ball. Let the dough rest, covered with a cloth, for about 10 minutes.

11. Butter 2 baking sheets.

12. To shape the loaves, pat each portion of dough into a 1-inch thick round and fold it in half. Place each semicircle on a baking sheet.

If you prefer round loaves, shape each portion of dough into a sphere and place in a buttered 5-cup charlotte mold, saucepan with an ovenproof handle, or 2-pound coffee can.

13. Brush the surface of the dough with melted butter, sprinkle the remaining ½ cup of almonds over the

tops of both breads, cover with a cloth, and let the breads rise until almost double in bulk, about 45 minutes.

14. Heat the oven to 350°. Bake the breads until the crusts are brown and the bottoms sound hollow when tapped, about 1 hour and 10 minutes. Remove the breads from the baking sheets immediately and let cool on wire racks. Serve warm.

Yeast-raised Peanut Doughnuts

ABOUT 2 DOZEN DOUGHNUTS EACH WITH ABOUT 5 GRAMS USABLE PROTEIN

For variety use any nuts in place of peanuts, and decorate the doughnuts with coconut or cinnamon-sugar.

1 cup buttermilk	3 tablespoons soy flour
1 tablespoon butter	1 teaspoon mace
½ cup honey	2 cups whole wheat
1 tablespoon molasses	flour (preferably soft
1 teaspoon salt	wheat or pastry flour)
2 tablespoons yeast	1¼ cups peanuts
½ cup warm water	½ cup wheat germ
2 eggs	1 quart oil (for frying)
1 egg yolk	¼ cup honey
About 2 cups unbleached	Melted butter
white wheat flour	

1. Warm the buttermilk in a saucepan until small bubbles form around the rim of the pan. Remove the pan from the heat and add the butter, honey, molasses, and salt. Stir until the butter melts and the honey and molasses dissolve. Transfer to a large bowl and let cool to wrist temperature.

2. In the cup in which the honey was measured, dissolve the yeast in the water. Let the yeast stand until bubbly, about 5 minutes.

3. When the milk mixture has cooled, add to it the dissolved yeast, eggs, egg yolk, and 1½ cups of the white wheat flour. Stir with a wooden spoon or rubber spatula until the dough is well mixed. Beat the dough 100 strokes.

4. In a small bowl sift together the soy flour, mace, and 1 cup of the soft whole wheat flour. Add to the bowl any particles that did not go through the sifter. The sifting is to distribute the soy flour and mace evenly. Stir these sifted ingredients into the dough in the large bowl.

5. Grind ¾ cup of the peanuts to a coarse powder in a blender. Without a blender either chop the nuts fine with a knife or place the nuts in a plastic bag or between two sheets of waxed paper, and roll into a powder with a rolling pin.

6. Stir the nuts, wheat germ, and the remaining 1 cup of whole wheat flour into the dough. Then stir in just enough white wheat flour to make a soft dough.

7. Scrape the dough out of the bowl onto a floured board and knead it until it is smooth, springy, and no longer sticky, about 10 minutes. Add more flour if the dough feels wet. Try to avoid tearing the dough as you knead.

8. Place the dough in a large buttered bowl and brush the surface with melted butter. Cover the bowl with a cloth and let the dough rise in a warm, draft-free place until it is double in bulk, about 1½ hours.

9. Punch down the dough and knead it briefly in the bowl or on a lightly floured board to press out all the air. Return the dough to the bowl, brush the surface with melted butter, cover, and let it rise again until double in bulk, about 1 hour.

10. Punch the dough down, knead it briefly on a lightly floured board, and round it into a ball. Let it rest, covered with a cloth, for about 10 minutes.

11. In a 2- or 3-quart kettle or deep fat dryer, heat 1 quart of oil slowly to 370°. Without a thermometer, test the oil temperature by frying a 1-inch

cube of bread. It should take 1 minute to become brown.

12. Pat or roll the dough out on a lightly floured board to about ½-inch thickness. Cut doughnut shapes with a floured doughnut cutter, or improvise a cutter using floured glasses, bottle caps, or tin cans. The doughnuts should be about 3½ inches across with a 1-inch hole. I find that the lids from widemouthed canning jars are a good size for the outer circle.

When all the cuts have been made, gather the scraps of dough, knead them briefly, and let them rest, covered with a cloth, for about 10 minutes. Pat and then cut more doughnuts from the scraps.

13. Fry 3 or 4 doughnuts and holes until brown on one side, about 1 minute. Turn and fry until brown on the other side, about ½ minute. Fry as many doughnuts as will fit into the kettle without crowding. Scoop the doughnuts out of the oil with a slotted spoon or fork. Let the oil return to the high temperature before frying the next doughnut batch. Drain and cool the doughnuts on paper towels.

14. Chop the remaining ½ cup of peanuts coarse. Dip one side of each doughnut in honey and then press the honeyed surface into the bowl of chopped peanuts. Serve the doughnuts warm.

Quick Breads

GENERAL INSTRUCTIONS

Quick breads, such as fruit and nut loaves and muffins, are sweet crumbly-textured breads made with leavening that rises more quickly than yeast—baking powder, baking soda, or eggs. To produce the crumbly texture, quick breads are baked with pastry or soft wheat flour, which is low in gluten. Non-wheat whole-grain flour and bean flours make good quick bread ingredients because they are low in gluten and therefore crumbly by nature. Begin with all ingredients at room temperature. To obtain a light texture that is not chewy, do not overmix the batter. Any quick bread batter will make fine muffins.

BASIC MIXING TECHNIQUES

Quick breads are usually more moist and heavier than cakes, but the mixing techniques are similar.

Creaming the Shortening with the Sweetener

Warm all ingredients to room temperature; the mixing will be faster and will make more small air pockets, which help to raise the bread to an even grain and smooth texture. However, when you warm the shortening to room temperature, make sure that it does not melt and become oily.

Beat the shortening with a fork or rotary beater until it is creamy and light colored. Gradually add the sweetener, continuing to beat the mixture well. Bakers call this the "cream."

Beating Egg Whites

Warm the eggs to room temperature. Separate the egg whites carefully from the yolks, and place the whites in a large, clean, deep bowl. Moisture, grease, or egg yolk in the bowl will prevent the whites from whipping. Begin beating the whites slowly with a large wire whisk, fork, or rotary beater. After about a half minute, when the whites are foamy, add a pinch of cream of tartar (if you have it), which is an acid that strengthens the egg protein so that it can hold a little more air. Beat the eggs faster until white peaks form. The egg whites should stand by themselves, with gracefully curled peaks.

Folding In the Egg Whites

Folding is a gentle scooping and stirring motion that mixes whipped ingredients into a batter without deflating the air.

Slide the egg whites onto the top of the batter.

Use a large spoon, a rubber spatula, or your hand in a slow, down, across the bottom, up and over the top motion. Stir gently, until the egg whites are all mixed in but not deflated.

METHODS FOR MIXING QUICK BREADS

The Cake Method

Cream the shortening and sweetener in a large bowl.

Add the eggs. For fruit and nut loaves, add whole beaten eggs, one at a time. For a cakier texture add only the yolks and reserve the whites. Mix in each egg thoroughly to give the mixture time to absorb the moisture. The moisture from the eggs becomes coated with the sweetener-shortening blend, creating a mixture of small liquid bubbles in a film of fat. If the eggs are added too quickly, or too many eggs are added, the fat-coated moisture bubbles will burst and the mixture will curdle—separate into water and oily parts. To prevent this, add a tablespoon or two of flour before you add the eggs—soy flour is particularly good.

Combine the flour with the other dry ingredients—baking powder, baking soda, salt, spices, sugar, dry milk—in a small bowl. *Sift* the dry ingredients if you wish. Sifting makes a bread lighter because it separates the flour particles with air; it also insures that the ingredients are well mixed. Sifting is not, however, a necessary step. If you do sift, the large particles of bran and germ can be returned to the batter. More siftings make a finer batter. Stir in any dry ingredients that are not sifted such as wheat germ or chopped nuts.

Add moist ingredients—fruit and liquids—alternately with the dry ingredients to the sweetener-shortening-egg mixture in the large bowl. Mixing with a wooden spoon or rubber spatula, add a third of the dry ingredients, then a third of the wet ingredients, alternating until the batter is thoroughly mixed. Begin and end with dry ingredients. This prevents curdling and lumps. Mix the batter only until all the dry ingredients are stirred in. Do not overmix.

For a light cakelike bread, now add stiffly beaten egg whites reserved when the yolks were added. Stir them gently into the batter. For cake batters, which are often thinner than quick bread batters, beat well with a rotary beater.

The Muffin Method

This method is generally used for plain, not-so-rich quick breads, such as cornbread.

Combine the dry ingredients—flour, baking powder, baking soda, salt, spices, sugar, dry milk—in a large bowl. Sift them if you wish and add to the bowl any particles that did not go through the sifter.

Combine the eggs, liquids, and melted, cooled shortening in a small bowl.

Mix the wet and the dry ingredients all at once. Stir with a wooden spoon or rubber spatula only until all the ingredients are moistened. The batter will look lumpy; let it rest a minute to thicken.

FOR BOTH THE CAKE METHOD AND THE MUFFIN METHOD

Prepare the pans. Butter the pans or muffin tins with unsalted shortening. Dust flour on the bottom of the buttered pan to act as a buffer to keep the bread from sticking during and after baking. Or cut a piece of waxed paper to fit the bottom of the pan and brush melted butter over the waxed paper.

Heat the oven to 350°. Most quick breads and cakes bake at 350°. If the recipe contains ingredients that tend to burn, heat the oven to 325°.

Heat the oven before you put the bread or cake in, to encourage the moisture in a bread to turn to steam, which helps breads to rise.

Pour the batter into the pans and fill two-thirds full. For cake batters fill the pans half full; they are lighter and will rise higher than quick breads.

Bake the breads. Place the loaves near the center of the oven and, if possible, all on the same shelf. There should be an inch or two of space between the loaves, and between the pans and the oven walls, so that heat can circulate. If the breads are on more than one shelf, stagger the pans so that they do not interfere with each other's heat.

Try not to peek at the bread until after it has risen and until it has a light brown color—about two-thirds of the total time. With cakes it is even more important to wait: a sudden rush of cold air into the oven can cause a cake to fall.

To test the breads for "doneness," gently press the surface of the bread in the center. If it is still wet and your fingerprint remains, the bread is not baked. If the bread springs back, leaving little or no fingerprint, the bread is done. Another test is to insert a toothpick, a clean broom straw, or a very thin knife into the center of the bread. If it comes out with no batter sticking to it, the bread is done. Also, expect the bread to shrink slightly from the sides of the pan. Loaves should bake in about 1 hour, muffins in about 20 minutes. The time will vary according to the pan, the size of the bread, and the ingredients. Dense, heavy breads with many fruit and nuts will take longer to bake than plain breads.

Cool quick breads in the pan on a wire rack or on a burner of the stove so that air can circulate. During this time the bread is still baking in the hot pan. Let the bread cool in the pan until it can be comfortably held in your hand. Then take the bread out of the pan and cool it right-side-up on a wire rack. If it sticks to the sides of the pan, loosen it with a knife. Do not tug at the bread; quick breads, especially when they are warm, are very fragile. As the bread cools, the texture becomes firm enough to support its own weight. The deep center crack in quick breads that are heavy in fruit and nuts is natural. Serve warm or at room temperature.

To store. Many quick breads taste better if they are stored for a day or more. This is particularly true of breads that are rich in fruit, yogurt, buttermilk, or nuts. After maturing, the flavor is more mellow and the loaf slices more easily. Loaves should be thoroughly cooled and wrapped in aluminum foil or plastic wrap to ripen. Breads age more slowly in the refrigerator, faster at room temperature.

Try not to serve breads directly from the refrigerator; the texture will be grainy and gritty. Either warm to room temperature or reheat in the oven.

To reheat quick breads or muffins, wrap them in aluminum foil and heat in a 350° oven for about 15 minutes for loaves and about 5 minutes for muffins.

FREEZING QUICK BREADS

Unbaked Batter

Batter will freeze well only if double-acting baking powder has been used. Wrap the bowl or pan in plastic wrap, tie securely, and freeze. When ready to bake, thaw overnight in the refrigerator.

Baked Breads

Freezing seems to dry and tighten the grain of baked quick breads, except for very fruity loaves which ripen in the freezer. Breads that are rich in shortening seem to survive freezing best. Wrap cooled quick breads in plastic bags, tie securely, and set on a flat shelf. Thaw the breads at room temperature or in the refrigerator. To reheat directly from the freezer, wrap the breads in aluminum foil and leave one end open for moisture to escape so the bread does not get soggy. Heat at 350° for about 25 minutes.

RECIPES

Banana Bread

1 LOAF WITH ABOUT 43 GRAMS USABLE PROTEIN

This is a smooth, moist, cakelike bread. Make it partially or totally with white wheat flour for a delicate crumb; with whole wheat flour for a more coarse crumb. Try other mashed fruits to replace the bananas —like apricots, for instance. For a crunchy texture, add grated coconut or chopped nuts.

½ cup butter
1¼ cups brown sugar
⅔ cup whole wheat flour (preferably soft wheat or pastry flour)
⅔ cup unbleached white wheat flour
½ teaspoon salt

½ cup wheat germ
2 eggs
1 teaspoon baking soda
⅓ cup yogurt
1 cup mashed overripe bananas, about 2 bananas

1. Heat the oven to 350°. Butter a medium-size loaf pan.

2. In a large bowl beat the butter with a fork or rotary beater until it is creamy. Gradually add the sugar.

3. In a small bowl sift together the whole wheat flour, white wheat flour, and salt. Add to the bowl any particles that did not go through the sifter. Stir in the wheat germ.

4. Add about two tablespoons of the dry ingredients to the butter mixture, then beat in the eggs one at a time, beating well after each one.

5. In a cup dissolve the baking soda in the yogurt. When it begins to foam add to the butter mixture in the large bowl.

6. With a wooden spoon or rubber spatula stir in the dry ingredients alternately with the bananas. Mix well.

7. Pour the batter into the loaf pan. Bake the bread until the center springs back when gently pressed or a toothpick or broom straw inserted in the center comes out clean, about 1 hour. Do not mistake pieces of mashed banana for unbaked dough. Cool the bread in the pan on a wire rack.

The flavor of this bread ripens and improves after 1 or 2 days.

Chocolate Applesauce Spice Bread

1 LOAF WITH ABOUT 54 GRAMS USABLE PROTEIN

This is dark, sweet, and compact bread. It is moist, particularly if made with chunky or homemade applesauce. If sweetened applesauce is used, reduce the amount of sugar. The recipe is based on the Cornell Triple-Rich formula. (See page 69.)

6 tablespoons butter
1¼ cups brown sugar
2 tablespoons soy flour
2 eggs
1¼ cups unbleached white wheat flour
¼ teaspoon salt
2 tablespoons milk powder
1 teaspoon baking soda
1½ tablespoons cocoa
½ teaspoon ground cinnamon
¼ teaspoon ground nutmeg
¼ teaspoon ground allspice
2 tablespoons wheat germ
½ cup walnuts
1 cup unsweetened applesauce
½ cup raisins
1 tablespoon unbleached white wheat flour
1 tablespoon cognac

1. Heat the oven to 350°. Butter a medium-size loaf pan.

2. In a large bowl beat the butter with a fork or rotary beater until it is creamy. Gradually add the

sugar. Sift in the soy flour. Mix well to make sure that no lumps of soy flour remain. Beat in the eggs one at a time, beating well after each one.

3. In a small bowl sift together the white wheat flour, salt, milk powder, baking soda, cocoa, and spices. Stir in the wheat germ.

4. Chop the nuts coarse and set them aside. With a wooden spoon or rubber spatula stir the dry ingredients alternately with the applesauce into the butter mixture in the large bowl. Chunky or homemade applesauce with pieces of apple left in it gives the bread a very moist texture.

5. Stir in the chopped nuts.

6. In a small bowl toss the raisins in the 1 tablespoon white wheat flour and mix them into the batter. Add the cognac and mix well.

7. Pour the batter into the loaf pan and bake until the center springs back when gently pressed or a toothpick or broom straw inserted in the center comes out clean, about 50 minutes. Cool the bread in the pan on a wire rack.

Whole Wheat Gingerbread

1 BREAD WITH TOPPING WITH ABOUT 60 GRAMS USABLE PROTEIN

This is a strong, flavorful gingerbread served with a dollop of meringue.

¼ cup butter	1½ teaspoons baking soda
⅓ cup molasses	1½ teaspoons ground ginger
⅓ cup brown sugar	or a 2-inch slice of
¼ cup soy flour	fresh ginger root
1 egg	1½ teaspoons ground
2 cups whole wheat flour	cinnamon
(preferably soft wheat	¼ cup wheat germ
or pastry flour)	¾ cup buttermilk

1. Heat the oven to 350°. Butter an 8-inch square pan.

2. In a large bowl beat the butter with a fork or rotary beater until it is creamy. Gradually add the molasses and sugar. Sift in the soy flour. Mix well to make sure that no lumps of soy flour remain. Beat in the egg. Beat well.

3. In a small bowl sift together the flour, baking soda, and spices. If fresh ginger root is used squeeze in a garlic press to extract the juice and stir the juice into the butter mixture. Add to the bowl any particles that did not go through the sifter. Stir in the wheat germ.

4. With a wooden spoon or rubber spatula stir the dry ingredients alternately with the buttermilk into the butter mixture in the large bowl. Mix well.

5. Pour the batter into the pan. Bake the bread until the center springs back when gently pressed or a toothpick or broom straw inserted in the center comes out clean, about 30 minutes. Cool the bread in the pan on a wire rack.

TOPPING

3 egg whites   ¼ teaspoon vanilla extract
3 tablespoons honey

In a large bowl beat the egg whites with a wire whisk or rotary beater until they are stiff. Gently fold in the honey and vanilla extract, trying not to deflate the eggs. Serve a square of gingerbread with a dollop of meringue on top.

Date Nut Bread

1 LOAF WITH ABOUT 46 GRAMS USABLE PROTEIN

This is a dark, rich breakfast or dessert bread with softened pieces of dates and raisins in each slice. I like to bake it in 1-pound coffee cans so it will slice into thick circles or half-moons. If served with cottage or ricotta cheese, the protein value is almost doubled.

1 cup dates
½ cup nuts
1 cup boiling water
½ cup raisins
¾ cup brown sugar
1 teaspoon baking soda
2 tablespoons butter

1 egg
½ cup whole wheat flour (preferably soft wheat or pastry flour)
½ cup unbleached white wheat flour
¾ cup wheat germ

1. Heat the oven to 350°. Butter a 1-pound coffee can or medium-size loaf pan. Chop the dates and nuts coarse.

2. In a large bowl pour the boiling water over the dates, nuts, raisins, sugar, baking soda, and butter, and stir. Let it cool to room temperature and stir in the egg.

3. In a small bowl sift together the whole wheat flour and white wheat flour. Add to the bowl any particles that did not go through the sifter. Stir in the wheat germ.

4. With a wooden spoon or rubber spatula stir the dry ingredients into the date-nut mixture in the large bowl. Mix well.

5. Pour the batter into the coffee can or loaf pan.

Bake the bread until the center springs back when gently pressed or a toothpick or broom straw inserted in the center comes out clean, about 45 minutes. Cool the bread in the pan on a wire rack.

Lemon Bread

1 BREAD WITH ABOUT 52 GRAMS USABLE PROTEIN

A delicate, crumbly breakfast or dessert bread.

6 tablespoons butter	½ cup wheat germ
1 cup brown sugar	⅓ cup nuts
1¼ cups whole wheat flour (preferably soft wheat or pastry flour)	2 eggs
	Rind of one lemon
1½ teaspoons baking powder	¼ cup milk
	Juice of 1 lemon
¼ teaspoon salt	¼ cup brown sugar

1. Heat the oven to 350°. Butter an 8-inch square pan. This bread will not bake thoroughly if a loaf pan is used.

2. In a large bowl beat the butter with a fork or rotary beater until it is creamy. Gradually add the sugar.

3. In a small bowl sift together the flour, baking powder, and salt. Add to the bowl any particles that did not go through the sifter. Stir in the wheat germ.

4. Grind the nuts to a coarse powder in a blender. Without a blender either chop the nuts fine with a knife, or place the nuts in a plastic bag or between two sheets of waxed paper and roll into a powder with a rolling pin. Stir the nuts into the sifted ingredients.

5. Add about 2 tablespoons of the dry ingredients to the butter mixture. Beat in the eggs, one at a time, beating well after each one. Grate the lemon rind and stir it in.

6. With a wooden spoon or rubber spatula stir the dry ingredients alternately with the milk into the butter mixture in the large bowl. Mix well.

7. Pour the batter into the pan. Bake the bread until the center springs back when gently pressed or a toothpick or broom straw inserted in the center comes out clean, about 40 minutes.

8. To make the glaze, in a cup dissolve the sugar in the lemon juice. When the bread is finished and you take it from the oven, prick the surface gently with a fork. Pour the glaze over the bread. Let the bread cool in the pan on a wire rack.

Peanut Bread

1 LOAF WITH ABOUT 67 GRAMS USABLE PROTEIN

This cake/bread has a sweet molasses taste with chunky peanuts on the outside and peanut flour on the inside. The peanut flour is easily made at home from whole peanuts.

PEANUT TOPPING

⅜ cup peanuts	1½ tablespoons honey
3 tablespoons butter	1½ tablespoons molasses

1. Chop the peanuts coarse and set them aside. In a large bowl beat the butter with a fork or rotary beater until it is creamy. Gradually add the honey and

molasses. Spread this mixture on the inside of a small-size loaf pan, and sprinkle the peanuts on the bottom and sides.

BATTER

¼ cup butter	¾ teaspoon ground cinnamon
2 tablespoons honey	
½ cup brown sugar	¼ teaspoon ground ginger or a ½-inch slice of fresh ginger root
3 tablespoons soy flour	
2 eggs	
1¼ cups whole wheat flour (preferably soft wheat or pastry flour)	⅜ cup wheat germ
	3 tablespoons peanuts
	¼ teaspoon baking soda
⅛ teaspoon salt	¾ cup buttermilk
1½ teaspoons baking powder	

2. Heat the oven to 350°.

3. In the bowl that was used to prepare the peanut topping (it is not necessary to wash it), beat the butter with a fork or rotary beater until creamy. Gradually add the honey and brown sugar. Sift in the soy flour. Mix well to make sure that no lumps of soy flour remain. Beat in the eggs, one at a time, beating well after each one.

4. In a small bowl sift together the whole wheat flour, salt, baking powder, and spices. If fresh ginger root is used, squeeze in a garlic press to extract the juice. Stir the juice into the butter mixture. Add to the bowl any particles that did not go through the sifter. Stir in the wheat germ.

5. Grind the peanuts to a coarse powder in a blender. Without a blender either chop the nuts fine with a knife, or place the nuts in a plastic bag or between two sheets of waxed paper and roll into a powder with a rolling pin. Stir the nuts into the sifted ingredients.

6. In a cup dissolve the baking soda in the buttermilk. With a wooden spoon or rubber spatula stir the

dry ingredients alternately with the buttermilk mixture into the butter mixture in the large bowl. Mix well.

7. Pour the batter into the loaf pan that was coated with the peanut topping. Bake the bread until the center springs back when gently pressed or a toothpick or broom straw inserted in the center comes out clean, about 1 hour. Set the pan on a wire rack for about 2 minutes, then invert the bread onto the rack to cool.

Persimmon Bread

1 LOAF WITH ABOUT 52 GRAMS USABLE PROTEIN

Persimmons are smooth, orange, heart-shaped fruits that should only be eaten when fully ripened and soft. They are my favorite fruit. This bread brings out their sweet, almost nutlike taste.

½ cup oil (preferably corn, cottonseed, or safflower)
½ cup brown sugar
2 tablespoons soy flour
2 eggs
2 cups whole wheat flour (preferably soft wheat or pastry flour)
¼ teaspoon salt
1½ teaspoons baking powder
½ teaspoon baking soda
½ cup wheat germ
1 cup persimmon pulp, about 2 persimmons

1. Heat the oven to 350°. Oil a medium-size loaf pan.

2. In a large bowl beat together the oil and sugar with a fork or rotary beater. Sift in the soy flour. Mix well to make sure that no lumps remain. Beat in the eggs one at a time, beating well after each one.

3. In a small bowl sift together the whole wheat flour, salt, baking powder, and baking soda. Add to the bowl any particles that did not go through the sifter. Stir in the wheat germ. For a soft, wet, fruitier loaf use only 1½ cups of flour.

4. Peel and pit the persimmons. Force the pulp through a sieve. With a wooden spoon or rubber spatula

stir the dry ingredients alternately with the persimmon pulp into the oil mixture in the large bowl.

5. Pour the batter into the loaf pan. Bake the bread until the center springs back when gently pressed or a toothpick or broom straw inserted in the center comes out clean, about 45 minutes. Cool the bread in the pan on a wire rack.

Buttermilk-Sesame Seed Corn Bread

1 LOAF WITH ABOUT 84 GRAMS USABLE PROTEIN

This is a moist corn bread.

½ cup sesame seeds
1 cup wheat germ
3 eggs
2 cups buttermilk
⅓ cup brown sugar
⅔ cup oil (preferably corn, cottonseed, or safflower)

½ cup unbleached white wheat flour
1¼ teaspoons baking soda
1 teaspoon salt
2 cups cornmeal

1. Heat the oven to 375°. Oil a 9-inch square pan.

2. Toast the sesame seeds and wheat germ together in a frying pan over low heat until they are brown, about 5 minutes. Stir frequently to prevent burning. Set aside.

3. In a large bowl beat together the eggs, buttermilk, sugar, and oil with a fork or rotary beater.

4. In a small bowl sift together the flour, baking soda, and salt. Stir in the sesame seed–wheat germ mixture and the cornmeal.

5. With a wooden spoon or rubber spatula stir the dry ingredients into the liquid ingredients in the large bowl. Mix well.

6. Pour the batter into the loaf pan. Bake the bread until the center springs back when gently pressed or a

toothpick or broom straw inserted in the center comes out clean, about 55 minutes. Cool the bread in the pan on a wire rack. Serve warm.

Walnut Barley Bread

1 LOAF WITH ABOUT 78 GRAMS USABLE PROTEIN

This bread is sweet and crumbly. Any low-gluten flour—millet, oat, rice, for instance—can be substituted for barley; any nut can be substituted for walnuts.

½ cup oil (preferably corn, cottonseed, or safflower)	¼ teaspoon salt
⅓ cup honey	1½ teaspoons baking powder
½ cup brown sugar	¼ teaspoon baking soda
1¼ cups barley flour	1½ cups walnuts
3 eggs	½ cup wheat germ

1. Heat the oven to 350°. Oil an 8-inch square pan. This bread will not bake thoroughly if a loaf pan is used.

2. In a large bowl beat together the oil, honey, and sugar with a fork or rotary beater. Sift in ¼ cup of the flour and mix well to make sure that no lumps remain. Beat in the eggs, one at a time, beating well after each one.

3. In a small bowl sift together the remaining 1 cup of flour, salt, baking powder, and baking soda.

4. Grind half the nuts to a coarse powder in a blender. Without a blender either chop the nuts fine with a knife, or place the nuts in a plastic bag or between two sheets of waxed paper and roll into a powder with a rolling pin. Stir the powdered nuts and the wheat germ into the sifted ingredients. Chop the other half of the nuts coarse with a knife or chopper and set aside.

5. With a wooden spoon or rubber spatula stir the dry ingredients into the butter mixture. Stir in the chopped nuts. Mix well.

6. Pour the batter into the pan. Bake the bread until the center springs back when gently pressed or a toothpick or broom straw inserted in the center comes out clean, about 40 minutes. Cool the bread in the pan on a wire rack.

Carob or Chocolate Brownies

ABOUT A DOZEN BROWNIES EACH WITH ABOUT 6 GRAMS USABLE PROTEIN

These brownies are rich, compact, and sweet.

1 cup carob or cocoa	⅔ cup whole wheat flour
1 cup butter	(preferably soft wheat or
1 cup brown sugar	pastry flour)
⅔ cup honey	A pinch of salt
1 teaspoon vanilla	½ cup wheat germ
2 eggs	1 cup nuts

1. Heat the oven to 350°. Butter an 8-inch square pan for cakelike brownies, or a larger pan for thinner, crispier, cookielike brownies.

2. If carob is used, toast it in a frying pan over low heat until dark brown, about 5 minutes. Stir frequently to prevent burning.

3. Melt the butter. In a large bowl beat together the carob or cocoa and melted butter with a fork or rotary beater. Gradually beat in the sugar, honey, and vanilla. Beat in the eggs, one at a time, beating well after each one.

4. In a small bowl sift together the flour and salt. Toast the wheat germ in a frying pan over low heat until brown, about 5 minutes. Stir frequently to prevent burning. Stir the wheat germ into the sifted ingredients. Chop the nuts coarse and set them aside.

5. With a wooden spoon or rubber spatula stir the dry ingredients into the butter mixture in the large bowl. Stir in the nuts. Mix well.

6. Pour the batter into the pan. Bake the brownies until the center is firm and a toothpick or broom straw inserted in the center comes out clean, about 35 minutes for the 8-inch square pan, less time for a larger pan. Cool the brownies in the pan on a wire rack.

Johnny Cake

1 CAKE WITH ABOUT 69 GRAMS USABLE PROTEIN

This was the "journey cake" of the early American travelers. When baked in a heavy, hot frying pan, it has a crisp crust and crumbly inner texture.

1 cup milk
⅓ cup honey
¼ cup butter
½ cup milk powder
1 cup cornmeal
3 eggs

1 cup whole wheat flour (preferably hard wheat flour or bread flour)
2 tablespoons baking powder
¾ teaspoon salt
½ cup wheat germ
1 tablespoon butter

1. Heat the oven to 425°.
2. Warm the milk in a saucepan until small bubbles form around the rim of the pan. Remove it from the heat and add the honey, butter, milk powder, and cornmeal. Stir until the butter melts and the honey dissolves. Make sure no lumps of milk powder remain. Transfer to a large bowl and let cool to wrist temperature.
3. When the milk mixture has cooled, beat in the eggs with a fork or rotary beater.
4. In a small bowl sift together the flour, baking powder, and salt. Add to the bowl any particles that did not go through the sifter. Stir in the wheat germ.
5. Butter an 8-inch square pan or put 1 tablespoon of butter into an 8-inch cast-iron frying pan. Place the

frying pan in the oven until the butter melts and the pan is hot. Brush the butter around the bottom and sides.

6. With a wooden spoon or rubber spatula stir the dry ingredients into the liquid ingredients in the large bowl. Mix just enough to moisten.

7. Pour the batter into the pan. Bake until the bread is crisp and firm, or a toothpick or broom straw inserted in the center comes out clean, about 25 minutes. Serve hot with honey or jam.

Yogurt Coffee Cake

1 CAKE WITH ABOUT 72 GRAMS USABLE PROTEIN

This is a moist breakfast or dessert cake.

⅓ cup butter	3 eggs
1¼ cups brown sugar	1 teaspoon baking soda
2 cups unbleached white wheat flour	1½ cups yogurt

1. Heat the oven to 325°. Butter an 8-inch square pan.

2. In a large bowl beat the butter with a fork or rotary beater until it is creamy. Gradually add the sugar. Sift in ¼ cup of the flour and mix well to make sure that no lumps remain. Separate the eggs. Reserve the whites and beat in the egg yolks. Beat well.

3. In a small bowl sift together the remaining 1¾ cups flour and the baking soda.

4. With a wooden spoon or rubber spatula stir the dry ingredients alternately with the yogurt into the butter mixture in the large bowl. Mix well.

5. In a large bowl beat the egg whites with a rotary beater or wire whisk until they are stiff. With a large spoon or rubber spatula stir them gently into the batter.

TOPPING

¾ cup pecans	2 teaspoons ground
½ cup wheat germ	cinnamon
½ cup brown sugar	

6. Chop the nuts coarse. Toast the nuts and wheat germ in a frying pan over a low heat until brown, about 5 minutes. Stir frequently to prevent burning. Remove the pan from the heat and stir in the sugar and cinnamon.

7. Pour the batter into the pan and sprinkle the topping over the batter. With a spoon or fork, draw swirls and lines in the batter to streak the topping into the cake.

8. Bake until the center springs back when gently pressed or a toothpick or broom straw inserted in the center comes out clean, about one hour. If the topping begins to darken, cover the pan with aluminum foil. Cool the cake in the pan on a wire rack. Serve warm or at room temperature.

Dark Brown Irish Soda Bread

1 LOAF WITH ABOUT 44 GRAMS USABLE PROTEIN

This is a part whole wheat, part white wheat version of an Irish soda bread. It slices most easily when it has matured for at least 6 hours; so plan accordingly.

1 cup buttermilk	1 cup whole wheat flour
2 tablespoons honey	(preferably soft wheat or
3 tablespoons oil	pastry flour)
2 teaspoons caraway seeds	1¼ cups unbleached white
or 1½ teaspoons ground	wheat flour
caraway seeds	1½ teaspoons baking soda
A 1-inch by 2-inch piece of	½ teaspoon salt
orange rind or	½ cup wheat germ
2 teaspoons grated	½ cup currants
orange rind	

1. Heat the oven to 350°. Oil a baking sheet.

2. In a blender combine the buttermilk, honey, oil, caraway seeds, and orange rind. Blend until the caraway seeds and orange rind are finely ground. Without a blender either use commercially ground caraway seeds and grated orange rind, or grind the caraway seeds in a coffee grinder, spice mill, or with a pestle. (If the seeds are used whole the bread will still be palatable, but the caraway seeds will be more obvious.) Then grate the orange rind and combine with the seeds, buttermilk, oil, and honey in a small bowl. Beat with a fork or rotary beater.

3. In a large bowl sift together the whole wheat flour, the white wheat flour, baking soda, and salt. Add to the bowl any particles that did not go through the sifter. Stir in the wheat germ and currants.

4. With a wooden spoon or rubber spatula stir the liquid ingredients into the dry ingredients in the large bowl. Mix well with the spoon or spatula and then continue mixing in the bowl by hand with a pulling or kneading motion. The dough will be very wet.

5. Scrape the dough off your hands and coat them with flour. Shape the dough into a ball and place on the baking sheet. Dip a sharp knife in flour and make a large cross on the surface of the loaf. Bake the bread until the crust is brown and the loaf feels firm to the touch, about 45 minutes. Remove the bread from the pan and wrap in a kitchen towel. Let the loaf cool and rest for at least 6 hours before slicing.

Steamed Brown Bread

4 SMALL LOAVES EACH WITH ABOUT 17 GRAMS
USABLE PROTEIN

Fruited, moist, and rich, this bread is made from the traditional rye, corn, and wheat formula and steamed in 16-ounce tin cans.

2 tablespoons butter
2 eggs
2 cups buttermilk
½ cup molasses
¼ cup brown sugar
1 tablespoon cognac
¾ cup whole wheat flour
 (preferably soft wheat
 or pastry flour)

¾ cup unbleached white
 wheat flour
½ cup whole rye flour
⅜ cup soy flour
2 teaspoons baking soda
1 teaspoon salt
½ cup cornmeal
⅔ cup currants
2 tablespoons unbleached
 white wheat flour

1. Butter four 16-ounce tin cans. To steam the breads prepare a 4- or 5-quart covered kettle as a steamer. Place a wire rack inside and fill with about 4 inches of water. Heat the water until it is gently bubbling.

2. Melt the butter and let it cool. In a large bowl beat together the butter, eggs, buttermilk, molasses, sugar, and cognac with a fork or rotary beater.

3. In a small bowl sift together the whole wheat flour, white wheat flour, rye flour, soy flour, baking soda, and salt. Add to the bowl any particles that did not go through the sifter. Stir in the cornmeal.

4. With a wooden spoon or rubber spatula stir the dry ingredients into the liquid ingredients in the large bowl. Mix well.

5. In a small bowl toss together the currants and the 2 tablespoons white wheat flour. Stir the currants gently into the batter.

6. Pour the batter into the cans, fill them two-thirds full and cover with foil. Steam the breads in the covered kettle until the center springs back when gently pressed or a toothpick or broom straw inserted in the center comes out clean, about 2 hours. Maintain the water level in the kettle to half the height of the cans and keep the heat low so that the water simmers evenly. Cool the breads in the cans on a wire rack.

Fresh Fruit Wheat Germ Muffins

ABOUT A DOZEN MUFFINS EACH WITH ABOUT 5 GRAMS
USABLE PROTEIN

*These are not-too-sweet, quick breakfast muffins.
Frozen or canned fruit is fine if fresh fruit is out of
season.*

⅓ cup butter
1 cup wheat germ
2 eggs
1 cup milk
3 tablespoons brown sugar
1 tablespoon molasses
1 cup unbleached white
  wheat flour

1 tablespoon baking
  powder
¾ teaspoon salt
1 cup chopped fresh fruit
  (for instance, peaches,
  apricots, or berries)

1. Heat the oven to 375°. Butter a 12-cup muffin tin.
Melt the butter and set it aside to cool.

2. Toast the wheat germ in a frying pan over low
heat until brown, about 5 minutes. Stir frequently to
prevent burning. Set the wheat germ aside.

3. In a large bowl beat together the butter, eggs,
milk, sugar, and molasses with a fork or rotary beater.

4. In a small bowl sift together the flour, baking
powder, and salt. Stir in the wheat germ.

5. With a wooden spoon or rubber spatula stir the
dry ingredients into the liquid ingredients in the large
bowl. Mix just enough to moisten. Stir in the fruit.

6. Spoon the batter into the tin. Fill each cup three-
quarters full. Bake the muffins until the center springs
back when gently pressed or a toothpick or broom straw
inserted in the center comes out clean, about 20 minutes. Cool the muffins in the tin on a wire rack. Serve
warm.

Nut Muffins

ABOUT A DOZEN MUFFINS EACH WITH ABOUT 8 GRAMS
USABLE PROTEIN

*Any nut butter plus nut combination—peanut butter
and peanuts, walnut butter and walnuts, sesame butter
(tahini) and sesame seeds—can be used. My favorite
combination is cashew butter and cashews.*

¼ cup butter
1 egg
1 cup milk
¼ cup brown sugar
½ cup nut butter
(see page 317)

1¼ cups whole wheat flour
(preferably soft wheat or
pastry flour)
1 tablespoon baking powder
¼ teaspoon salt
½ cup wheat germ
1 cup nuts

1. Heat the oven to 375°. Butter a 12-cup muffin
tin. Melt the butter and set it aside to cool.
2. In a large bowl beat together the butter, egg, milk,
sugar, and nut butter with a fork or rotary beater.
3. In a small bowl sift together the flour, baking
powder, and salt. Return to the bowl any particles that
did not go through the sifter. Use ¼ teaspoon more
salt if the nuts or nut butter are unsalted. Stir in the
wheat germ. Chop the nuts coarse. Stir them in.
4. With a wooden spoon or rubber spatula stir the
dry ingredients into the liquid ingredients in the large
bowl. Mix just enough to moisten.
5. Spoon the batter into the tin. Fill each cup three-
quarters full. Bake the muffins until the center springs
back when gently pressed or a toothpick or broom straw
inserted in the center comes out clean, about 20 minutes. Cool the muffins in the tin on a wire rack. Serve
warm.

Orange Muffins

**ABOUT A DOZEN MUFFINS EACH WITH ABOUT 4 GRAMS
USABLE PROTEIN**

*A whole orange is used in these easy-to-make muf-
fins. Try using another citrus fruit like a lemon or a
lime, in place of the orange.*

¼ cup butter	1½ cups whole wheat flour
1 orange	(preferably soft wheat or
About ⅔ cup milk	pastry flour)
2 eggs	2 teaspoons baking powder
½ cup brown sugar	½ teaspoon salt
	½ cup wheat germ

1. Heat the oven to 375°. Butter a 12-cup muffin tin. Melt the butter and set it aside to cool.

2. Squeeze the juice from the orange and add enough milk to make 1 cup of liquid. In a blender combine the butter, orange juice mixture, pulp and rind, eggs, and sugar. Blend until the orange rind is finely grated. Without a blender, cut the pulp as fine as possible, grate the rind, and beat with the butter, eggs, sugar, and the orange juice mixture in a small bowl.

3. In a large bowl sift together the flour, baking powder, and salt. Add to the bowl any particles that did not go through the sifter. Stir in the wheat germ.

4. With a wooden spoon or rubber spatula stir the orange mixture into the dry ingredients in the large bowl. Mix just enough to moisten.

5. Spoon the batter into the tin. Fill each cup three-quarters full. Bake the muffins until the center springs back when gently pressed or a toothpick or broom straw inserted in the center comes out clean, about 20 minutes. Cool the muffins in the tin on a wire rack. Serve warm.

Rye Cheese Muffins

ABOUT A DOZEN MUFFINS EACH WITH ABOUT 5 GRAMS
USABLE PROTEIN

*These muffins are perfect to accompany soup or
salad. For a grainier muffin use whole wheat flour in
place of the white wheat.*

¼ cup chopped
green peppers
¼ cup chopped onions
About 1 cup milk
2 eggs
1 tablespoon brown sugar
¼ cup oil
½ cup grated cheese, about
1½ ounces (for instance
Swiss or cheddar)

1 cup unbleached white
wheat flour
1 cup whole rye flour
2½ teaspoons baking
powder
1½ teaspoons salt
½ cup wheat germ

1. Heat the oven to 375°. Oil a 12-cup muffin tin.
2. Chop the peppers and onion coarse. Cook them
in a saucepan with enough milk to cover them, until
soft, about 10 minutes. Stir frequently to prevent the
milk from burning, and do not let it boil. Drain the
vegetables, save the milk, and set both aside.
3. In a large bowl, beat together the eggs, ¾ cup
milk, sugar, and oil with a fork or rotary beater. Use
the milk in which the vegetables have been cooked and
add to it, if necessary, to make ¾ cup. Stir the cheese
and the drained vegetables into the milk mixture.
4. In a small bowl sift together the white wheat flour,
rye flour, baking powder, and salt. Add to the bowl any
particles that did not go through the sifter. Stir in the
wheat germ.
5. With a wooden spoon or rubber spatula stir the
dry ingredients into the liquid ingredients in the large
bowl. Mix just enough to moisten.
6. Spoon the batter into the tin. Fill each cup three-
quarters full. Bake the muffins until the center springs

back when gently pressed or a toothpick or broom straw inserted in the center comes out clean, about 20 minutes. Serve hot.

Whole Wheat Popovers

ABOUT A DOZEN POPOVERS EACH WITH ABOUT 3 GRAMS
USABLE PROTEIN

These popovers are quick to make, light to eat, and high in protein. Fill with an egg for breakfast or with fruit for dessert.

1 cup whole wheat flour	½ teaspoon salt
(preferably hard wheat or	2 eggs
bread flour)	1½ cups milk

1. Heat the oven to 450°. Butter a 12-cup muffin tin or 12 three-inch custard cups.
2. In a large bowl sift together the flour and salt.
3. Add the eggs and milk to the flour and beat well to develop the gluten in the batter—about 5 minutes with a hand rotary beater or 3 minutes with an electric beater. This is a thin, smooth batter. Place the muffin tin or custard cups in the oven for a few moments.
4. Pour the batter into the hot cups and fill them half full. Bake the popovers in the 450° oven for 10

minutes and then reduce the heat to 350° and bake until the popovers are dark brown, about 30 minutes longer. Do not open the door of the oven during the first half hour of baking.

5. Take the popovers out of the cups and puncture each with a fork to let the trapped steam escape so that they will not get soggy. Serve hot.

Biscuits

The quickest way to have homemade bread is to bake biscuits—ready for the table in just 20 minutes.

MIXING

In a small bowl sift together the dry ingredients—flour, salt, and baking powder. Return to the bowl any particles that did not go through the sifter.

Cut a solid shortening—like butter or margarine—into the dry ingredients. (For instructions see page 214.)

Mix the eggs (if any) into the flour and shortening mixture. Mix lightly with a fork or use your hand or a wooden spoon to push the flour gently from the edges of the bowl just until the dry ingredients are moistened. Overstirring will make rubbery biscuits.

Any biscuit dough can be prepared as either cut or drop biscuits.

MAKING CUT BISCUITS

Add only enough milk to dampen all the flour and make a soft, dry dough.

Knead the dough lightly in the bowl or on a floured

table to mix the ingredients and make the dough smooth—only 10 to 15 folds. (For kneading instructions see page 45.) Use your fingertips instead of the palms of your hands.

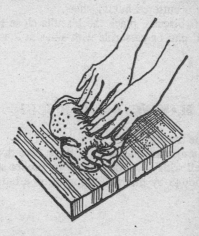

Heat the oven to 400°.

Pat or roll the dough ½ inch thick.

Cut into squares with a floured knife or spatula, or into rounds with a floured biscuit cutter, cup, or glass. When round biscuits are cut, there will be scraps

of dough which should be gathered, kneaded briefly, patted, and cut again into biscuits. Handle the dough as little and as lightly as possible.

For crusty biscuits, place the cut biscuits well separated on a buttered baking sheet.

For soft biscuits, place the biscuits close together in a buttered pan or casserole with sides at least 2 inches high.

MAKING DROP BISCUITS

Heat the oven to 400°.
Add enough milk to make a thick, wet dough.
Mix well with a wooden spoon or rubber spatula.
Drop dough by the tablespoonful on a buttered baking sheet.

BAKING CUT OR DROP BISCUITS

Bake the biscuits until the tops are golden brown and the center of each biscuit is firm—about 12 minutes. Serve biscuits hot.

RECIPES

Basic Whole Wheat Biscuits

ABOUT A DOZEN BISCUITS EACH WITH ABOUT 7 GRAMS USABLE PROTEIN

This substantial hot roll recipe lends itself to variation. By adding herbs, cheese, nuts, or fruit you can make hors d'oeuvres, rolls, teacakes, or desserts.

2½ cups whole wheat flour (preferably soft wheat or pastry flour)

1½ tablespoons baking powder

1 teaspoon salt

3 tablespoons cold butter

About 1½ cups milk

2 eggs

2 tablespoons honey

⅓ cup soy grits

⅓ cup wheat germ

½ cup milk powder

2 tablespoons water

1. Heat the oven to 400°.

2. In a large bowl sift together the flour, baking powder, and salt. Add to the bowl any particles that did not go through the sifter. Cut the butter into the sifted ingredients with a pastry blender or two knives, or crumble the butter into the flour mixture by rubbing them together quickly with your fingertips.

3. In a small bowl mix together ¾ cup of the milk, 1 of the eggs, the honey, soy grits, wheat germ, and milk powder. Make sure no lumps of milk powder remain. Let the mixture stand for about 5 minutes to soften the soy grits and wheat germ. Tossing lightly with a fork, add gradually to the sifted ingredients in the large bowl.

4. Add only enough milk to make a dry dough. Knead the dough briefly in the bowl or on a lightly floured board to mix the ingredients and make a smooth dough.

5. Pat the dough to ½-inch thickness. Cut in squares with a floured knife or spatula, or cut into rounds with a floured biscuit cutter, cup, or glass. When round biscuits are cut, there will be scraps of dough which should be gathered, kneaded briefly, patted, and cut into biscuits. Handle the dough as little and as lightly as possible.

6. For crusty biscuits butter a baking sheet and place the cut biscuits well separated on it. For soft biscuits butter a pan or casserole and place the cut biscuits close together in it.

7. In a cup beat together the remaining egg and the

water and brush this egg wash on the biscuits. Bake the biscuits until they are golden brown and feel firm when gently pressed, about 12 minutes. Break apart the soft biscuits. Serve hot.

Currant Scones

ABOUT A DOZEN SCONES EACH WITH ABOUT 7 GRAMS USABLE PROTEIN

The basic biscuit recipe can easily be adapted to create flavored scones.

1 recipe Basic Whole Wheat Biscuits	1 teaspoon lemon extract Melted butter
1 tablespoon grated lemon rind	1 egg 2 tablespoons water
½ cup currants	

1. Heat the oven to 400°. Butter an 8-inch square pan.

2. Prepare BASIC WHOLE WHEAT BISCUITS from step 1 through 3. Stir in the lemon rind, currants, and lemon extract.

3. Add only enough milk to make a dry dough. Knead the dough briefly in the bowl or on a lightly floured board to mix the ingredients and make a smooth dough.

4. Pat the dough into the pan. Cut the dough into 12 squares with a spatula or bench scraper dipped in melted butter.

5. In a cup beat together the egg and the water and brush this egg wash on the scones. Bake the scones until they are golden brown and feel firm when gently pressed, about 12 minutes.

6. Separate the scones. Serve hot.

Olive Cheese Biscuits

ABOUT A DOZEN BISCUITS EACH WITH ABOUT 5 GRAMS
USABLE PROTEIN

*These compact biscuits are particularly good with
soup or cut in half and served as snacks.*

2 cups whole wheat flour
    (preferably soft wheat or
    pastry flour)
1½ tablespoons baking
    powder
½ teaspoon salt
2 tablespoons brown sugar
3 tablespoons cold butter

3 egg yolks
1 cup grated cheese, about
    3 ounces (for instance,
    Swiss)
¼ cup minced olives,
    black or green
About ½ cup milk
2 tablespoons water

1. Heat the oven to 400°.

2. In a large bowl sift together the flour, baking powder, and salt. Add to the bowl any particles that did not go through the sifter. Stir in the sugar.

3. Cut the butter into the sifted ingredients with a pastry blender or two knives, or crumble the butter into the flour mixture by rubbing them together quickly with your fingertips.

4. Set aside 1 tablespoon egg yolk. In a small bowl mix together the remaining egg yolks, cheese, and olives. Tossing lightly with a fork add gradually to the flour mixture in the large bowl.

5. Add enough milk to make a wet, sticky dough, the consistency of modeling clay.

6. Pat the dough into a 2-inch cylinder, and cut into 1-inch slices.

7. For crusty biscuits butter a baking sheet and place the cut dough well separated on it. For soft biscuits butter a pan or casserole and place the cut dough close together on it.

8. In a cup beat together the reserved egg yolk and

the water and brush this egg wash on the biscuits. Bake until they are golden brown and feel firm when gently pressed, about 12 minutes. Separate the soft biscuits. Serve hot.

Sesame Drop Biscuits

ABOUT A DOZEN BISCUITS EACH WITH ABOUT 5 GRAMS USABLE PROTEIN

Buttermilk makes these biscuits light. For variety, use chopped nuts to replace the sesame seeds.

½ cup sesame seeds
2 cups whole wheat flour (preferably soft wheat or pastry flour)
¼ cup soy flour
1½ tablespoons baking powder

1 teaspoon salt
¼ cup cold butter
2 eggs
2 teaspoons molasses
About ¾ cup buttermilk
Melted butter

1. Heat the oven to 400°. Butter a baking sheet.

2. Toast the sesame seeds over low heat until they are brown, about 5 minutes. Stir frequently to prevent burning. Set aside 1 tablespoon of the seeds and in a blender grind the remainder into a gritty powder. Without a blender chop as fine as possible with a nut chopper.

3. In a large bowl sift together the wheat flour, soy flour, baking powder, and salt. Add to the bowl any particles that did not go through the sifter. Stir in the powdered sesame seeds.

4. Cut the butter into the sifted ingredients with a pastry blender or two knives, or crumble the butter with the flour mixture by rubbing them together quickly with your fingertips.

5. In a cup beat together the eggs and molasses. Tossing lightly with a fork add gradually to the flour mixture in the large bowl.

6. Add enough buttermilk to make a wet, thick dough. Mix well with a wooden spoon or rubber spatula.

7. Drop the dough by the tablespoonful onto the baking sheet. Brush the biscuits with melted butter and sprinkle with the reserved sesame seeds. Bake the biscuits until they are golden brown and feel firm when gently pressed, about 12 minutes.

Rye Drop Biscuits

ABOUT A DOZEN BISCUITS EACH WITH ABOUT 4 GRAMS
USABLE PROTEIN

These biscuits are dark, flaky, and compact.

2 cups whole rye flour	2 tablespoons cumin or
¾ cup soy flour	caraway seeds
1½ tablespoons baking	⅜ cup oil
powder	About 1 cup milk
1 teaspoon salt	Oil
2 tablespoons brown sugar	

1. Heat the oven to 400°. Oil a baking sheet.

2. In a large bowl sift together the whole rye flour, soy flour, baking powder and salt. Add to the bowl any particles that did not go through the sifter. Stir in the sugar and add the caraway or cumin seeds. Add the oil, drop by drop, stirring briskly and lightly with a fork to make a crumbly mixture.

3. Add enough milk to make a wet, thick dough. Mix well with a wooden spoon or rubber spatula.

4. Drop the dough by the tablespoonful on the baking sheet.

5. Brush the biscuits with oil. Bake until they are golden brown and feel firm when gently pressed, about 12 minutes. Serve hot.

Orange Strawberry Shortcake

ABOUT A DOZEN SHORTCAKES EACH WITH ABOUT 6 GRAMS USABLE PROTEIN

As soon as the shortcakes come out of the oven, arrange an assembly line to put them together so that the shortcake is hot and the yogurt topping is cold when served. The yogurt often takes an hour to prepare, so plan accordingly.

TOPPING

1 quart fresh strawberries	¼ cup honey
2 cups drained yogurt	3 egg whites

1. Set aside 12 whole, nicely shaped strawberries, and slice the remaining ones.

2. Drain the yogurt in a funnel or sieve lined with a paper towel or filter paper or hang the yogurt in a cheesecloth bag. Set the funnel in a glass or the sieve in a bowl to catch the water (whey) that drains out, and place this entire apparatus in the refrigerator. (Save the whey for yeast bread-baking.) Let the yogurt drain until it is of thick pudding consistency, about 1 hour. The amount of yogurt needed initially to make 2 cups drained yogurt and the amount of time it takes to drain depend upon the original thickness of the yogurt. When it is ready, beat it with the honey in a small bowl until smooth. Refrigerate. Prepare the shortcakes.

3. While the shortcakes are in the oven, in a large bowl beat the egg whites with a wire whisk or rotary beater until stiff. With a large spoon or rubber spatula fold the egg whites gently into the yogurt mixture.

SHORTCAKES

1 cup unbleached white wheat flour	½ cup wheat germ
1 cup whole wheat flour (preferably soft wheat or pastry flour)	⅓ cup cold butter
	2 eggs
	⅓ cup honey
	2 tablespoons grated orange rind
1½ tablespoons baking powder	About ¼ cup milk
¼ teaspoon salt	Melted butter

1. Heat the oven to 400°. Butter a baking sheet.

2. In a large bowl sift together the white wheat flour, whole wheat flour, baking powder and salt. Stir in the wheat germ.

3. Cut the butter into the sifted ingredients with a pastry blender or two knives, or crumble the butter into the flour mixture by rubbing them together quickly with your fingertips.

4. In a small bowl beat the eggs with the honey and add the orange rind. Tossing lightly with a fork add gradually to the flour mixture in the large bowl.

5. Add enough milk to make a wet, thick dough. Mix well with a wooden spoon or rubber spatula.

6. Drop the dough by the tablespoonful onto the baking sheet.

7. Brush the dough with melted butter. Bake the shortcakes until they are golden brown and feel firm when gently pressed, about 12 minutes.

8. To assemble, open each shortcake with a knife or fork. Place several spoonfuls of the yogurt and several strawberry slices on the inside. Cover with the top half of the shortcake. Spoon on a dollop of the yogurt mixture and top with a whole strawberry.

Pancakes

GENERAL INSTRUCTIONS

Pancakes are thin fried cakes made from a poured batter or flattened dough. They are particularly good for holding a high-protein filling, are often inexpensive, and are quick to make.

Most but not all of the batter pancake recipes in this chapter follow the mixing and frying method outlined below. For dough pancakes, follow the individual recipe.

MIXING PANCAKE BATTER

In a large bowl mix together, with a fork or rotary beater, the liquid ingredients—the eggs, milk, syrupy sweeteners, and oil or melted butter.

In a small bowl sift together the dry ingredients—the flour, baking soda or powder, and salt. Add to the bowl any particles that did not go through the sifter. Stir in the dry ingredients that are not sifted—wheat germ or nuts, for instance.

Combine the liquid and the dry ingredients. With a wooden spoon or rubber spatula mix just enough to moisten.

If time permits, refrigerate the batter for about an hour.

For lighter pancakes, separate the eggs. Add the yolks to the liquids, and beat the egg whites until they are stiff. (For instructions see page 158.) With a large spoon or rubber spatula, stir the beaten egg whites gently into the batter after it has been refrigerated.

FRYING PANCAKES

Fry the pancakes on a hot griddle or frying pan. The griddle is hot enough when a drop of water bounces on the surface before it evaporates. If the frying surface is not well seasoned you may want to brush butter on the griddle for the first batch of pancakes to prevent sticking; thereafter it should not be necessary to butter the griddle if some shortening was added to the batter.

Pour or ladle the batter onto the griddle in one motion. Use about ¼ cup for an average-size pancake. Fry until bubbles form on the surface and the edges are dry, about 2 minutes. Turn once and fry until brown, about ½ minute.

If the pancakes are not cooked in the center, or if the browning is uneven, the griddle is probably too hot.

If the pancakes are too thick, or when the batter thickens as you reach the bottom of the bowl, add milk or water and stir.

To keep the pancakes hot until all the batter has been fried, stack and wrap them in a kitchen towel, in aluminum foil, or in a covered casserole. Place in a 200° oven.

ADDITIONAL INFORMATION

Unused batter will keep well in the refrigerator for about a week.

Any pancake batter will make fine waffles. Just add 2 or 3 tablespoons of melted butter or oil to the batter and bake on a waffle iron.

RECIPES

Basic Whole Grain Pancakes with Cranberry Syrup

ABOUT A DOZEN PANCAKES EACH WITH ABOUT
5 GRAMS USABLE PROTEIN

Any whole-grain flour—wheat, rye, barley, oat—or combination of flours will make a successful pancake. Because the pancake is not strongly flavored, the taste of each grain is distinct.

2 eggs	½ cup soy flour
1½ cups milk	1 teaspoon baking soda
2 tablespoons honey	½ teaspoon salt
2 tablespoons oil	¼ teaspoon nutmeg
1 cup whole-grain flour	½ cup wheat germ

1. In a large bowl beat together the eggs, milk, honey, and oil with a fork or rotary beater.
2. In a small bowl sift together the whole-grain flour, soy flour, baking soda, salt, and nutmeg. Add to the bowl any particles that did not go through the sifter. Stir in the wheat germ.
3. Combine the liquid and the dry ingredients. With a wooden spoon or rubber spatula mix just enough to moisten. Refrigerate the batter while you prepare the syrup.

4. On a hot, ungreased frying pan or griddle, fry about ¼ cup batter until bubbles form on the surface and the edges are dry, about 2 minutes. Turn once and fry until brown, about ½ minute. Continue with the rest of the batter. Keep the pancakes hot wrapped in a kitchen towel and placed in a 200° oven. If the pancakes are too thick, or when the batter thickens as you reach the bottom of the bowl, add milk and stir.

5. Reheat the syrup, spoon over hot pancakes, and serve.

CRANBERRY SYRUP

1 cup fresh cranberries	2 tablespoons frozen orange
1 cup water	juice concentrate
¼ cup honey	

1. In a saucepan cook the cranberries in the water, covered, over low heat until the cranberries are soft, about 10 minutes. Put the berries through a food mill or force them through a sieve.

2. Combine the cranberry liquid with the honey and orange juice concentrate. Boil until syrupy, about 15 minutes.

Baked Pancakes with Fruit

2 LARGE PANCAKES EACH WITH ABOUT 14 GRAMS
USABLE PROTEIN

These are large puffy pancakes you can enjoy without having to stand at the griddle. This batter also makes fine popovers if baked in a muffin tin or in custard cups.

2 eggs	2 tablespoons soy flour
½ cup milk	½ teaspoon salt
⅓ cup whole wheat flour (preferably soft wheat or pastry flour)	3 tablespoons wheat germ
	2 tablespoons butter

1. Heat the oven to 425°.
2. In a large bowl beat together the eggs and milk with a fork or rotary beater.
3. In a small bowl sift together the wheat flour, soy flour, and salt. Add to the bowl any particles that did not go through the sifter. Stir in the wheat germ.
4. Combine the liquid and the dry ingredients. With a wooden spoon or rubber spatula, mix just enough to moisten. If time permits, refrigerate the batter for about an hour.
5. Melt a tablespoon of butter in each of two 8-inch round ovenproof dishes or frying pans. Pour half the batter into each dish.
6. Bake the pancakes until they are golden brown, puffy, and firm, about 15 minutes. Do not peek at the pancakes until they have baked for at least 10 minutes.

FRUIT

4 cups sliced fresh fruit (for instance peaches, apples, pears, berries)	**Juice of ½ lemon** **¼ cup maple syrup**

Slice the fruit. Combine the fruit, lemon juice, and maple syrup in a saucepan. Cover and cook until the fruit is softened, about 5 minutes. Spoon fruit over hot pancakes and serve.

Raised Pancakes with Fruit Cream Syrup

ABOUT A DOZEN PANCAKES WITH SYRUP EACH WITH ABOUT 5 GRAMS USABLE PROTEIN

Prepare this batter at night and fry the pancakes for breakfast. The oat flour can easily be made at home in a blender. Refer to page 42 for yeast instructions.

1 tablespoon yeast

A drop of honey

¼ cup water

2¼ cups milk

1 tablespoon honey

2 teaspoons molasses

½ cup milk powder

⅔ cup whole wheat flour

(preferably soft wheat or pastry flour)

⅔ cup oat flour

⅔ cup wheat germ

1 teaspoon salt

1 teaspoon baking soda

2 eggs

2 tablespoons oil

1. In a cup dissolve the yeast and a drop of honey in the water. Let stand until bubbly, about 5 minutes.

2. Warm 2 cups of the milk in a saucepan until small bubbles form around the rim of the pan. Remove the pan from the heat and add the honey, molasses, and milk powder. Stir until the honey and molasses dissolve and no lumps of milk powder remain. Transfer to a large bowl and let cool to wrist temperature.

3. When the milk mixture has cooled add to it the dissolved yeast, the wheat flour, and the oat flour. To make oat flour at home, whirl rolled oats in the blender until they are powdery. Beat the mixture well with a wooden spoon or rubber spatula.

4. Cover the bowl with a plate and let the mixture rise at least 2 hours and not more than overnight. In the morning, mix the batter until the bubbles disappear and all the air is stirred out. Prepare the syrup.

5. Add the wheat germ, salt, baking soda, eggs, and oil to the batter. Stir well. Make sure that there are no lumps of baking soda in the batter. Add the remaining ¼ cup milk to make a thin batter.

6. On a hot, ungreased frying pan or griddle, fry about ¼ cup batter until bubbles form on the surface and the edges are dry, about 2 minutes. Turn once and fry until brown, about ½ minute. Continue with the rest of the batter. Keep the pancakes hot wrapped in a kitchen towel and placed in a 200° oven. If the pancakes are too thick, or when the batter thickens as you reach the bottom of the bowl, add milk and stir.

7. Pour the syrup over hot pancakes and serve.

Unused batter will keep in the refrigerator for about 4 days. Stir every day.

FRUIT CREAM SYRUP

2 tablespoons lemon juice
¾ cup orange juice
¼ cup honey

A pinch of salt
2 egg yolks

In the top of a double boiler, heat and stir together the lemon juice, orange juice, honey, salt, and egg yolks until thickened, about 5 minutes.

Yogurt Pancakes

ABOUT A DOZEN PANCAKES EACH WITH ABOUT
5 GRAMS USABLE PROTEIN

These pancakes look thick and heavy on the griddle but actually have a delicate light texture.

4 eggs
1½ cups yogurt
½ cup milk
2 tablespoons honey
1 tablespoon oil
¾ cup whole wheat flour

(preferably soft wheat or
pastry flour)
1 teaspoon baking soda
½ teaspoon salt
¼ cup rolled oats
¼ cup wheat germ
Butter

1. In a large bowl beat together the eggs, yogurt, milk, honey, and oil with a fork or rotary beater.
2. In a small bowl sift together the flour, baking soda, and salt. Add to the bowl any particles that did not go through the sifter. Stir in the rolled oats and wheat germ.
3. Combine the liquid and the dry ingredients. With a wooden spoon or rubber spatula mix just enough to moisten. If time permits refrigerate for about an hour.
4. On a hot, greased frying pan or griddle, fry about

¼ cup batter until bubbles form on the surface and the edges are dry, about 2 minutes. Turn once and fry until brown, about ½ minute. Continue with the rest of the batter. Keep the pancakes hot wrapped in a kitchen towel and placed in a 200° oven. If the pancakes are too thick, or when the batter thickens as you reach the bottom of the bowl, add milk and stir. After several pancakes have been fried, it may no longer be necessary to grease the griddle. Serve hot.

Buckwheat Crepes with a Choice of Fillings

ABOUT A DOZEN CREPES, WITH RICOTTA-SPINACH FILLING, EACH WITH ABOUT 5 GRAMS USABLE PROTEIN; WITH NUT-CHEESE FILLING, EACH WITH ABOUT 4 GRAMS USABLE PROTEIN

For a meal, fill these thin pancakes with one of these substantial fillings; for dessert, spread them with honey or jam.

1 egg	1 cup buckwheat flour
¼ teaspoon salt	About 1¼ cups water
A pinch of pepper	Butter

1. In a large bowl beat the egg well with a wooden spoon or rubber spatula. Add the salt and pepper.

2. Gradually add flour to the egg, beating thoroughly until the egg cannot absorb any more flour—about ¼ cup. Beat well. Gradually add the water, alternating with the remaining flour. Beat well with each addition. Add water until the batter is the consistency of heavy cream. Refrigerate the batter while you prepare the filling.

3. Heat an 8-inch cast-iron frying pan and brush with butter. When the butter just begins to smoke, pour slightly less than ¼ cup of batter into the pan. Rotate the pan so that a thin film of batter covers the entire

surface. Fry until dry, about 1 minute. Turn once and fry the other side until brown, about ½ minute. Make sure that the pan remains an even, hot temperature. Continue with the rest of the batter.

For crispy crepes, stack them in aluminum foil, partially covered, in a 200° oven. For soft crepes, stack them on a plate covered with an inverted bowl.

If the crepes are too thick, or when the batter thickens as you reach the bottom of the bowl, add water and stir.

RICOTTA-SPINACH FILLING

3 pounds fresh spinach or
2 packages frozen
chopped spinach
Water
6 large fresh mushrooms
¼ cup butter

2 tablespoons flour,
any kind
2 cups milk
1 cup ricotta cheese
¼ teaspoon nutmeg
Salt and pepper

1. Clean the spinach, remove the thick stems, chop, and cook in a covered saucepan over medium heat in 1 inch of water until soft, about 5 minutes; or prepare the frozen spinach according to the directions on the package. Drain well and set aside.

2. Slice the mushrooms. In a saucepan, cook them in the butter until soft, about 2 minutes. Scoop the mushrooms out of the butter with a slotted spoon and combine them with the spinach in a small bowl.

3. Stir the flour into the mushroom butter with a fork or wire whisk and cook over a medium flame, stirring constantly until all the butter is absorbed, about 2 minutes. Gradually add the milk and continue stirring until the sauce is thick.

4. Pour the sauce over the spinach and mushrooms. Stir in the ricotta cheese and nutmeg. Add salt and pepper to taste.

5. To serve, place the crepe on a plate and spoon about ½ cup filling along the center third. Fold the

right third over the filling; fold the left third over the right. Serve hot.

NUT-CHEESE FILLING

1 cup pecans or walnuts	6 ounces (for instance,
2 cups grated cheese, about	cheddar or Danish tilsit)

1. Chop the nuts. Set them aside.
2. Place a fried crepe on the frying pan and sprinkle the center third with about 2½ tablespoons cheese and about 1½ tablespoons nuts. While it is still in the frying pan cover the crepe and the pan with an inverted bowl until the cheese melts, about 2 minutes. Then, fold the right third over the filling; fold the left third over the right. Continue with the rest of the crepes. Serve hot.

Cheese Blintzes

ABOUT A DOZEN BLINTZES EACH WITH ABOUT 15 GRAMS
USABLE PROTEIN

These cheese-filled pancakes can be made in quantity and frozen in plastic bags. To thaw and reheat, just fry the frozen blintzes. Blintzes are particularly good served with sour cream or yogurt and fruit.

4 eggs	(preferably soft wheat or
1 cup milk	pastry flour)
1 cup whole wheat flour	1 teaspoon salt
	Butter

1. In a large bowl beat together the eggs and milk with a fork or rotary beater.
2. In a small bowl sift together the flour and salt. Add to the bowl any particles that did not go through the sifter.
3. Combine the liquid and the dry ingredients. With a wooden spoon or rubber spatula mix just enough to

moisten. Refrigerate the batter while you prepare the filling.

4. Heat an 8-inch cast-iron frying pan and brush with butter. When the butter just begins to smoke, pour slightly less than ¼ cup of batter into the pan and rotate the pan so that a thin film of batter covers the entire surface. Fry until dry, about 1 minute. Make sure that the pan remains an even, hot temperature. Continue with the rest of the batter.

If the pancakes are too thick, or when the batter thickens as you reach the bottom of the bowl, add milk and stir.

Do not turn the pancake over. Take it from the frying pan gently with a spatula. Continue with the rest of the batter. Stack the pancakes on a kitchen towel with the fried side up.

5. Place about ⅓ cup cheese filling in the center of the fried side of the pancake. Fold the bottom of the pancake over the filling; fold the sides of the pancake over the filling to meet in the center. Roll the pancake away from you to close the small packet. The blintze should look like an egg roll.

If time permits refrigerate the blintzes until chilled, about 2 hours, so the cheese filling will not melt when it is fried.

6. Fry the blintzes until brown on both sides in a frying pan with enough butter to prevent sticking. Serve hot.

FILLING

4 cups cottage cheese or ricotta	1 tablespoon honey
2 eggs	¼ teaspoon nutmeg
	Salt

Press the cottage cheese through a sieve or use ricotta cheese directly from the container. In a bowl combine the cheese, eggs, honey, and nutmeg. Add salt to taste. Mix well.

Chinese Steamed Pancakes

ABOUT A DOZEN FILLED PANCAKES EACH WITH ABOUT
7 GRAMS USABLE PROTEIN

*Any combination of vegetables in the filling, plus the
protein ingredients—the eggs and bean curd—seasoned
with soy sauce will make a fine Oriental-style meal.*

2 cups unbleached white wheat flour	1 teaspoon salt About ½ cup water

1. Stir the flour and salt together in a large bowl.
Gradually add water just until the dough comes together
into a dry ball.

2. Begin to knead the dough on a lightly floured
board, adding water with your fingertips if necessary to
make a firm dough. Knead the dough well, until it is
smooth and springy, about 15 minutes. Cut off a lump
of dough about the size of a small egg and round it into
a ball. Repeat this 11 times to make a dozen pancakes.

3. Roll out each ball of dough into a thin circle. It
will probably be easiest to begin rolling directly on the
dough, but as it gets thinner and stickier, put it between
two pieces of plastic wrap. With a sharp knife, trim the
dough into about an 8-inch circle.

4. To steam the pancakes, prepare a 4- or 5-quart
covered kettle as a steamer. Place a wire rack inside
and fill with about 1 inch of water. Heat the water
until it is gently bubbling, place the pancake on the
rack, and cover the pot. Steam the pancakes one at
a time until the surface is dry, about 3 minutes. Turn
and steam the other side, about ½ minute. Stack the
pancakes between pieces of plastic wrap and cover with
a kitchen towel. Prepare the filling.

5. To serve, bring the vegetables and pancakes to the
table separately. Diners can then assemble their own
meals.

FILLING

2 tablespoons sesame oil	2 2-inch square cubes
1-inch slice of fresh	bean curd
ginger root	½ cup bean sprouts
2 cloves garlic	½ pound chopped
1 shredded carrot	fresh spinach
6 chopped scallions	¼ teaspoon dry mustard
½ cup sliced water	or ½ teaspoon prepared
chestnuts	mustard
2 eggs	¼ cup soy sauce (preferably
	tamari soy sauce)

1. Have all the vegetables cut and waiting in small bowls so that they can be added quickly.

2. Heat the oil in a wok or cast-iron frying pan. Stir in the ginger and garlic. Stir briskly for 2 minutes with a spatula or wooden spoon. Scoop out the ginger and garlic.

3. Stir in the carrot, scallions, and water chestnuts. When they are slightly cooked and still crisp push them to the side of the wok or frying pan.

4. Beat the eggs and fry in the same pan, stirring briskly, until cooked like scrambled eggs.

5. Stir the bean curd cubes, bean sprouts, spinach, and the fried vegetables that were on the side of the pan into the eggs. Add oil if necessary to prevent sticking. Stir lightly. Fry until the bean curd and bean sprouts are hot and the spinach is wilted.

6. In a cup mix the mustard into the soy sauce, and pour over the vegetables. Stir well.

Indian Dosai with Fresh Coconut-Cheese Chutney

ABOUT A DOZEN PANCAKES WITH CHUTNEY EACH WITH ABOUT 6 GRAMS USABLE PROTEIN

The pancakes are sour and the chutney is hot. It is a meal for those who enjoy powerful tastes.

2 cups uncooked brown rice	Water
½ cup uncooked black beans	½ teaspoon baking soda
1 teaspoon salt	Oil

1. Put the rice, beans, and salt in a bowl and cover with water. Soak overnight covered with a plate or plastic wrap.

2. Put the rice, beans, and enough soaking water to make blending easy in a blender and grind until they are a smooth paste. Add enough soaking water to make the paste into a thin batter. Without a blender, pound the rice and beans with a pestle in a mortar or bowl.

3. Let the batter stand, covered, overnight to ferment.

4. Prepare the chutney. Stir the baking soda into the batter. On a hot, greased frying pan or griddle, fry about ¼ cup batter until bubbles form on the surface and the edges are dry, about 2 minutes. Turn once and fry until brown, about 1 minute. Continue with the rest of the batter. Keep the pancakes hot wrapped in a kitchen towel and placed in a 200° oven. If the pancakes are too thick, or when the batter thickens as you reach the bottom of the bowl, add water and stir.

5. Spoon chutney over hot dosai and serve.

Unused batter will keep for weeks in the refrigerator. It simply sours more the longer it stands.

FRESH COCONUT-CHEESE CHUTNEY

2 tablespoons oil	½ teaspoon dry mustard
1 cup grated fresh coconut	or 1 teaspoon prepared mustard
½ cup minced green chili peppers	A pinch curry powder
1 tablespoon mint leaves	1½ cups farmer cheese
4 cloves pressed garlic	Salt

1. Heat the oil in a frying pan. Add the coconut,

peppers, mint, garlic, mustard, and curry. Mix well. Cook over low heat until the coconut softens, about 5 minutes. Remove the pan from the heat.

2. Stir in the farmer cheese. Add salt to taste.

Tortillas with a Choice of Filling

ABOUT A DOZEN TORTILLAS, WITH BEAN-CHEESE FILLING EACH WITH ABOUT 6 GRAMS USABLE PROTEIN; WITH PEPPER-CHEESE FILLING EACH WITH ABOUT 5 GRAMS USABLE PROTEIN

Tortillas are Mexican corn or wheat flour pancakes that make an envelope for a variety of foods. The two fillings suggested here should be modified or changed to use any leftover foods you may have. To serve most simply, place each food in a bowl and allow each diner to assemble his or her own dish.

1½ cups masa harina
  (Mexican corn flour)
⅓ cup unbleached white
  wheat flour

¼ cup wheat germ
2 tablespoons oil
About 1 cup water

1. Combine the masa, wheat flour, wheat germ, and oil in a large bowl. Gradually add water until the dough comes together into a soft ball. Knead well until the dough is smooth and firm, about 5 minutes. The dough should have the consistency of modeling clay. Cut off a lump of dough, about the size of a small egg, and round into a ball. Repeat this 11 times to make a dozen tortillas.

2. Roll out the ball of dough into a thin circle between two pieces of plastic wrap. Then, with a sharp knife, trim the dough into about an 8-inch circle.

3. On a hot ungreased frying pan or griddle, fry the tortilla until puckered and brown, about 3 minutes.

Turn once and fry until brown, about 1 minute. Keep the tortillas warm wrapped in a kitchen towel.

Unbaked tortilla dough can be stored in the refrigerator in a plastic bag for about 2 weeks. Unfilled, fried tortillas can be stored in the refrigerator in a plastic bag for about 4 weeks.

To soften stiff tortillas, place them in a casserole with 1 teaspoon of water. Cover and bake in a preheated 300° oven until the tortillas are soft, about 5 minutes.

BEAN-CHEESE FILLING (BURRITOS)

2 cups uncooked kidney beans and 8 cups of water or 6 cups cooked beans	Sliced tomatoes Sliced avocados Chopped scallions Shredded lettuce
4 tablespoons oil	1½ cups grated cheese,
1 tablespoon salt	about 5 ounces (for
4 cloves minced garlic	instance Monterey Jack
1 teaspoon cumin	or cheddar)

1. Heat the oven to 350°.
2. In a covered saucepan over low heat cook the beans in the water until soft, about 2 hours. Add water if necessary to keep the beans from burning. Cooking time can be reduced by about half if the beans are first soaked overnight. Omit this step if canned or cooked kidney beans are used.
3. Combine the beans, oil, salt, garlic, and cumin in a frying pan and heat. Mash into a thick paste. Prepare the vegetables.
4. Fill each tortilla with about ½ cup of the bean mixture and about 2 tablespoons cheese, and garnish with tomatoes, avocados, scallions and lettuce.
5. Fold the bottom of the tortilla over the filling; fold the sides of the tortilla over the filling to meet in the center. Roll the tortilla away from you to close the small packet. The tortilla should look like an egg roll.

6. Place the tortillas with the open edge down in a casserole and bake, uncovered, until the filling is warm and the cheese melts, about 10 minutes. Serve hot.

PEPPER-CHEESE FILLING (QUESADILLAS)

3 cups grated cheese, about 10 ounces (for instance, Monterey Jack or cheddar)

Shredded letuce
Oil
Jalapeno pepper relish

1. Place a tortilla in a hot, well-oiled frying pan. Fill the tortilla with about ¼ cup cheese and garnish with relish and lettuce.

2. Fold the tortilla in half and fry on both sides until the cheese begins to melt and the tortilla is crisp. Drain on a paper towel. Serve hot.

Pies and Crusted Pastries

GENERAL INSTRUCTIONS

A pastry crust is made by first mixing the flour with the shortening and then adding the water or liquid. This makes a flaky dough, especially if soft wheat or pastry flour (which is low in stretchy gluten) is used.

I prefer unbleached white wheat flour to whole wheat flour for pie crusts, and solid shortening to oil, because the crusts are easier to handle. Respectable crusts certainly can be made with whole wheat and oil—it just takes more skill and patience, and the crusts are not as fine.

MIXING A PIE CRUST

Chill all the utensils and ingredients, particularly if the weather is warm, or if you have had problems making crusts before. The most important ingredient to chill is the shortening.

Mix the shortening into the flour by one of these methods:

1. *Cut the shortening into the flour.* Use a pastry blender or two strong butter knives. Hold a knife in each hand with blades touching and draw the blades in opposite directions, like the blades of a pair of scissors.

214

2. *Crumble the shortening into the flour by rubbing them together between your fingertips.* Work quickly so that the heat from your hands does not melt the shortening.

With either method you want to achieve small pieces of shortening coated with a film of flour, which will look like coarse cornmeal. When the crust is baked and the shortening melts, the pastry will be layered with pockets of crispy flour and air.

If you want to use oil for the shortening, place the oil in a sprinkling bottle (if available), like the ones used for dampening clothes before ironing. In this way only a fine spray of oil adheres to the flour. Without a

sprinkling bottle, add the oil by droplets. As you add the oil, stir briskly with a fork. Try to avoid wet lumps of oil and flour.

Add the chilled liquid gradually (usually water, but fruit juice is a good substitute), a spoonful at a time, tossing the flour lightly with a fork until a soft dough forms. Work gently to prevent activating the gluten. When two-thirds of the suggested amount of liquid is added, gather all the moistened dough into your hands and form it into a ball. Take it out of the bowl. Continue to stir liquid into the flour remaining in the bowl, adding as little as possible—just enough to make the flour mixture into dough. Too much liquid will make the crust soggy. Gather this last bit of dough into a ball and join the two portions together, pressing gently with your hands. Try not to let the warmth of your hands melt the shortening.

When the dough is properly mixed, it will be lumpy and slightly sticky.

Wrap the dough in plastic wrap or waxed paper and refrigerate it for at least an hour, preferably a few hours. The dough will keep well in the refrigerator for about a week. Chilling the dough makes it easier to handle, tenderizes it, and keeps it from shrinking during baking.

To roll the dough, work on a smooth surface—formica, or, even better, marble, which is cold and therefore prevents the shortening from softening.

ROLLING A PIE CRUST

Three ways to roll a pie crust are listed here. I prefer the first because it requires the least equipment, and I can feel the texture of the dough as it is rolled.

The main advantage of the waxed paper method and the pastry cloth method is that they prevent too much flour from being absorbed into the dough as it is rolled, which would make a dry, tough crust.

1. *On a floured table:* Spread a thin layer of flour on the table. Form the dough into a patty and smooth the edges so there are no cracks. Turn the dough so that each surface is lightly floured, and dust flour on the rolling pin. Begin rolling outward from the center of the patty, pressing gently in all directions to roll a circle (or the shape of the pie tin in which the crust will go). Keep the surface of the dough lightly floured while keeping the inside moist. Do not press the rolling pin too deeply into the dough or the moist dough inside will stick to the pin. Try not to roll over the edge of the dough, which will make it too thin.

After a few rolls, lift the dough to make sure it is not sticking to the table. Turn the dough over and lightly dust this new "top surface" with flour. Continue rolling in all directions. Start from the middle and make sure the dough is not sticking. Dust the table lightly with flour when necessary. When the dough is 2 inches larger than the size of the pan to be covered, and about ⅛ inch thick, fold it into quarters. Lift and put into the pie tin and unfold. Or drape the circle of dough gently over the rolling pin to transfer it to the pie plate.

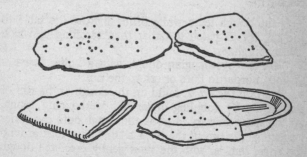

2. *Between sheets of waxed paper:* Lightly dust the surface of a sheet of waxed paper with flour. Place the dough patty on the sheet, dust with flour, and cover

with another sheet of waxed paper. Roll the dough as on a floured table, but without adding any more flour. When the dough is 2 inches larger than the pan to be covered, peel off the top sheet of waxed paper. Place the dough in the pie tin, and peel off the second piece of waxed paper.

3. *On a pastry cloth with a cloth rolling-pin cover:* Rub the pastry cloth and the rolling-pin cover with flour. Place the dough on the pastry cloth and roll as on a floured table. You should not need to add as much flour as in the first method. When the dough is 2 inches larger than the pan to be covered, turn the dough onto the pie tin.

If the dough tears while lifting it from the table to the tin, try to patch it rather than rerolling it, which causes toughness.

Trim the overhanging dough with a knife. Leave a ½-inch border to flute or crimp the rim.

To crimp the crust, build up the dough at the rim of the pie tin by doubling under the overhanging dough. At the same time try to hook the dough onto the under surface of the rim of the tin. Crimp with a fork around the edge, that is, with the tines gently press the dough onto the rim all the way around the pie.

For a fancier trim and to build up the crust to contain custard fillings, flute the crust by pinching the

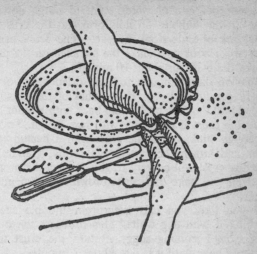

dough at the rim. Use the thumb and index finger of one hand on the outside of the rim and the knuckle or fingertip of the index finger of the other hand on the inside of the rim.

Chill the crust in the refrigerator for an hour if time permits. The crust will keep for 4 or 5 days in the refrigerator if it is sealed well in a plastic bag.

BAKING A PIE

Prepare the filling.

To prebake the bottom crust of a pie, heat the oven to 425°. "Dock" the pie dough—make tiny holes with a fork or toothpick—which lets out the steam so that large bubbles do not form.

Place a piece of buttered aluminum foil on the pastry, butter side toward the dough. Cover the aluminum foil with dried beans, clean pebbles, or a pie tin with an ovenproof cup of water on it to weigh down the crust so that bubbles do not form and the crust does not shrink or slide from the pan. (The beans can still be used for cooking.) Bake the pie shell on the middle rack of the oven for about 10 minutes.

Remove the aluminum foil and dried beans or pebbles or pie tin and cup. If the sides of the crust have slipped into the pan, press them back with a blunt knife. Patch the crust if necessary with raw dough. To make the dough stick, brush the crust with a beaten egg or water and attach the raw dough gently. Handle with care; the crust will be very fragile. Return the pastry to the oven and bake until light brown, about 5 minutes longer.

If you like, you can waterproof the pie shell by brushing it with egg white. This prevents the bottom crust from becoming soggy. Return the crust to the oven and bake until it is dry, about 2 minutes.

For a one-crust pie: fill the shell with the filling.

For a two-crust pie: fill the bottom shell, roll the top crust as you did the bottom, slash petal-like vents in the dough or cut a small circle in the center for steam to escape. Place the top crust over the filling, trim the overhanging dough, fold the edge of the top crust over the rim of the bottom crust and secure to the underside of the rim of the pie tin. Press the rim with a fork or flute it.

Heat the oven to 425°. Bake the pie on the middle rack of the oven. After 15 minutes, lower the oven temperature to 350°.

To glaze the top crust of a two-crust pie, brush the surface with egg white or a honey-water mixture. Both will make a shiny, golden brown crust.

As the pie bakes, if the crust begins to brown too much, cover the top of the crust with a sheet of aluminum foil, or cover the rim of the pie with a strip of aluminum foil.

Bake a one-crust pie until the filling is done. For

instance, the filling of a custard pie should be firm when the pie has baked about 30 minutes.

A two-crust pie is done when the crust is brown and crisp and the filling is cooked, about 1 hour.

FREEZING PIE CRUST DOUGH

Wrap raw, unrolled dough, or rolled dough in the tin, in airtight plastic bags and freeze. When ready to use, defrost in the refrigerator—about 4 hours for a one-crust ball of dough. To defrost an unbaked shell, follow the directions on page 219 for prebaking the bottom crust of a pie, except for the time; bake the crust for 15 minutes before removing the aluminum foil.

To freeze prebaked pie shells, wrap individually in plastic bags and stack them gently in the freezer. To use, simply fill and bake.

RECIPES

Basic Whole Wheat Pie Crust

This pastry dough can be used for sweet or salty fillings, open or covered pies, turnovers, tarts, and quiches. For a 2-crust pie, double the quantities. For a flakier crust or if the whole wheat dough is difficult to handle, use unbleached white wheat flour in place of the whole wheat.

¾ cup whole wheat flour
   (preferably soft wheat or
   pastry flour)
2 tablespoons soy flour
½ teaspoon salt

2 tablespoons wheat germ
⅓ cup cold butter
About 4 tablespoons
   cold water

1. In a small bowl sift together the wheat flour, soy flour, and salt. Add to the bowl any particles that did not go through the sifter. Stir in wheat germ.

2. Cut the butter into the sifted ingredients with a pastry blender or two knives, or crumble the butter into the flour mixture by rubbing them together quickly with your fingertips. The mixture should resemble coarse cornmeal. Tossing the flour lightly with a fork, gradually add enough water to make a soft dough. If time permits, wrap the dough in waxed paper and refrigerate until chilled, about 2 hours.

3. Roll the dough into a 10-inch circle. Place the dough in an 8-inch pie tin, trim the overhanging dough, and pinch the edges with your fingertips or a fork to attach the crust to the rim of the pie tin. If time permits, place the crust in the refrigerator until chilled, about 1 hour.

4. Heat the oven to 425°. Prick the bottom of the pie shell with a fork, place a piece of buttered aluminum foil over the crust, butter side towards the crust, and cover the aluminum foil with clean pebbles or dried beans.

5. Bake the crust for 10 minutes. Then remove the foil and beans or pebbles, and repair any damaged portions of the crust. If the sides of the crust have slipped into the pan, press them back with a blunt knife. Return the crust to the oven and bake until light brown, about 5 minutes longer. The crust is now ready for filling.

Apple Pie

1 PIE WITH ABOUT 37 GRAMS USABLE PROTEIN

Any fresh fruit will make a fine pie. Try peaches, pears, rhubarb, pitted cherries, or blueberries.

A double recipe Basic
Whole Wheat Pie Crust

1. Prepare a double recipe of the BASIC WHOLE WHEAT PIE CRUST or a substitute. Roll out and pre-bake the bottom crust. Set aside the rest of the dough for the top crust.

APPLE FILLING

About 5 apples
½ cup sunflower seeds
½ cup wheat germ
½ cup honey
½ cup raisins
1 tablespoon grated orange rind

2 teaspoons ground cinnamon
½ teaspoon ground nutmeg
½ teaspoon ground mace
½ teaspoon salt
2 tablespoons butter
1 tablespoon honey
1 tablespoon water

2. Peel, core, and slice the apples thin. In a large bowl, combine the apples, sunflower seeds, wheat germ, honey, raisins, orange rind, spices, and salt. Mix well. Spoon the filling into the baked pie crust, fill to over-flowing, and press to pack it tightly. Cut the butter into small pieces and place over the apples.

3. Heat the oven to 425°.

4. Roll the second half of the dough into a 10-inch circle. Slash petal-like vents in the dough or cut a small circle in the center for steam to escape. Place the dough over the apple filling, trim the overhanging dough, and fold the edge of the top crust over the rim of the bottom crust and secure it to the underside of the rim of the pie tin. Press the rim with a fork or flute it.

5. In a cup, combine the 1 tablespoon each of honey and water. Brush this glaze on the pie crust.

6. Bake the pie for 10 minutes, then lower the oven temperature to 350° and bake until the crust is golden brown and the filling is bubbly, about 50 minutes longer. If the crust begins to brown too much, cover the top with a sheet of aluminum foil or cover the rim of the pie with a strip of aluminum foil. Cool in the tin on a wire rack. Serve warm or at room temperature.

Vegetable Pie with Ricotta Topping

1 PIE WITH ABOUT 92 GRAMS USABLE PROTEIN

Any group of vegetables that combines the protein ingredients—soybeans and nuts—with the ricotta cheese topping will make a high-protein vegetable pie meal.

**1 recipe Basic Whole
Wheat Pie Crust**

1. Prepare 1 recipe of the BASIC WHOLE WHEAT PIE CRUST or a substitute. Roll out and bake the dough in a deep pie tin or casserole.

VEGETABLE FILLING

¼ cup uncooked soybeans and 2 cups water, or ½ cup cooked soybeans	2 fresh tomatoes ½ cup nuts ½ teaspoon salt
2 onions	¼ teaspoon thyme
1 carrot or turnip	¼ teaspoon basil
½ pound spinach	¼ teaspoon oregano

2. In a covered saucepan over low heat cook the soybeans in the water until the beans are soft, about 2½ hours. Add water if necessary to keep the beans from burning. Cooking time can be reduced by about half if the beans are first soaked overnight. Omit this step if cooked soybeans are used.
3. Cut the onions into wedges, and slice the carrot or turnip, clean the spinach and remove the thick stems, quarter the tomatoes, chop the nuts and soybeans coarse.
4. In a large saucepan combine the onions and carrot or turnip with 1 inch of water. Cover the pan and simmer the vegetables until they are barely tender, about 15 minutes.
5. Stir in the soybeans, spinach, tomatoes, and nuts.

Cover and cook until the spinach and tomatoes are soft, about 5 minutes. Drain the vegetables well. Mix in the seasonings.

6. Heat the oven to 425°.

RICOTTA TOPPING

2 cups milk	**2 eggs**
¼ cup butter	**1 cup ricotta cheese**
3 tablespoons flour,	
any kind	

7. In a saucepan heat the milk to boiling and remove the pan from the heat. Melt the butter in another saucepan over low heat. Stir the flour into the butter with a fork or wire whisk. Continue stirring about 2 minutes. Gradually add the milk to the flour-butter mixture and continue stirring. Cook over low heat until the sauce is thick, about 5 minutes. Remove the pan from the heat and let it cool to warm.

8. In a small bowl beat the eggs. Stir them into the sauce. Stir in the ricotta.

9. Spoon the vegetables into the pie shell and cover them with ricotta topping. Bake the pie for 10 minutes, then lower the oven temperature to 350° and bake until the topping is firm and light brown, about 30 minutes longer. If the crust begins to brown too much, cover the rim of the pastry with a strip of aluminum foil. Cool in the tin or on a wire rack. Serve hot, warm, or at room temperature.

The flavor of this pie improves after a day. Reheat or serve at room temperature.

Pecan Pie

1 PIE WITH ABOUT 46 GRAMS USABLE PROTEIN

This is a very sweet pie. Try walnuts for variety.

¾ cup unbleached white
  wheat flour
⅜ cup soy flour
½ teaspoon salt

6 tablespoons cold butter
About ¼ cup cold
  orange juice

1. In a small bowl sift together the wheat flour, soy flour, and salt. Add to the bowl any particles that did not go through the sifter.

2. Cut the butter into the sifted ingredients with a pastry blender or two knives, or crumble the butter into the flour mixture by rubbing them together quickly with your fingertips. The mixture should resemble coarse cornmeal. Tossing the flour lightly with a fork, gradually add enough orange juice to make a soft dough. If time permits wrap the dough in waxed paper and refrigerate until chilled, about 2 hours.

3. Roll the dough into a 10-inch circle. Place the dough in an 8-inch tin, trim the overhanging dough, and pinch the edges with your fingertips or a fork to attach the crust to the rim of the pie tin. If time permits, place the crust in the refrigerator until chilled, about 1 hour.

4. Heat the oven to 375°. Prick the bottom of the pie shell with a fork, place a piece of buttered aluminum foil over the crust, butter side towards the crust, and cover the aluminum foil with clean pebbles or dried beans.

5. Bake the crust for 10 minutes. Then remove the foil and beans or pebbles, and repair any damaged portions of the crust. If the sides of the crust have slipped into the pan, press them back with a blunt knife, return the crust to the oven, and bake until light brown, about 5 minutes longer. The crust is now ready for filling.

FILLING

3 tablespoons butter	3 eggs
¾ cup brown sugar	¾ teaspoon vanilla
¾ cup dark corn syrup	2¼ cups pecans

6. Lower the oven temperature to 350°.

7. In a bowl, beat the butter with a fork or rotary beater until it is creamy. Gradually stir in the sugar, syrup, eggs, and vanilla. Mix well. Add the pecans.

8. Pour the pecan filling into the pie shell. Wrap a strip of aluminum foil around the rim of the crust to prevent it from burning. Bake the pie until the filling is golden brown and firm, about 45 minutes. Let cool in the tin on a wire rack. Serve warm or at room temperature.

Pumpkin Pie with Nut-Wheat Germ Crust

1 PIE WITH 63 GRAMS USABLE PROTEIN

The crust of this pie is easy to make because it is simply pressed into the pan. To vary this basic recipe change the nuts in the crust or use a different custard filling.

⅓ cup butter	1 tablespoon honey
1 cup nuts	1 egg white
1 cup wheat germ	

1. Heat the oven to 250°. Melt the butter and set it aside.

2. Grind the nuts to a coarse powder in a blender. Without a blender either chop nuts fine with a knife, or place the nuts in a plastic bag or between two sheets of

waxed paper and roll into a powder with a rolling pin. Toast the nuts and the wheat germ in a frying pan over low heat until brown, about 5 minutes. *Stir frequently to prevent burning.*

3. In a small bowl dissolve the honey in the butter. Add the wheat germ and nuts and stir until moistened.

4. Press this crust mixture into an 8-inch pie tin. Do not form a crust on the rim of the pie tin; build the pie shell only on the sloping sides of the pan.

5. Brush the crust with egg white for waterproofing, and bake 5 minutes. The crust is now ready for filling.

FILLING

2 tablespoons butter	¼ teaspoon ground mace
1½ cups cooked pumpkin	¼ teaspoon ground cloves
2 eggs	½ teaspoon ground ginger
½ cup honey	or a 1-inch slice of
½ cup milk powder	fresh ginger root
½ teaspoon salt	¾ cup evaporated milk
½ teaspoon ground	1 teaspoon vanilla
cinnamon	

6. Heat the oven to 425°. Melt the butter and set it aside.

7. In a bowl mix together the pumpkin, eggs, honey, milk powder, salt, and spices. If fresh ginger root is used, squeeze in a garlic press to extract the juice. Stir in the butter, evaporated milk and vanilla.

8. Pour the filling into the pie shell up to the rim of the tin. Bake the pie for 15 minutes, then lower the oven temperature to 325° and bake until the filling is firm, about 30 minutes longer. If the edge of the filling or the crust begins to brown too much, cover the rim of the pie with a strip of aluminum foil.

9. Cool in the tin on a wire rack. Chill at least 1 hour in the refrigerator before serving. Pumpkin pie is particularly good served with ice cream or yogurt.

Papaya Custard Tart

1 TART WITH ABOUT 39 GRAMS USABLE PROTEIN

This is a rich dough with an exotic fruit filling. If fresh papaya is out of season, substitute a bottled (not canned) papaya that is preserved in light syrup. If papaya is not available, or you are not a papaya lover, substitute peaches or apricots.

⅓ cup nuts
1 cup unbleached white
   wheat flour
½ teaspoon salt
½ cup cold butter

1 tablespoon honey
1 egg yolk
About 5 tablespoons
   cold water

1. Grind the nuts to a coarse powder in a blender. Without a blender either chop the nuts fine with a knife, or place the nuts in a plastic bag or between two sheets of waxed paper and roll into a powder with a rolling pin. Set the nuts aside.

2. In a small bowl, sift together the flour and salt. Stir in the nuts.

3. Cut the butter into the dry ingredients with a pastry blender or two knives, or crumble the butter into the flour mixture by rubbing them together quickly with your fingertips. The mixture should resemble coarse cornmeal.

4. In a cup combine the honey with the egg yolk. Tossing the flour mixture lightly with a fork, add the honey-egg mixture. Gradually add enough cold water to make a soft dough. If time permits, wrap the dough in waxed paper and refrigerate until chilled, about 2 hours.

5. Roll the dough into a 10-inch circle. Place the dough in an 8-inch tart tin, pie plate, or layer-cake pan. Trim the overhanging dough, and pinch the edges with

your fingertips or a fork to attach the crust to the rim of the pie tin. Handle gently since the dough is delicate; however, it does mend easily, so do not hesitate to patch where necessary. If time permits, place the crust in the refrigerator until chilled, about 1 hour.

6. Heat the oven to 425°. Prick the bottom of the pie shell with a fork, place a piece of buttered aluminum foil over the crust, butter side toward the crust and cover the aluminum foil with clean pebbles or dried beans.

7. Bake the crust for 10 minutes. Then remove the foil and beans or pebbles, and repair any damaged portions of the crust. If the sides of the crust have slipped into the pan, press them back with a blunt knife, return the pie to the oven and bake until light brown, about 5 minutes longer. The crust is now ready for filling.

FILLING

1 ripe papaya
About ½ cup honey
1 egg

¼ cup unbleached white wheat flour
¼ cup milk powder
½ cup milk

8. Lower the oven temperature to 375°. Clean, peel, and slice the papaya.

9. In a saucepan heat ½ cup honey until it is hot but not boiling. Remove the pan from the heat. Soak the papaya in the honey for at least 15 minutes, turning it occasionally to make sure it absorbs the honey flavor.

10. Brush some of the heated honey on the inside of the pie shell. It will act as waterproofing.

11. Scoop the papaya out of the honey and let the excess liquid drip off. Arrange the slices in the shell. Bake for 15 minutes.

12. Lower the oven temperature to 325°.

13. In a small bowl beat together the egg and ⅓ cup

honey. Use the honey in which the papaya was soaked and add to it if necessary to make ⅓ cup. Sift in the flour. In a cup dissolve the milk powder in the milk and add this to the honey-egg mixture. Stir well.

14. Pour the custard over the baked papaya and return the pastry to the oven. Bake until the custard is firm and light brown, about 20 minutes. If the crust begins to brown too much, cover the rim of the pie with a strip of aluminum foil. Cool in the tin on a wire rack. Serve chilled or at room temperature.

Bertha's Split Pea Turnovers

ABOUT A DOZEN TURNOVERS EACH WITH ABOUT
7 GRAMS USABLE PROTEIN

These small pastries can be eaten as snacks or a meal. The bean filling (any bean can be used) complements the wheat protein in the crust.

1¼ cups whole wheat flour (preferably soft wheat or pastry flour)	½ teaspoon salt
	2 eggs
	½ cup oil
1¼ cups unbleached white wheat flour	About 2 tablespoons cold water
1 teaspoon baking powder	Oil

1. In a large bowl sift together the whole wheat flour, the white wheat flour, the baking powder, and the salt. Add to the bowl any particles that did not go through the sifter.

2. In a cup beat the eggs with a fork. Tossing the flour lightly, gradually add the eggs to the flour. Add the oil, drop by drop, stirring briskly and lightly to make a crumbly mixture. Gradually add enough water to make a soft dough. If time permits, wrap the dough in waxed paper and refrigerate it until chilled, about 2 hours. Prepare the filling.

3. Heat the oven to 400°. Oil 2 baking sheets.

4. On a board lightly floured with white wheat flour, roll the dough into a ¼-inch-thick rectangle. With a knife, trim the ragged edges, and cut the dough into 24 squares of about 3 by 3 inches.

5. On 12 of the squares spoon about ¼ cup of filling each. Wet the edges of the filled squares of dough with a finger dipped in water, and place an unfilled square of dough over the filling. Pinch the 4 sides between your fingers or with a fork to seal well.

6. Place the turnovers on the baking sheets and brush their surfaces with oil. Bake the turnovers until golden brown, about 35 minutes. Serve hot or warm.

FILLING

1 cup uncooked split peas	⅓ cup oil
2½ cups water	2 eggs
A large onion	1½ teaspoons salt
	Pepper

1. In a covered saucepan over low heat cook the peas in the water until the peas are soft, about 1½ hours. Let stand until the peas are just warm. Drain.

2. Chop the onion fine. Mash the peas with the onion, oil, eggs, and salt. Add pepper to taste.

Baklava (Greek Fillo Pastry with Nut Filling)

ABOUT 2 DOZEN SERVINGS OF BAKLAVA EACH WITH
ABOUT 5 GRAMS USABLE PROTEIN

Baklava is a honey-soaked, rich, high-protein dessert made from fillo pastry leaves, paper-thin sheets of dough that are sold in Middle Eastern and gourmet food shops.

BAKLAVA

1½ cups wheat germ
4 cups mixed nuts (for instance pistachios, walnuts, almonds, macadamia nuts)
¾ teaspoon ground cinnamon
¾ teaspoon ground cloves
¾ cup brown sugar
½ cup butter
½ cup oil (preferably corn, cottonseed, or safflower)
A 1-pound package fillo pastry dough

1. Toast the wheat germ in a frying pan over low heat until brown, about 5 minutes. Stir frequently to prevent burning. Grind the nuts to a coarse powder in a blender. Without a blender either chop the nuts fine with a knife, or place the nuts in a plastic bag or between two sheets of waxed paper and roll into a powder with a rolling pin.

2. In a large bowl combine the wheat germ, nuts, spices, and sugar. Mix well.

3. Heat the oven to 350°. In a small saucepan melt the butter. Remove the pan from the heat and stir in the oil. Brush the bottom and sides of a 9-by-12-by-2-inch pan with some of this mixture.

4. Open the package of fillo. Remove the dough and unfold it gently. Cover the pastry leaves with plastic wrap or a damp cloth to prevent the dough from drying and keep the unused dough covered until you need it. Cut the fillo leaves in half with scissors to fit the size of the pan. Most fillo leaves come in 12-by-18-inch sheets.

5. Place about 15 layers of dough on the bottom of the pan, one by one, brushing with the butter mixture between layers. Spread about ½ cup of the nut filling over the pastry.

6. Layer with about 6 layers of pastry and butter. Small pieces of pastry can be included in the layering; a whole sheet is not necessary. Again spread about ½ cup of the original amount of nut filling over the pastry, and again layer with about 6 sheets of buttered fillo. Continue layering with nuts and sheets of pastry until

all the filling and fillo is used up. Finish with about 15 layers of fillo. If the butter mixture becomes too thick to spread easily, add oil and stir.

7. Brush the surface with the butter mixture and trim the edges of any overhanging dough. With a sharp knife, cut the pastry into diamonds. Wrap unused fillo sheets in a plastic bag, seal securely, and refrigerate.

8. Bake the pastry until the top layers of dough are golden brown and flaky, about 1 hour. If the top is not yet brown then, increase the baking temperature to 400° and bake for a few minutes longer. While the pastry is in the oven, make the syrup.

SYRUP

1½ cups honey	A slice of lemon
2 cups water	A cinnamon stick

9. In a saucepan, combine the honey, water, lemon, and cinnamon. Cook over low heat until the mixture boils. Boil gently until it thickens, about 10 minutes. Scoop out the lemon and cinnamon stick and remove the pan from the heat. Let the syrup cool to warm.

10. When the pastry has finished baking, spoon the syrup over the hot baklava. If you let the baklava stand for a few hours, the honey will soak in.

Spanakotiropita
(Greek Fillo Pastry with Spinach-Feta Filling)

ABOUT A DOZEN SPANAKOTIROPITA EACH WITH ABOUT 16 GRAMS USABLE PROTEIN

You may want to add escarole to these pastries in place of some of the spinach; some say that it is always included in authentic spanakotiropita.

3 pounds fresh spinach or
  2 packages frozen
  chopped spinach
A large onion
1½ pounds feta cheese,
  about 4 cups, crumbled
2 cups cottage cheese
4 eggs
¼ cup chopped fresh dill or

2 tablespoons dried
  dill weed
½ cup butter
½ cup oil (preferably corn,
  cottonseed, or safflower)
1 cup wheat germ
A 1-pound package of
  fillo pastry dough

1. Clean the spinach, remove the thick stems, and chop. Chop the onion. Cook the spinach and the onion in a covered saucepan over medium heat in 1 inch of water until both vegetables are just soft, about 10 minutes; or prepare the frozen spinach according to the directions on the package and include the onion in the pan. Drain well. Let cool to room temperature.

2. In a large bowl mix together the spinach and onions, feta cheese, cottage cheese, 3 of the eggs, and the dill. Mix well.

3. In a small saucepan melt the butter. Remove the pan from the heat and stir in the oil. Butter 2 baking sheets with some of this mixture. Then let the mixture cool to room temperature, and beat in the remaining egg.

4. Open the package of fillo. Remove the dough and unfold it gently. Cover the pastry leaves with plastic wrap or a damp cloth to prevent the dough from drying, and keep the unused dough covered until you need it.

5. Place a layer of fillo on the worktable. Brush it with the egg-butter mixture. Place another layer of pastry on the first and brush it with the egg-butter mixture. Continue layering until there are 5 sheets. Sprinkle about 3 tablespoons of wheat germ on the last layer.

6. With scissors cut the layers of fillo into two 18-by-6-inch strips. Most fillo leaves come in 12-by-18-inch sheets. Place about ½ cup of the spinach-cheese filling on the lower right-hand corner of one strip of pastry. Fold the corner of the dough up and over to

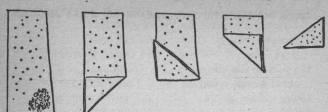

meet the left-hand edge, making a triangle. Continue folding triangles back and forth from right to left along the strip of dough (in the manner that the American flag is folded). Repeat the layering, cutting, filling, and folding. There should be about a dozen pastries. If the butter mixture becomes too thick to spread easily, add oil and stir.

To make smaller, hors d'oeuvres-size pastries, cut the layered sheets of fillo into four 4½-by-12-inch strips. Fill each with about ¼ cup of filling and fold into triangles.

Other ways of assembling and filling the fillo are rolling the filling in the pastry like a tube of strudel or layering it between pastry sheets like baklava.

7. Wrap unused fillo sheets in a plastic bag, seal securely, and refrigerate. Unused filling is very good eaten as is.

8. Heat the oven to 425°. Place the spanakotiropita on the baking sheets and brush the tops with the butter mixture. Bake the pastries until the tops are golden brown and flaky, about 15 minutes. Serve hot or warm.

Unbaked pastries freeze well. Wrap individually in plastic wrap or in plastic bags. When ready to use, unwrap, place the frozen pastries on baking sheets, brush with melted butter and bake.

Cheese Strudel

1 STRUDEL WITH ABOUT 266 GRAMS USABLE PROTEIN

Once you get the knack of stretching the strudel dough, this recipe can be easily used to roll up many fillings for main dishes or desserts. Prepare either the salty or the sweet filling to add to the cheese. If you plan to use drained cottage cheese, it often takes about 2 hours to prepare, so plan accordingly.

3 cups unbleached white wheat flour	About ¾ cup water
1 egg	¼ cup butter
1 tablespoon·oil	1 tablespoon honey
2 teaspoons vinegar or wine	½ cup wheat germ
1 teaspoon salt	2 tablespoons butter

1. Sift the flour into a large bowl. Make a well in the center of the flour and add the egg, oil, vinegar or wine, salt, and ¼ cup of the water. Mix the dough with your fingers or a fork until it begins to hold together. Gradually add enough water to make a soft dough.

2. Knead the dough on a lightly floured board until it is soft and springy. Add water on your fingertips or a little flour on the table to adjust the consistency of the dough. Knead until the dough has a firm, smooth feel, about 15 minutes.

3. Heat an empty saucepan. Butter the surface of the dough, invert the pan and cover the dough with it. Let the dough rest for about ½ hour. Meanwhile, prepare the filling.

STRETCHING THE DOUGH

4. Melt the butter. Spread a tablecloth or sheet over the table and sprinkle it with flour. You will need a large space because the dough will stretch into a 3-foot square. Brush the surface of the dough with butter.

5. Begin to stretch the dough by pressing the ball into a flat round. Then take the dough in your hands and pinch and press the circle into a thinner circle. When the round is large enough, place the dough over the backs of your hands, and gently pull and stretch the dough with your knuckles. The dough should stretch easily if you work slowly and with sureness. Do not be fearful that the dough is too delicate to be stretched. Anyway, if it does tear, holes are easily patched.

6. Continue stretching on the backs of your hands until the weight of the dough pulls the dough from your hands. The circle will be about 1½ feet across.

7. Place the dough on the table and continue to stretch it by taking a small piece of dough in both hands and pulling your hands gently in opposite directions. First work your way around the rim of the circle. Then, lift the dough and using the back of your hands, as before, stretch the center portions. Stretch the dough until it is paper-thin and about a 3-foot circle. Some say that to assure a flaky strudel you should be able to read a newspaper through the dough. Patch holes by pinching the dough together, but avoid stretching the area around the patch because it will tear again. Do not expect the dough to be an even thickness. Cut off the thickened rim of the circle of dough.

FILLING THE DOUGH

8. Heat the oven to 375°. Butter a large baking sheet. Stir the honey into the butter. Heat if necessary to dissolve.

9. Brush the surface of the dough with the butter mixture. Sprinkle the dough with the wheat germ.

10. Spoon the cheese filling onto the dough, arranging it in a long band about 6 inches from the edge of the dough nearest to you and about 3 inches from each side. Cut the 2 tablespoons of butter into small pieces and distribute it over the filling.

11. Roll the strudel into a tube by lifting the cloth under the front edge of the dough. The 6-inch flap of

dough closest to you will fold itself over the filling. Fold the 3-inch side flaps of dough over the filling. Continue gently to lift the cloth until the strudel has rolled itself up. Bend the strudel roll into a horseshoe shape or circle to fit the baking sheet. Brush the surface with the remaining butter mixture.

12. Bake the pastry until the crust is golden brown and flaky, about 35 minutes. Cool on the baking sheet on a wire rack. Serve warm or at room temperature.

CHEESE FILLING

5 cups farmer cheese or drained cottage cheese	2 cups nuts
	4 eggs

ADDITIONS FOR A SALTY FILLING

2 teaspoons salt	½ teaspoon thyme
½ teaspoon basil	

OR

ADDITIONS FOR A SWEET FILLING

½ cup brown sugar	1 cup white raisins
½ cup honey	1 teaspoon salt

1. If you are using cottage cheese, drain it in a funnel or sieve lined with a paper towel or filter paper. Set the funnel in a glass or the sieve in a bowl to catch the water (whey) that drains out. (Save the whey for yeast bread-baking.) Let the cottage cheese drain until it is dry and cakey, about 2 hours. The amount of cottage cheese needed initially to make 5 cups after draining and the amount of time it takes depend upon how watery the cottage cheese was.

2. Grind the nuts to a coarse powder in a blender. Without a blender either chop the nuts fine with a knife, or place the nuts in a plastic bag or between two

pieces of waxed paper and roll into a powder with a rolling pin.

3. Combine the cheese, nuts, and eggs in a bowl.

4. Add to the cheese mixture the ingredients for either the salty or the sweet filling. Mix well and refrigerate.

Cakes

These cakes are lighter and fancier desserts than the quick breads but are more substantial than commercial cakes because they are made with whole grains. Since the amount of protein is high, these desserts can be considered an essential part of the meal. A slice of cheesecake makes a good breakfast or supplies the protein food for a soup and salad dinner.

Make these cakes plain or fancy—in loaves, shallow pans, or as frosted layers.

Leftover cake batter can make cupcakes.

Several different methods of mixing cakes are used in the recipes, so see each recipe for the details. For basic mixing techniques, see the Quick Breads chapter.

RECIPES

Basic Whole Wheat Butter Cake

1 CAKE WITH ABOUT 50 GRAMS USABLE PROTEIN

This is a moist, sweet, butter cake that can be made into many kinds of cakes and cookies. See page 260 for cookie variations.

½ cup butter
¼ cup honey
⅔ cup brown sugar
¼ cup soy flour
3 eggs
1½ cups whole wheat flour

(preferably soft wheat or pastry flour)
1¾ teaspoons baking powder
¾ teaspoon salt
¾ cup milk

1. Heat the oven to 350°. Line an 8-inch square pan with waxed paper and butter the paper.

2. In a large bowl beat the butter with a fork or rotary beater until it is creamy. Gradually add the honey and brown sugar. Sift in the soy flour. Mix well to make sure that no lumps of soy flour remain. Beat in the eggs, one at a time, beating well after each one.

3. In a small bowl sift together the whole wheat flour, baking powder, and salt. For a lighter cake, resift. Add to the bowl any particles that did not go through the sifter.

4. Stir the dry ingredients alternately with the milk into the butter mixture. Beat well.

5. Pour the batter into the pan and bake until the center springs back when gently pressed or a toothpick or broom straw inserted in the center comes out clean, about 40 minutes. Cool the cake in the pan on a wire rack until it is cool enough to hold in your hand. Then take the cake out of the pan, peel off the waxed paper, and cool right-side-up on the rack.

Three Variations of the Basic Cake

PINEAPPLE-GINGER UPSIDE-DOWN CAKE

1 CAKE WITH ABOUT 50 GRAMS USABLE PROTEIN

Any fresh fruit can be substituted for the pineapple. Sweetened canned fruit can be used, but in that case do not soak the fruit in honey.

4 slices fresh pineapple
3 tablespoons honey
½ cup water
¼ cup butter
½ cup brown sugar
1½ teaspoons molasses
1 tablespoon water
½ teaspoon vanilla
¼ teaspoon salt
¼ teaspoon ground
  cinnamon
¼ cup sliced candied
  ginger
1 recipe Basic Whole Wheat
  Butter Cake

1. Peel, core, and slice the pineapple into thin rings. In a cup dissolve two tablespoons of the honey in the water. Put the pineapple slices in a shallow bowl and pour the honey-water over them. Let the pineapple soak for about 10 minutes. Turn the slices once or twice to make sure that all the slices are sweetened.

2. In a small bowl beat the butter with a fork or rotary beater until it is creamy. Gradually add the remaining 1 tablespoon honey, the sugar, molasses, water, vanilla, salt, and cinnamon. Beat well after each addition.

3. Spread the mixture on the bottom and sides of an 8-inch square pan. Blot the pineapple slices on a piece of paper toweling. Arrange the pineapple in an attractive pattern on the butter-sugar mixture. I like to place a full circle of pineapple in the center of the pan and place quarter-pieces around the circle like flower petals. Place the ginger between the pineapple slices.

4. Follow all the steps for the BASIC WHOLE WHEAT BUTTER CAKE and pour the batter over the pineapple. Bake the cake until the center springs back when gently pressed or a toothpick or broom straw inserted in the center comes out clean, about 40 minutes. Cool the cake in the pan on a wire rack for 5 minutes, then invert on a plate before the caramel hardens.

SPICE CAKE

Prepare the BASIC WHOLE WHEAT BUTTER CAKE and sift with the flour two teaspoons of a mixture of some of the following ground spices: cinnamon, nutmeg, ginger, cloves, mace, or cardamom; then add a handful of raisins to the batter before pouring it into the pan.

CHOCOLATE CAKE

Add 3 ounces of melted unsweetened chocolate to the BASIC WHOLE WHEAT BUTTER CAKE batter following the eggs.

Maple Sponge Loaf

1 LOAF WITH ABOUT 51 GRAMS USABLE PROTEIN

This eggy, not-too-sweet cake makes good breakfast toast or dessert cake/bread with ice cream.

2 egg yolks
2 eggs
1 cup maple syrup
1 teaspoon vanilla
⅓ cup milk
½ cup oil (preferably corn, cottonseed, or safflower)

1¾ cups whole wheat flour
   (preferably soft wheat or
   pastry flour)
¼ cup wheat germ
1½ tablespoons cornstarch
1 teaspoon baking powder

1. Heat the oven to 375°. Line a medium-size loaf pan with waxed paper and oil the paper.
2. In a large bowl over a kettle of boiling water warm the egg yolks, eggs, maple syrup, and vanilla. While heating, beat well with a rotary beater—hand or electric—until light and foamy. Do not overheat and cook the eggs. Remove from the heat.
3. In a small saucepan heat the milk and oil. Gradually add half of this to the mixture in the bowl. Set aside the other half. Beat the egg mixture until it is thick, about 10 minutes with a hand beater or 5 minutes with an electric beater.
4. In a small bowl sift together the whole wheat flour, wheat germ, cornstarch, and baking powder. Resift them into the mixture in the large bowl. Add to the

bowl any particles that did not go through the sifter. Beat well.

5. Add the remaining half of the milk-oil mixture to the batter and beat well.

6. Pour the batter into the loaf pan and bake until the center springs back when gently pressed or a toothpick or broom straw inserted in the center comes out clean, about one hour. Cool the loaf in the pan on a wire rack until cool enough to hold in your hand. Take the cake out of the pan, peel off the waxed paper, and cool on the rack.

Rye Orange Spice Cupcakes

ABOUT 1 DOZEN CUPCAKES EACH WITH ABOUT 3 GRAMS USABLE PROTEIN

These cupcakes are particularly moist and rise only slightly because rye is the sole flour used. Substitute whole wheat or white wheat flour for a drier, higher-rising cake.

¼ cup orange juice	1½ cups whole rye flour
1 teaspoon anise seeds	2 eggs
2 teaspoons grated orange rind	2 teaspoons baking powder
	¾ teaspoon salt
⅓ cup butter	1 teaspoon cinnamon
1 cup brown sugar	1 cup milk

1. Heat the oven to 350°. Butter a 12-cup muffin tin.

2. In a small saucepan heat together the orange juice, anise seeds, and orange rind over low heat for 5 minutes.

3. In a large bowl beat the butter with a fork or rotary beater until it is creamy. Gradually add the sugar. Sift in ¼ cup of the flour and mix well to make sure that no lumps remain. Beat in the eggs, one at a time, beating well after each one.

4. In a small bowl sift together the remaining 1¼ cups of flour, the baking powder, salt, and cinnamon. Add to the bowl any particles that did not go through the sifter.

5. With a wooden spoon or rubber spatula stir the sifted ingredients alternately with the milk into the butter mixture in the large bowl. Mix well.

6. With a rotary beater or fork beat in the orange juice mixture.

7. Spoon the batter into the tin. Fill each cup ¾ full. Bake until the center springs back when gently pressed or a toothpick or broom straw inserted in the center comes out clean, about 20 minutes. Cool the cupcakes in the pan on a wire rack.

Yeast-Raised Carob or Chocolate Layer Cake with Maple Syrup Frosting

1 FROSTED CAKE WITH ABOUT 96 GRAMS USABLE PROTEIN

When frosted, this cake is an elegant dessert. It must rise overnight in the refrigerator, so plan your time accordingly. Once baked, this cake will keep fresh for at least a week. Refer to page 42 for yeast instructions.

10 tablespoons butter
⅜ cup cocoa or carob
⅔ cup honey
¼ cup soy flour
2 eggs
1½ cups whole wheat flour
   (preferably soft wheat or
   pastry flour)
1 teaspoon salt

½ cup wheat germ
1 tablespoon yeast
¼ cup warm water
½ cup milk powder
⅔ cup milk
¾ teaspoon baking soda
⅜ cup warm water
1½ teaspoons vanilla

1. Melt 5 tablespoons of the butter. In a cup or small bowl mix together the cocoa or carob and butter.

2. In a large bowl, beat 5 tablespoons of butter with

a fork or rotary beater until it is creamy. Gradually add the honey. Sift in the soy flour. Mix well to make sure that no lumps of soy flour remain. Beat in the eggs, one at a time, beating well after each one.

3. In a small bowl sift together the flour and salt. Add to the bowl any particles that did not go through the sifter. Stir in the wheat germ.

4. In the cup in which the honey was measured, dissolve the yeast in the water. Let it stand until bubbly, about 5 minutes.

5. Stir the chocolate or carob mixture into the butter mixture in the large bowl. Then add the dissolved yeast. Beat well.

6. In a cup dissolve the milk powder in the milk. Then add to the batter in the large bowl. Finally, add the flour mixture and beat well.

7. Cover the bowl with a plate or plastic wrap and place it in the refrigerator for at least 6 hours and not more than overnight.

8. Heat the oven to 350°. Line two 8-inch round layer pans with waxed paper and butter the paper.

9. In a cup combine the baking soda, warm water, and vanilla. Stir this into the batter and beat well.

10. Pour the batter into the pans. Bake the cake until the center springs back when it is gently pressed or a toothpick or broom straw inserted in the center comes out clean, about 30 minutes. Cool the layers in the pan on wire racks until cool enough to hold. Then take the layers out of the pan, peel off the waxed paper, and cool right-side-up on the racks.

MAPLE SYRUP FROSTING WITH NUTS

¾ cup maple syrup
3 egg whites
A pinch of salt

Several drops of lemon
   juice
½ cup walnuts

1. In a small saucepan boil the syrup gently until a drop from a spoon forms a wispy hair, about 20 min-

utes. Meanwhile, in a large bowl beat the egg whites and the salt with a rotary beater or a wire whisk until foamy.

2. Pour the *hot* maple syrup in a thin stream into the egg whites and continue beating until all the maple syrup is incorporated. An extra pair of hands is helpful.

Add the lemon juice and beat well. The frosting should now be of spreading consistency.

If the maple syrup has boiled too long and the frosting begins to harden, beat in about 1 tablespoon of boiling water. If the maple syrup has not boiled long enough and the frosting does not thicken, continue beating holding the bowl over a bowl of boiling water.

3. When the frosting and the cakes have cooled, place a layer on a large plate. Spread the frosting between the two layers and on the top and sides of the cake. Decorate with nuts.

Orange Pound Cake

1 LOAF WITH ABOUT 62 GRAMS USABLE PROTEIN

This cake is made with no leavening except eggs, and uses the old-fashioned proportions of equal weights of flour, sugar, and butter to make a true "pound for pound" cake. For variety, add a handful of raisins. The wheat germ flour can be made at home in a blender.

1 cup butter	¼ teaspoon salt
1 cup brown sugar	¼ teaspoon mace
¼ teaspoon vanilla	5 eggs
1½ cups unbleached white wheat flour	¼ cup frozen orange juice concentrate
½ cup wheat germ flour	

1. Heat the oven to 325°. Line a medium-size loaf pan with waxed paper and butter the paper.

2. In a large bowl beat the butter with a fork or

rotary beater until it is creamy. Gradually add the sugar and vanilla.

3. In a small bowl sift together the white wheat flour, wheat germ flour, salt, and mace. Add to the bowl any particles that did not go through the sifter. To make wheat germ flour at home, whirl raw or toasted wheat germ in the blender until it is powdery.

4. Beat about ¼ cup of the sifted mixture into the butter mixture. A rotary beater, hand or electric, is helpful in making this cake. Set aside the remaining sifted mixture.

5. Beat in the eggs one at a time, beating well after each one. Resift the remainder of the flour mixture and add it slowly to the mixture in the large bowl.

6. Beat the orange juice concentrate into the batter. Make sure as you are beating that the batter at the sides and the bottom of the bowl is mixed in.

7. Pour the batter into the loaf pan. Bake the loaf until the center springs back when it is gently pressed or a toothpick or broom straw inserted in the center comes out clean, about 1 hour. There should be an even split along the center of the loaf. Cool the loaf in the pan on a wire rack.

Fruit Cake

3 LOAVES EACH WITH ABOUT 57 GRAMS USABLE PROTEIN

This is a dark, sweet, fruit cake which lends itself to experimentation. Substitute fruits for fruits and nuts for nuts.

2 whole oranges, seeded
1 whole lemon, seeded
¼ grapefruit, seeded
½ cup stewed kumquats
⅔ cup pickled
    watermelon rind
1 cup filberts
1 cup blanched almonds
1 cup Brazil nuts
1 cup pecans
½ cup mashed fresh
    apricots
½ cup diced citron
2 cups raisins
2 cups currants
⅔ cup chopped dates
2 tablespoons vinegar
3 tablespoons honey
⅓ cup molasses
⅓ cup rum
1 cup butter

1½ cups brown sugar
5 eggs
½ teaspoon vanilla extract
½ teaspoon almond extract
3 tablespoons yeast
½ cup warm water
1 cup whole wheat flour
    (preferably hard wheat or
    bread flour)
⅓ cup milk powder
½ teaspoon salt
2 teaspoons ground
    cinnamon
1 teaspoon ground allspice
1 teaspoon ground cloves
1 teaspoon ground ginger or
    a 2-inch slice of fresh
    ginger root
¼ teaspoon ground nutmeg
1½ cups wheat germ
1 cup cashews

1. Heat the oven to 300° and place a shallow pan of water on the oven floor. Line 3 medium-size loaf pans with waxed paper and butter the paper.

2. Grind the oranges, lemon, and grapefruit in a blender. Without a blender chop them into fine pieces. Chop the kumquats, watermelon rind, filberts, almonds, Brazil nuts, and pecans coarse. In a large bowl combine all the fruit, the chopped nuts, the vinegar, honey, molasses, and rum. Mix well.

3. In a small bowl beat the butter with a fork or rotary beater until it is creamy. Gradually add the sugar. Beat in the eggs, vanilla extract, and almond extract.

4. In the cup in which the honey was measured dissolve the yeast in the warm water. Let it stand until bubbly, about 5 minutes.

5. In a small bowl sift together the flour, milk powder, salt, and spices. If fresh ginger root is used, squeeze in a garlic press to extract the juice and stir that juice into the butter mixture. Add to the bowl any particles that did not go through the sifter.

6. Mix the butter mixture, the dissolved yeast, the sifted ingredients, and the wheat germ into the fruit and nut mixture in the large bowl.

7. Grind the cashew nuts to a coarse powder in a blender. Without a blender either chop the nuts fine with a knife, or place the nuts in a plastic bag or between two sheets of waxed paper and roll into a powder with a rolling pin. Stir this cashew meal into the batter.

8. Pour the batter into the loaf pans. Bake the cakes until firm or a toothpick or broom straw inserted in the center comes out clean, about 2 hours. Do not mistake pieces of mashed fruit for unbaked dough. If the crust begins to brown too much, cover the breads with a tent of aluminum foil. Cool the cakes in the pans on wire racks.

9. For special occasions, take the loaves out of the pans and wrap them in rum-soaked cheesecloth. Place them in metal tins or wrap in aluminum foil and store the breads for at least a month. Keep the cheesecloth moistened with more rum if it dries.

Cheesecake

1 CAKE WITH ABOUT 138 GRAMS USABLE PROTEIN

This creamy cheesecake can be the protein food for a meal that is otherwise low in protein. It resembles Italian soft cheesecake; for German-style, substitute cream cheese for the ricotta. That, however, will have less protein.

CRUST

⅓ cup butter
1 cup wheat germ

1 cup graham cracker
    crumbs, about 8 crackers

1. Heat the oven to 250°.
2. Melt the butter. Toast the wheat germ in a frying pan over low heat until brown, about 5 minutes. Stir frequently to prevent burning. Crush the graham crackers in a plastic bag with a rolling pin until they are fine-ground. In a small bowl combine the butter, wheat germ, and graham cracker crumbs. Mix until the dry ingredients are moistened.
3. Press this crust mixture firmly into the bottom and sides of a 9-inch springform mold or a deep round cake tin. Bake this crust for 5 minutes.

FILLING

10 ounces cream cheese
4 eggs
2 cups ricotta cheese

⅔ cup honey
1 teaspoon vanilla extract

4. Heat the oven to 325°.
5. Warm the cream cheese to room temperature. Separate the eggs. Set the whites aside. In a large bowl combine the cream cheese, egg yolks, ricotta, and honey. Blend the mixture until it is creamy. Try to mix in all the cream cheese since large pieces will make the

cake lumpy. A blender, a rotary beater, or an electric mixer is helpful in making this cake. Fold in the vanilla extract.

6. In another large bowl beat the egg whites with a wire whisk or rotary beater until they are stiff. Fold them gently into the cheese mixture.

7. Pour the cheese mixture into the crust. Bake the cake until the filling is firm, about 50 minutes. If the filling browns too quickly, cover it with aluminum foil.

TOPPING

1 cup yogurt	½ tablespoon vanilla
1 tablespoon honey	extract

8. In a small bowl blend the yogurt, honey, and vanilla extract. Pour this topping over the cake. Return the cake to the oven for 10 minutes. Turn off the oven and open the oven door slightly. Let the cake cool in the oven. Chill the cake in the refrigerator overnight before serving.

Nut Cake or Filled Nut Roll

1 CAKE WITHOUT FILLING WITH ABOUT 76 GRAMS USABLE PROTEIN; WITH FILLING WITH ABOUT 91 GRAMS USABLE PROTEIN

This no-flour nut cake can be cut into small squares for everyday eating (it will keep fresh for several days), or rolled with a creamy filling for a special dessert. A soft, substantial nut like walnuts or pecans seems to work best. If you prefer, fill the roll with whipped cream.

1½ cups ground	7 eggs
walnuts or pecans, about	¾ cup brown sugar
2 cups whole nuts	1 teaspoon baking powder

1. Heat the oven to 350°. Butter a 12-by-18-inch baking sheet, with ¾-inch sides. Line with waxed paper and butter the paper.

2. Grind the nuts to a coarse powder in a blender. Without a blender place the nuts in a plastic bag or between two sheets of waxed paper and roll into a powder with a rolling pin.

3. Separate the eggs. Set the whites aside. In a large bowl beat the egg yolks with a rotary beater or wire whisk until foamy and light-colored. Gradually add the sugar, beating until it becomes thick, lemon colored, and forms a slowly descending ribbon when the beater is lifted.

4. Beat in the nuts and baking powder.

5. In a large bowl beat the egg whites with a wire whisk or rotary beater until they are stiff. With a large spoon or rubber spatula gently fold the egg whites into the egg-nut mixture.

6. Pour the batter into the pan and spread it to an even thickness. Bake the cake until it is brown and firm, about 20 minutes. Cool the cake covered with a damp cloth in the pan on a wire rack.

For small cakes, when the cake is cool cut it into 24 3-inch squares. Spread a thin layer of honey or jam on one square and set another square on top of it.

FILLING

4 egg yolks   ⅓ cup brown sugar

1. In a small bowl beat the egg yolks with a rotary beater or wire whisk until foamy and light-colored. Gradually add the sugar just as you did for the cake.

2. To form the nut roll, turn the cake over onto a large piece of waxed paper. Peel off the waxed paper backing. Spread the filling on the entire surface and roll the cake gently and loosely, like a jelly roll, from the wider side. Serve immediately, because the egg filling quickly seeps into the cake.

Carrot Cake with Cream Cheese Frosting

**1 SMALL FROSTED LOAF WITH ABOUT 43 GRAMS
USABLE PROTEIN**

*This is an elegant, crumbly cake dessert. For variety,
try using beets to replace the carrots. The frosting also
makes a good spread for toast.*

¼ cup oil (preferably corn,
   cottonseed, or safflower)
¼ cup brown sugar
¼ cup honey
¾ cup whole wheat flour
   (preferably soft wheat or
   pastry flour)

1 teaspoon baking powder
¼ teaspoon baking soda
⅛ teaspoon salt
½ teaspoon ground nutmeg
¼ cup wheat germ
1 egg
¾ cup grated carrots

1. Heat the oven to 350°. Line a small-size loaf pan
with waxed paper and oil the paper.
2. In a large bowl beat together the oil, sugar, and
honey with a fork or rotary beater.
3. In a small bowl sift together the flour, baking
powder, baking soda, salt, and nutmeg. Add to the
bowl any particles that did not go through the sifter.
Stir in the wheat germ.
4. Add about 2 tablespoons of the dry ingredients
to the oil mixture, then beat in the egg. Beat well.
5. With a wooden spoon or rubber spatula stir the
dry ingredients into the oil mixture in the large bowl.
Stir in the carrots. Mix well.
6. Pour the batter into the loaf pan. Bake the cake
until the center springs back when gently pressed or a
toothpick or broom straw inserted in the center comes
out clean, about 45 minutes. Cool the cake in the pan on
a wire rack until it is cool enough to hold in your
hand. Take the cake out of the pan. Peel off the waxed
paper, and cool right-side up on the rack. Spread with
frosting.

FROSTING

4 ounces cream cheese	½ cup ricotta cheese
½ cup dates	¼ cup honey
¼ cup pecans	

Warm the cream cheese to room temperature. Chop the dates and pecans fine. In a small bowl combine the frosting ingredients and mix well. Spread on the cooled cake.

Cookies

Cookies usually are rich in butter and very sweet. The easiest cookies to make are small lumps of a very stiff batter dropped onto a baking sheet. There are several ways to combine the ingredients. See each recipe for the mixing method and the Quick Breads chapter for specific techniques.

Bake cookies on flat baking sheets at about 350°. They are done when lightly browned and crisp at the edges. They do not have to be hard, since they harden as they cool. Since all the cookies will not fit on one or two baking sheets, you will have to make several batches.

When experimenting with cookie recipes, mix the dough and bake one batch; let these cookies cool on a wire rack to see if they are a pleasing consistency—watch particularly to see that they do not spread too much on the baking sheet. Add flour or liquid to the batter to adjust it to the right thickness.

When cooling cookies, do not stack them; they will become misshapen.

To keep baked cookies moist, add an orange rind to the cookie jar.

RECIPES

Almond Butter Cookies

ABOUT 2 DOZEN COOKIES WITH ABOUT 76 GRAMS
USABLE PROTEIN

*To make peanut butter cookies, substitute peanut
butter and unsalted peanuts for almond paste and almonds. Add a little extra honey.*

4 ounces almond paste
½ cup honey
⅔ cup butter
2 eggs
1 cup whole wheat flour
(preferably soft wheat or
pastry flour)
¼ teaspoon baking powder
A pinch of salt
½ cup wheat germ
¾ cup almonds

1. Butter a baking sheet.
2. In a large bowl beat together the almond paste
and the honey with a fork or rotary beater. Beat in the
butter until the mixture is creamy. Add the eggs and
beat well.
3. In a small bowl sift the flour, baking powder, and
salt together. Add to the bowl any particles that did not
go through the sifter. Stir in the wheat germ. Add the
dry ingredients to the almond paste mixture in the large
bowl. Mix well with a wooden spoon or rubber spatula.
4. Drop the batter by the teaspoonful onto the baking sheet. Press whole or large pieces of almonds onto
the top of the cookies.
5. Heat the oven to 350°. Set the baking sheet on
top of the stove while the oven is heating. Let the
cookies dry this way for about 15 minutes. Bake
until the cookies are light brown and the edges are
crisp, about 15 minutes. Cool the cookies on a wire
rack.

Peter's Chocolate Chip-Mint Cookies

ABOUT 2 DOZEN COOKIES WITH ABOUT 31 GRAMS
USABLE PROTEIN

These are cakelike cookies with a slight taste of mint. Use whole wheat flour for a darker cookie, and for variety try raisins instead of the chocolate chips and mint.

⅓ cup butter
½ cup honey
1 egg
½ teaspoon vanilla
    extract
½ teaspoon mint extract
¾ cup unbleached white
    wheat flour

¾ cup soy flour
½ teaspoon baking soda
¾ teaspoon salt
1 cup semisweet
    chocolate chips, a
    6-ounce package

1. Heat the oven to 325°. Butter a baking sheet.
2. In a large bowl beat the butter with a fork or rotary beater until it is creamy. Gradually add the honey. Beat in the egg, vanilla extract, and mint extract. Beat well.
3. In a small bowl sift together the wheat flour, soy flour, baking soda, and salt. Add the dry ingredients to the butter mixture. Mix well with a wooden spoon or rubber spatula. Stir in the chocolate chips.
4. Drop the batter by the teaspoonful onto the baking sheet and bake until the cookies are brown and crisp at the edges, about 12 minutes. Cool the cookies on a wire rack.

Maple Rye Cookies

ABOUT 2 DOZEN COOKIES WITH ABOUT 39 GRAMS
USABLE PROTEIN

These cookies are crispy and crunchy.

½ cup butter
½ cup maple syrup
1 egg
½ teaspoon vanilla
1 cup whole rye flour

¼ teaspoon salt
½ teaspoon baking powder
½ cup wheat germ
½ cup walnuts

1. Heat the oven to 375°. Butter a baking sheet.
2. Gradually beat the maple syrup into the butter.
Then beat in the egg and the vanilla.
3. In a small bowl sift together the flour, salt, and
nutmeg. Add to the bowl any particles that did not go
through the sifter. Chop the nuts coarse.
4. Add the sifted ingredients to the maple mixture.
Mix well with a wooden spoon or rubber spatula. Stir
in the wheat germ and nuts.
5. Drop the batter by the teaspoonful onto the baking sheet and bake until the cookies are brown and crisp
at the edges, about 12 minutes. Cool the cookies on a
wire rack.

Raisin Soy Cookies or
Oatmeal Tahini Cookies

ABOUT 3 DOZEN COOKIES: RAISIN SOY WITH ABOUT
88 GRAMS USABLE PROTEIN; OATMEAL TAHINI WITH
ABOUT 140 GRAMS USABLE PROTEIN

*With only simple changes, one recipe can make many
kinds of cakes and cookies. This recipe begins with the
Basic Whole Wheat Butter Cake batter. The sweetening
is increased and then enough dry ingredients are added*

to make a cookie dough that holds its shape on a baking sheet. Use more honey if you have a sweet tooth.

RAISIN SOY COOKIES

⅓ cup honey
1 recipe Basic Whole Wheat
  Butter Cake batter
  (page 241)

1 cup soy grits
⅔ cup raisins

1. Heat the oven to 350°. Butter a baking sheet.
2. Stir the honey into the cake batter.
3. Add the soy grits to the batter and let them absorb the moisture for about 15 minutes. Stir in the raisins.

OATMEAL TAHINI COOKIES

1 cup soy nuts
⅓ cup honey
1 recipe Basic Whole Wheat
  Butter Cake batter
  (page 241)

½ cup tahini
4 cups rolled oats
1 tablespoon grated orange
  rind

1. Heat the oven to 350°. Butter a baking sheet. Chop the soy nuts coarse.

2. Stir the honey into the cake batter.

3. Stir the tahini into the batter, then add the rolled oats, soy nuts and orange rind.

BAKING THE COOKIES

4. Drop the batter by the teaspoonful onto the baking sheet. Bake the cookies until they are brown and crisp at the edges, about 15 minutes. The center may still remain soft. Cool the cookies on a wire rack.

Fresh Coconut Honey Macaroons

ABOUT 2 DOZEN MACAROONS WITH ABOUT 46 GRAMS
USABLE PROTEIN

Made with either fresh or dried coconut (see variations below), these macaroons are sweet and moist.

2½ cups fresh coconut, grated fine	¾ teaspoon baking soda
	½ teaspoon salt
⅔ cup brown sugar	4 egg whites
⅜ cup soy flour	½ cup honey
½ cup wheat germ	

1. Heat the oven to 325°. Butter a baking sheet and dust with white wheat flour.

2. In the top of a double boiler mix together all the ingredients except the honey. Stir to make sure there are no lumps of soy flour. Add the honey and mix well.

3. Heat the mixture over simmering water until it thickens, about 10 minutes. Stir constantly.

4. Drop the coconut batter by the teaspoonful onto the baking sheet. Bake the cookies until they are brown and crisp at the edges, about 20 minutes. Cool the cookies on a wire rack.

VARIATIONS

To make macaroons with dried, unsweetened coconut, add half the wheat germ. These cookies will be softer, less chewy, and appear more like the storebought kind. If dried coconut is used there will be about 97 grams usable protein in this recipe.

Add melted chocolate, pieces of dried fruit, nuts, or citrus-fruit rinds.

Sunflower Icebox Cookies

ABOUT 2 DOZEN COOKIES WITH ABOUT 47 GRAMS
USABLE PROTEIN

With this recipe you can make your own "slice-and-bake" cookies. The dough will keep refrigerated for about a week and will keep frozen for several months.

1½ cups whole wheat flour (preferably soft wheat or pastry flour)	½ cup sunflower seeds
	½ cup wheat germ
	¾ cup soft butter
¼ cup soy flour	½ cup brown sugar
3 tablespoons cocoa (if you wish to make chocolate cookies)	½ teaspoon vanilla extract

1. In a large bowl sift together the wheat flour and soy flour. Add the cocoa if you wish. Add to the bowl any particles that did not go through the sifter.
2. Grind the sunflower seeds to a coarse powder in a blender. Without a blender either chop the seeds fine with a knife, or place the seeds in a plastic bag or between two sheets of waxed paper and roll into a powder with a rolling pin.
3. Add the seeds, wheat germ, butter, sugar, and vanilla extract to the sifted ingredients and work them together with your hands until the dough is as smooth

as modeling clay. Form the dough into a long roll as wide around as a silver dollar.

4. Wrap the dough in waxed paper. Refrigerate the dough until chilled, about 2 hours.

5. Heat the oven to 325°. Butter a baking sheet.

6. Cut the dough into ⅓-inch-thick slices and place the cookies on the baking sheet. These cookies will not spread. Bake the cookies until they are crisp, about 15 minutes. Cool on a wire rack.

Bran Cookies

ABOUT 4 DOZEN COOKIES WITH ABOUT 66 GRAMS USABLE PROTEIN

These are light, crumbly cookies.

1 cup butter
1⅓ cups brown sugar
2 eggs
1¼ cups whole wheat flour (preferably soft wheat or pastry flour)
3 tablespoons soy flour
¼ teaspoon baking soda
2 teaspoons baking powder
¾ teaspoon salt
1½ teaspoons ground cinnamon
¾ teaspoon ground mace
1¼ cups wheat germ
1½ cups bran

1. Heat the oven to 400°. Butter a large baking sheet.

2. In a large bowl beat the butter with a fork or rotary beater until it is creamy. Gradually add the sugar. Beat in the eggs. Beat well.

3. In a small bowl sift together the wheat flour, soy flour, baking soda, baking powder, salt, and spices. Add to the bowl any particles that do not go through the sifter.

4. Toast the wheat germ and bran in a frying pan over low heat until brown, about 5 minutes. Stir frequently to prevent burning. Stir this mixture into the sifted ingredients.

5. With a wooden spoon or rubber spatula stir the dry ingredients into the butter mixture.

6. Drop the batter by the teaspoonful onto the baking sheets. Bake the cookies until they are brown and crisp, about 12 minutes. Gently take the cookies off the baking sheet with a spatula and let them cool and harden on a wire rack. Do not stack them or they will be misshapen.

Puddings

Puddings are like very wet cakes. Because these puddings are rich in whole grains, nuts, beans, eggs, and milk, the following recipes provide a surprisingly large proportion of your daily protein needs.

RECIPES

Banana Bread Pudding

ABOUT 8 SERVINGS EACH WITH ABOUT 13 GRAMS
USABLE PROTEIN

This is a soft, moist pudding that makes good use of dry bread and overripe bananas.

2 cups milk	1 cup nuts
1 cup milk powder	½ cup dates
6 slices bread	1 cup overripe mashed
1 tablespoon butter	bananas, about 2
½ cup maple syrup	bananas
½ teaspoon ground nutmeg	2 tablespoons brandy
¼ teaspoon salt	2 eggs

1. Heat the oven to 325°. Place a pan of water on the floor of the oven. Butter a 6-cup casserole, baking dish, or saucepan with an ovenproof handle.

2. Warm the milk in a saucepan until small bubbles form around the rim of the pan. Remove the pan from the heat and add the milk powder. Stir until it dissolves.

3. Cut the bread into cubes. Stir the bread, butter, syrup, nutmeg, and salt into the milk.

4. Chop the nuts and dates fine. Stir them into the milk-bread mixture, along with the bananas and the brandy.

5. Separate the eggs. Set the whites aside. Beat the egg yolks in a cup and add to them several tablespoons of the warm milk. Add the yolks to the milk mixture.

6. In a large bowl beat the egg whites with a wire whisk or rotary beater until they are stiff. With a large spoon or rubber spatula fold them gently into the mixture in the saucepan.

7. Pour the pudding into the baking dish. Bake until it is firm, the top is brown, and the edges are dry, about 1½ hours. Serve warm or at room temperature.

American Indian Pudding

ABOUT 8 SERVINGS EACH WITH ABOUT 4 GRAMS
USABLE PROTEIN

This is a creamy cornmeal-thickened custard.

4 cups milk	½ teaspoon vanilla
1 cinnamon stick, or	extract
½ teaspoon ground	3 tablespoons cornmeal
cinnamon	¼ teaspoon salt
A 1-inch piece fresh ginger	¼ cup molasses
root or ½ teaspoon	⅓ cup honey
ground ginger	1 tablespoon butter
1 vanilla bean or	1 egg

1. Heat the oven to 300°. Butter a 6-cup casserole, baking dish, or saucepan with an ovenproof handle.

2. Warm 3 cups of the milk and the flavorings in a

saucepan. Cook the mixture over low heat for about 3 minutes, being careful not to let it boil.

3. Gradually stir in the cornmeal. Add the salt, molasses, honey, and butter. Cook, stirring, over a low heat until the mixture thickens. Make sure it does not boil or burn. Scoop out the cinnamon stick, ginger root, and vanilla bean.

4. Let the milk mixture cool to warm. In a cup beat the egg and add to it several tablespoons of the warm milk. Then add the egg to the milk mixture.

5. Pour the pudding into the baking dish. Bake for a half hour, uncovered. Pour the remaining 1 cup of milk over the pudding and return it to the oven to bake until the pudding is firm, about 2 hours longer.

Cheese Spoonbread

ABOUT 8 SERVINGS EACH WITH ABOUT 8 GRAMS
USABLE PROTEIN

This is a hot corn pudding that can be served sweet-ened with maple syrup or honey or salted with a white sauce.

2 cups boiling water	1¾ cups milk
1½ cups cornmeal	1 tablespoon baking powder
½ cup soy grits	¾ cup grated cheese, about
5 tablespoons butter	2½ oz (for instance
1 tablespoon honey	cheddar or Monterey
½ teaspoon salt	Jack)
3 eggs	

1. Heat the oven to 350°.

2. In a large bowl pour the boiling water over the cornmeal and soy grits. Add 3 tablespoons of the butter, the honey, and salt. Stir until the butter melts and the honey dissolves. Let cool to warm.

3. Separate the eggs. Set the whites aside. Beat the

egg yolks with ½ cup of the milk in a small bowl. Stir this mixture into the cornmeal.

4. Stir the baking powder into the cornmeal mixture. Make sure there are no lumps. Add the remaining 1¼ cups of milk and the cheese. This will be a thin batter.

5. In a large bowl beat the egg whites with a wire whisk or rotary beater until they are stiff. With a large spoon or rubber spatula fold the egg whites gently into the batter.

6. Put the remaining 2 tablespoons of butter into a 2-quart casserole, baking dish, or saucepan with an ovenproof handle. Place the dish in the oven until the butter melts. Brush the butter around the bottom and sides of the dish.

7. Pour the batter into the dish. Bake the spoon-bread until it is firm and the edges are crisp, about 25 minutes. For a drier, more breadlike pudding, bake longer.

Cherry-Millet Pudding

ABOUT 8 SERVINGS EACH WITH ABOUT 6 GRAMS
USABLE PROTEIN

This is a variation of traditional rice pudding. Any grain would make a good substitute for the millet. Barley and bulgur are particularly good.

½ cup soy nuts
½ cup fresh cherries
½ cup millet
1 quart milk
½ cup honey

1 vanilla bean or 1 teaspoon
   vanilla extract
½ teaspoon salt
½ teaspoon ground nutmeg

1. Heat the oven to 300°. Chop the soy nuts coarse. Pit the cherries and cut them in half.

2. Combine all the ingredients in a 6-cup casserole, baking dish, or saucepan with an ovenproof handle.

3. Bake the pudding uncovered until most of the milk is absorbed, about 3 hours. Stir the pudding every half hour. Scoop out the vanilla bean, if used. To reduce the baking time by about 1 hour, combine all the ingredients and let them stand in the refrigerator overnight.

4. Take the pudding from the oven and cover with waxed paper to prevent a skin from forming. Serve warm or chilled.

Frumenty

ABOUT 8 SERVINGS EACH WITH ABOUT 9 GRAMS
USABLE PROTEIN

Long, slow cooking brings out the sweetness of wheat in this medieval grain pudding.

1 cup wheat berries	½ teaspoon ground nutmeg
About 4 cups water	A pinch saffron
1 cup milk powder	2 eggs
2 cups milk	¼ cup walnuts
⅔ cup honey	¼ cup filberts
1 tablespoon molasses	⅓ cup currants
½ teaspoon salt	⅓ cup raisins

1. In a covered 2-quart saucepan over low heat cook the wheat berries in the water until the berries burst, about 4 hours. For a chewier pudding, cook only until the berries are soft. Add water if necessary to keep the berries from burning. Cooking time can be reduced by about half if the berries are first soaked overnight.

2. In a small bowl dissolve the milk powder in the milk. Mix until there are no lumps. Add the milk and the honey, molasses, salt, nutmeg, and saffron to the wheat berries. Continue to cook over low heat.

3. Beat the eggs in a cup and add to them several tablespoonsful of the hot liquid. Then add the yolks to the pudding.

4. Chop the nuts coarse. Stir in the nuts, currants, and raisins. Stir well and cook to a porridge-like consistency, about 1 hour. Serve the pudding warm, hot, or chilled.

Grandma Bessie's Noodle Pudding

ABOUT 8 SERVINGS EACH WITH ABOUT 11 GRAMS
USABLE PROTEIN

This makes a sweet side dish or a heavy dessert. Many combinations of dried and fresh fruits can be substituted for the apples and apricots.

12 ounces ½-inch egg noodles, about 4½ cups cooked noodles	½ cup dried apricots
	½ cup honey
	½ cup wheat germ
3 eggs	3 tablespoons butter
1 large apple	

1. Cook the noodles according to the directions on the package. Rinse and drain.

2. Separate the eggs. Peel and core the apple and cut it into small chunks. Chop the apricots. In a large bowl mix together the noodles, egg yolks, apple, apricots, honey, wheat germ, and 2 tablespoons of the butter.

3. In a large bowl beat the egg whites with a wire whisk or rotary beater until stiff. With a large spoon or rubber spatula, fold the egg whites gently into the noodle mixture.

4. Melt the remaining 1 tablespoon butter in an 8-inch cast-iron frying pan. Brush the butter around the bottom and sides of the pan.

5. Pour the noodle mixture into the frying pan and

cook, covered, over low heat until the pudding is firm, about 30 minutes.

6. Turn the pudding by reversing it onto a plate and slipping the pudding back into the pan. Fry to brown the underside, about 15 minutes. Serve hot.

Chick-pea Pudding

ABOUT 8 SERVINGS EACH WITH ABOUT 8 GRAMS USABLE PROTEIN

This half-pudding half-cake resembles a Mexican tor-ta de garbanzo. *The chick-peas give it a sweet taste and a grainy texture.*

2 cups uncooked chick-peas
   and 3 cups water
   or two 20-ounce cans of
   prepared chick-peas
4 eggs
½ cup evaporated milk

⅔ cup honey
⅔ cup maple syrup
¼ teaspoon salt
¼ teaspoon ground
   cinnamon
1 cup raisins

1. In a covered saucepan over low heat cook the chick-peas in the water until the peas are soft, about 3 hours. Add water if necessary to keep the peas from burning. Cooking time can be reduced by about half if the peas are first soaked overnight. Omit this step if canned or cooked chick-peas are used.

2. Heat the oven to 350°. Butter a 6-cup cas-serole, baking dish, or saucepan with an ovenproof handle.

3. Separate the eggs. Set the whites aside. In a blender combine the peas, egg yolks, milk, honey, maple syrup, salt, and cinnamon and blend into a smooth paste. Without a blender mash the chick-peas with a fork or force them through a sieve; then mix well with the egg yolks, milk, honey, maple syrup, salt, and cinnamon.

4. In a large bowl beat the egg whites with a fork or rotary beater until they are stiff. With a large spoon or rubber spatula fold the egg whites gently into the chick-pea mixture. Gently stir in the raisins.

5. Pour the pudding into the baking dish. Bake the pudding until it is firm and a toothpick or broom straw inserted into the center comes out clean, about 1½ hours. Cool the pudding in the casserole on a wire rack. Serve warm.

Protein

Proteins and Usable Proteins

Proteins are complex molecules made of small chemical building blocks called *amino acids*. The twenty different amino acids commonly found in proteins link together into long twisted chains to build an enormous variety of protein molecules. We eat these large protein molecules in foods which the body then breaks down into single amino acids. These small individual units are then recombined to form new body proteins such as hormones, enzymes, muscle, hair, and nails.

The human body needs all twenty amino acids. The body can make some amino acids for itself; others must be obtained from foods. The nine amino acids which must be supplied by food are called the *essential amino acids:* histidine, isoleucine, leucine, lysine, methionine, phenylalanine, threonine, tryptophane, and valine. The body easily converts these essential amino acids into the nonessential amino acids, so from only nine, all twenty can be made. This means that the best protein sources are those foods which contain many essential amino acids. Since chemical tests can determine the amount of each amino acid in any food, we can choose the best protein foods by looking at their essential amino acid composition.

To find good plant sources of protein, we must find foods that contain large amounts of the essential amino acids. The following list is ordered by the amount of

277

essential amino acids per ounce of food. The foods at the top of the list are rich in essential amino acids; those at the bottom of the list have practically none.

DRIED BEANS
NUTS AND SEEDS
GRAINS
BREWER'S YEAST
VEGETABLES (INCLUDING BEAN SPROUTS)
TUBERS (LIKE POTATOES)
FRUITS

The recipes in this book use plant foods with the greatest amount of essential amino acids—dried beans, nuts and seeds, and grains—as ingredients for high-protein breads.

Dried beans, nuts and seeds, and grains contain many essential amino acids; but a large percentage of these amino acids are not usable by the body. This is because the nine essential amino acids are needed in a specific proportion and this proportion is not found in plant foods. They may have more than enough of one or two of the amino acids and less than enough of the others.

Nutrition scientists believe that cow's milk and hen's eggs most nearly contain the proportion of amino acids that the human body needs. By comparing a food to the reference milk or egg amino acid content, we can evaluate its *protein quality*. If one essential amino acid is insufficient in quantity or missing from the diet, protein production in the body may fall to a low level or stop completely. Imagine that the body is building a protein and one of the essential amino acids is missing. The protein chain stops forming at the point where the missing amino acid is needed. This fragment of a protein chain is useless.

If the body has the right amounts of eight of the essential amino acids, but only half of the ninth, it can *use* only half of the first eight: the *usable protein* is reduced to the amount of the *limiting* amino acid; the remaining half of the amino acids are wasted as protein —they are used as carbohydrates or excreted. For example, if you wanted to make pancakes and had a bin full of flour but only a tablespoon of water you would only be able to make one small pancake.

The protein value of a food—its usable protein—depends on the *quantity* and *quality* of its amino acids —how many total essential amino acids it contains and in what ratio. Milk, eggs, meat, or fish (animal products) contain the essential amino acids in the proper proportions so most of the essential amino acids in them can be used and few are wasted. Animal foods are therefore called good quality or *complete* protein foods. Plant foods, because they lack one or more essential amino acid, are called poor quality or *incomplete* protein foods. Even though dried beans, nuts and seeds, and grains are rich in amino acids, most of the amino acids are wasted because one of the essential amino acids is not present in large enough amounts.

To use the valuable proteins in dried beans, nuts and seeds, and grains the amino acid content of these foods should be examined carefully. The charts which follow show the amino acid pattern of GRAINS, DRIED BEANS, and NUTS AND SEEDS in comparison to the reference egg protein. A check on the chart indicates that the food has a generally good balance of that amino acid compared with what we need; a plus on the chart indicates an abundance; a minus indicates a deficiency. A double plus or minus indicates that the food is extremely abundant or deficient in that amino acid.

The four amino acid groups that are likely to be deficient in plant foods are sulfur-containing amino acids, lysine, tryptophane, and isoleucine.

GRAINS	SULFUR-CONTAINING AMINO ACIDS	LYSINE	TRYPTOPHANE	ISOLEUCINE
Barley	√	—	++	—
Buckwheat	√	—	+	—
Corn	—	——	——	—
Millet	√	—	++	—
Oats	√	—	+	—
Rice, brown	—	—	√	√
Rice, white	—	—	√	√
Rye	√	—	—	√
Whole wheat	√	—	+	—
Wheat germ	√	+	+	√
Wheat bran	√	—	+	—
Unbleached white wheat flour	√	——	√	√

NUTS AND SEEDS				
Almonds	√	——	√	√
Brazil nuts	++	——	++	—
Carobs	—	++	—	—
Cashews	√	√	++	√
Coconuts	—	—	√	√
Hazelnuts	——	—	+	++
Pecans	—	√	+	√
Pistachios	—	√	√	√
Sesame seeds	+	——	++	—
Sunflower seeds	√	—	+	√
Walnuts	√	——	√	—

DRIED BEANS AND PEAS	SULFUR-CONTAINING AMINO ACIDS	LYSINE	TRYPTOPHANE	ISOLEUCINE
Beans	——	+	√	√
Chick-peas	——	+	—	√
Lentils	——	+	—	√
Lima beans	——	+	—	√
Peas	——	++	—	√
Peanuts*	—	—	√	√
Soy beans	——	+	√	√

YEAST				
Brewer's and baker's yeast	——	+	—	√

The charts show that grains, dried beans, and nuts and seeds do not contain amino acid in proportions that correspond well to human needs. Some of the amino acids are oversupplied and others are deficient. Barley, for instance, is high in tryptophane and low in leucine and isoleucine; while yeast is low in tryptophane and sulfur-containing amino acids and high in leucine. In the next section it will become apparent how, by combining the right foods, you can create balanced, complete proteins from these unbalanced, incomplete ones.

---

* Peanuts are not true nuts; they are legumes.

Complementing and Supplementing Proteins

By combining foods you can use the essential amino acids in grains, dried beans, and nuts and seeds to the best advantage. Complementary protein mixtures combine two plant protein foods that have opposite amino acid strengths (+) and weaknesses (−). An excess in one food compensates for a deficiency in the other. The combination of these two foods, then, creates a complete, highly usable protein.
For example:

	SULFUR-CONTAINING AMINO ACIDS	LYSINE	TRYPTOPHANE	ISOLEUCINE
Beans	——	+	√	√
Wheat	√	—	+	—
Beans & Wheat	√	√	√	√

Each *plus* amino acid is matched with a *minus* or *balanced* amino acid. Each *minus* amino acid is matched with a *plus* or *balanced* amino acid. In this way a complete protein food is made from two incomplete ones.
  To complement these foods, therefore, combine:

Grains (deficient in lysine and isoleucine)
   with

Dried beans or *wheat germ* (strong in lysine and balanced in isoleucine)

Dried beans (deficient in sulfur-containing amino acids and some tryptophane)
   with
Grains or *wheat germ* (strong in tryptophane and balanced in sulfur-containing amino acids)
   or nuts and seeds (strong in tryptophane)

Nuts and seeds (deficient in sulfur-containing amino acids and lysine)
   with

Dried beans or *wheat germ* (strong in lysine)
   or grains (balanced in sulfur-containing amino acids)
Protein complementarity is not new. Mexicans eat corn with beans, Italians eat pasta with beans, Japanese eat rice with soy—combinations that have proved through experience to provide the necessary protein in low-meat diets.

Supplementary protein mixtures combine an incomplete plant protein with a complete animal protein, such as milk or eggs. This makes available the unused amino acids in the plant foods.

Therefore, to increase the amount of usable protein:

Complement one plant food with another plant food, balancing their amino acid strengths and weaknesses;

Supplement a plant food with an animal food such as eggs or milk.

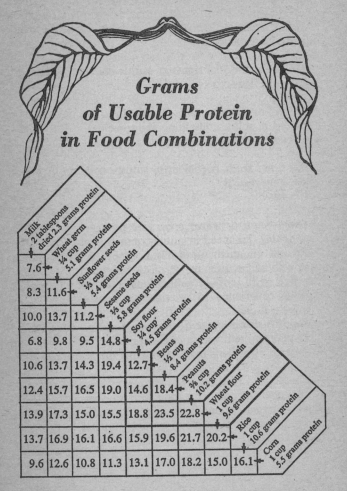

As a mileage chart shows the distance between two cities, this chart shows the protein advantage from complemented or supplemented combinations.

In the protein mileage chart the intersection of two foods indicates the number of grams of usable protein in the *combination*. For example, at the intersection of 1 cup of wheat flour and ¼ cup soy flour, the chart reads 18.8 grams usable protein—the protein from a wheat-soy mixture in these proportions. However, if you ate the wheat and soy separately, you would get only 14.1 grams usable protein since:

1 cup of wheat flour contains 9.6
    grams usable protein
¼ cup of soy flour contains 4.5
    grams usable protein   ——

                      14.1 grams usable protein when eaten separately. But when soy and wheat are eaten together in these proportions, usable protein increases from 14.1 to 18.8 grams, or by 33 percent.

To calculate the advantage from other protein mixtures, add the amount of protein in each of the two foods as though they were eaten separately, then compare this value to the value in the intersected square representing the foods eaten together.

Since foods within a food group are similar in their amino acid amounts and patterns, one grain may be substituted for another grain, or one bean substituted for another bean with only a small difference in usable protein yield. Check the balance charts to make sure the substituted foods are similar.

Protein Combinations

Complement GRAINS with:

Dried beans

Wheat germ

Complement DRIED BEANS with:

Grains

Nuts and seeds

Wheat germ

Complement NUTS AND SEEDS with:

Dried beans

Wheat germ

Supplement GRAINS, DRIED BEANS, and NUTS & SEEDS with:

Milk products

Eggs

How Much Is Enough?

The *average* adult protein need is based on body weight. Athletes and office workers each need about the same amount of protein *per pound* of normal body weight. To find your approximate *usable* protein need, multiply your weight in pounds by 0.26 if you are an adult male and by 0.24 if you are an adult female. For example, a 155-pound man would need 155 × 0.26 grams, or about 40 grams of usable protein a day. A 125-pound woman would need 125 × 0.24, or about 30 grams usable protein a day.

The chart lists the factor by which you must multiply your weight to calculate the safe level of usable protein to include in your diet each day.

Age Group	Multiplication Factor to find safe level of usable protein intake for 1 day
Infants	
6-11 months	.70
Children	
1-3 years	.54
4-6 years	.46
7-9 years	.40
Male adolescents	
10-12 years	.37
13-15 years	.33
16-19 years	.27

Female adolescents
    10-12 years   .35
    13-15 years   .29
    16-19 years   .25
Adult male   .26
Adult female   .24
Pregnant   Add 9 to total
    latter half
Lactating   Add 17 to total
    first 6 months

However, just as many adults need more or less than the often-recommended eight hours of sleep each night, every person has a slightly varying protein need; and many factors influence the amount. Infections, wound-healing, and stress often increase protein demands. People who are growing or nurturing growth—children and pregnant or nursing mothers—need much more protein per pound than average adults.

———
* Chart adapted from *Energy and Protein Requirements*. Reproduced by permission of The World Health Organization, from WHO Technical Report Series, No. 522, 1973.

Protein in the Kitchen

I hope you will use the charts to help choose foods and create high protein meals. I keep the "Protein Combinations" chart taped to the refrigerator door as a reminder. The value of the protein combinations will increase if the foods are combined in one meal. However, by complementing and supplementing the proteins in a single recipe, I feel confident that each individual food is well balanced.

Even when protein-complementing becomes a kitchen habit, it may not always be possible to produce a perfect usable protein. You can, however, improve protein utilization of plant foods as much as 50 percent over the protein use of the same foods eaten separately. Certainly, there is much more protein available if the foods are combined thoughtfully rather than at random.

Baking protein-rich breads means that bread becomes a staple food with more value than simply calories. Bread, or even dessert, can then supply much of the protein for an entire meal. The menu can be simple— bread, soup, and salad, or salad and cheesecake dessert. In each recipe in this book the total amount of usable protein is listed under the title.* With a little arithmetic, protein planning should now be easy.

---

* The amount of usable protein in each recipe is computed by the chemical score of the combination of ingredients. The value is obtained by calculating the content of each essential

amino acid in the recipe and comparing each amino acid quantity with the same amino acid in eggs. This gives percentages. The amino acid with the lowest percentage is called the limiting amino acid; and this percentage is the chemical score. The amount of usable protein is then computed by multiplying the total protein (both usable and nonusable) by the chemical score.

A Compendium of Ingredients

For comprehensive listing of stores and distributors where these ingredients can be found, consult *The Organic Directory,* Book Division, Rodale Press, Inc.; Emmaus, Pennsylvania 18049, $2.95.

Grains

WHEAT

Varieties of wheat are generally classified by the color (red or white) and by the amount of gluten protein contained. For baking, the gluten content is the more useful way to categorize the grain. High-gluten wheat is hard wheat; low-gluten wheat is soft wheat; there are many gradations in between. Environmental factors such as the nitrogen content of the soil, rainfall, and temperature as well as the strain of wheat determine the amount of gluten protein.

Hard wheat, in the United States, is raised mostly in the Northwest—Wyoming, the Dakotas, Montana—because it needs a long cool spring, although the highest gluten wheat comes from Deaf Smith County, Texas.

Soft wheat, in the United States, is grown in the Central, Southern, and Eastern states.

WHEAT BERRIES: the entire wheat kernel.

CRACKED WHEAT: kernels ground into coarse pieces without floury particles.

WHEAT GRITS: finer than cracked wheat.

ROLLED WHEAT: steamed and flattened kernels.

BULGUR, OR PARCHED WHEAT: steamed (parboiled) and toasted kernels, which are available in various grinds from whole kernels to fine-ground, with no powdery flour at all. Bulgur tastes toasted and has a chewy texture.

Wheat Flours

HARD WHEAT, BREAD, or HIGH-PROTEIN FLOUR is ground from hard wheat kernels that are high in gluten. This "strong" flour absorbs a lot of moisture and becomes stretchy and elastic so that it can expand and still hold the leavening gas released by the yeast, without tearing the dough. For this reason, hard wheat flour is primarily used for baking yeast breads. It often feels gritty and granular.

SOFT WHEAT or PASTRY FLOUR is made from soft wheat kernels that are finely milled and low in gluten. Soft wheat flour is delicate and used primarily for pastries, cakes, and tender, crumbly breads which do not require stretchy gluten. It often feels powdery and smooth.

ALL-PURPOSE FLOUR is a blend of hard and soft wheat which is used successfully for both yeast breads and pastries.

WHOLE WHEAT FLOUR is made from hard wheat, soft wheat, or a blend. It contains the entire wheat kernel—endosperm, bran, and germ—which can be ground to different degrees of coarseness.

GRAHAM FLOUR was named for Sylvester Graham, a nineteenth-century whole-grain bread enthusiast. Graham flour is whole wheat flour in which the starchy endosperm of the wheat kernel is fine-ground and the bran and germ layers are left flaky and coarse.

UNBLEACHED WHITE WHEAT FLOUR is made from hard wheat, soft wheat, or a blend. It contains only the starchy endosperm of the wheat kernel; the bran and germ have been sifted out. Unbleached white wheat flour makes very light, fine-grained breads because it lacks the coarse bran and germ, which interfere with the forming of the gluten strands. Unfortunately, it is these particles—the bran and the germ—that contain most of the proteins, vitamins, and minerals in wheat. However, by enriching a bread with wheat germ, most of the nutritive value is returned while retaining a light texture.

Add unbleached white flour to any whole-grain flour to make a bread less coarse or crumbly, and use it on the table when shaping loaves so that the crust is smooth and not gritty.

GLUTEN FLOUR is a low-starch flour made by washing the starch from hard wheat flour. The residue is dried and ground. Raw, wet gluten is tasteless, light gray, rubbery, and as sticky as chewing gum. Add gluten flour to flours low in gluten or with no gluten to help a yeast bread rise.

You can find the gluten content of wheat by chewing about a tablespoon of whole wheat berries. Swallow the juice until a small wad of gluten is left. Practice with hard and soft wheat will teach you how much gluten to expect. Gluten makes wonderful organic chewing gum. Children who grow up in wheat-farming country call this "wheat gum."

GLUTEN-FREE FLOUR or wheat starch is white wheat flour is often used by people who are allergic to the flour from which the gluten has been removed. This glutten protein.

Wheat Germ

This is the flaky embryo of the wheat kernel. Because it is rich in oil, it must be refrigerated to prevent it from becoming rancid.

RAW WHEAT GERM: 1 cup of wheat germ added to 5 to 6 cups flour will not significantly change the texture of a bread, but it will greatly increase the bread's nutritional value. Toast the wheat germ if you do not like the raw taste.

TOASTED AND/OR SWEETENED WHEAT GERM is the variety available in most supermarkets. I prefer raw wheat germ because it is flakier, less granular, and less expensive.

WHEAT GERM FLOUR OR POWDER is fine-ground raw

or toasted wheat germ. To make wheat germ flour at home, whirl whole wheat germ in the blender until it is powdery.

Bran Flakes

These are the outer dry layers of the grain kernel. To soften bran, which will make a bread moist, pour boiling water over the flakes or mix the batter or dough without the leavening and let the mixture stand overnight.

NON-WHEAT GRAINS

Non-wheat grains offer taste and texture variety to breads but are low in gluten. Flours low in gluten make a yeast bread that does not rise well, resulting in a crumbly, compact loaf. Therefore, use barley, buckwheat, corn, millet, oats, rice, and rye in combination with wheat or gluten flour to make a light yeast loaf. If the dough is less than two-thirds wheat, expect a compact bread. You can use more non-wheat flour in cookies, cakes, quick breads, biscuits, and pancakes because they do not depend primarily upon gluten for structure.

Barley

WHOLE BARLEY: the entire barley kernel, hull removed.

BARLEY GRITS: kernels cracked into coarse pieces.

PEARLED BARLEY: kernels polished by a process that leaves mostly starch.

BARLEY FLOUR: a fine-ground powder, particularly flavorful if toasted. It makes crumbly, cakey breads that keep well.

Buckwheat

WHOLE BUCKWHEAT: the entire buckwheat kernel.

BUCKWHEAT GRITS: kernels cracked into coarse pieces.

KASHA OR POACHED BUCKWHEAT: steamed (parboiled) and toasted grits which are available in various grinds—fine, medium, and coarse—with no powdery flour.

BUCKWHEAT FLOUR: a heavy, strong-tasting powder that is excellent for traditional American pancakes.

Corn

White corn is traditional in the South and in Rhode Island; yellow corn is traditional in the North; and blue, black, and red corn is traditional in the Southwest. There are no baking differences among them.

Most corn products are sold without the germ (degermed). Look for the variety that still retains the germ.

WHOLE CORN: the entire corn kernel.

CRACKED CORN, SAMP, HOMINY, GRITS: corn kernels cut or ground into small particles. The grind and the name differ from one locality or mill to another.

CORNMEAL: kernels ground to a sandy texture with no starchy powder. Cornmeal makes a crunchy, crumbly quick bread.

CORN FLOUR: a fine-ground starchy powder.

Masa harina: a Mexican, lime-treated, fine-ground corn flour used for tortillas and tamales; available in Latin American grocery stores.

FLAKED CORN: soaked and pressed kernels.

CORNSTARCH: a powder from the starch of the corn kernel used to thicken liquids such as pie fillings and sauces.

Millet

WHOLE MILLET: hulled kernels that look like tiny beads with a hole for stringing.

MILLET GRITS OR CRACKED MILLET: kernels cracked into coarse bits with no powdery flour.

MILLET MEAL: kernels ground to a rough texture with floury particles.

MILLET FLAKES: steamed and pressed kernels.

MILLET FLOUR: a fine-ground powder with a bland taste; it makes crunchy breads.

Oats

OAT GROATS: whole hulled kernels.

STEEL-CUT OATS OR SCOTCH OATMEAL: kernels cut into several cubelike pieces.

ROLLED OATS OR COMMERCIAL OATMEAL: oat flakes made by soaking and pressing whole kernels.

OAT FLOUR: a fine-ground powder that makes a light bread when combined with sticky flours like soy, rye, and buckwheat. To make oat flour at home, whirl rolled oats in the blender until they are powdery.

Rice

Long, medium, and short grain refer to the length of the kernel. Short grain rice is more chewy and sticky than long grain.

WHOLE BROWN RICE: hulled kernels with part of the bran removed.

WHITE RICE: kernels that are polished to remove the hull, the germ, and practically all of the bran.

PARBOILED OR CONVERTED RICE: whole kernels processed by steam pressure before milling, which forces the vitamins and minerals from the hull, bran, and germ into the starchy part of the grain.

RICE GRITS: kernels cracked into coarse bits with no powdery flour.

RICE FLOUR: fine-ground kernels that make a dense, moist, chewy, smooth cake. Use the non-waxy variety, which should be indicated on the package, since the waxy type is a "sweet rice flour" that is used as a thickener.

RICE BRAN: the outer dry layers of the brown rice kernel. To soften, see wheat bran flakes (page 296).

RICE POLISH: the inner bran layers and germ of brown rice, a byproduct of polishing brown rice into white.

Rye

WHOLE RYE: hulled kernels.

RYE GRITS: kernels ground into coarse pieces.

RYE MEAL: kernels ground finer than grits to a rough, floury texture. Rye meal is also called pumpernickel flour since the original pumpernickel breads were made from rye meal. Today, commercial pumpernickel is made primarily from white wheat flour; some rye flour is added for taste and texture and caramel is added to give the breads a dark color.

WHOLE RYE FLOUR: a sticky, but not elastic, fine-ground flour that makes a moist, compact loaf. Sourdough is a good leavener for rye bread because the acids in the sourdough seem to dissolve the gummy substance in rye flour that interferes with the gluten formation.

WHITE RYE FLOUR: a fine-ground rye powder which contains only the starchy white endorsperm of the rye kernel; the bran and germ have been sifted out.

Triticale (trit-ĭ ká'lé)

A new grain that is a cross between wheat and rye. Triticale tastes like rye but has the high gluten content of hard wheat, which makes it easy to handle, stretch, and rise.

Water

Water as the liquid in breads brings out the flavor of the grain and makes a crisp crust.

If you are having trouble with yeast-baking, perhaps your water is too hard or too soft. Hard water, due to dissolved salts, retards growing yeast. Soft water tends to dissolve gluten, weakening the gas-holding structure. Both hard and soft water, therefore, make a small compact loaf that does not rise well. Very soft water makes soggy, sticky breads.

Dairy Products

MILK

Milk gives bread and cakes a softer grain and increases the time that the bread will keep fresh. When brushed on the surface of a yeast bread before baking, it gives an overall brown color.

RAW MILK: direct from the cow without processing. Raw milk is available in health food stores and directly from the dairy farmer. After standing an hour or so the cream rises to the top and can be skimmed off. Scald raw milk before baking yeast breads to kill bacteria and inactivate certain milk proteins that might cause a dense or gummy bread.

PASTEURIZED, HOMOGENIZED WHOLE MILK: contains 4 percent butterfat, and for that reason is not used for dissolving yeast. The fat coats the yeast and prevents proper dissolving.

SKIMMED (NONFAT) MILK: contains no butterfat and therefore half the calories of whole milk, but retains all of the protein and minerals.

CREAM: the component of milk that is largely butterfat.

EVAPORATED MILK: evaporated, sterilized, cooled, and canned milk. Reconstitute it by adding 1 cup of water for every cup of evaporated milk or use it undiluted from the can for added protein.

SWEETENED CONDENSED MILK: evaporated milk with sugar added. To reconstitute, add 2½ cups water for every cup condensed milk.

Milk Powder, Whole and Skimmed (Nonfat), Instant and Noninstant: A white, powdery dehydrated milk in tiny flakes or powder. Powdered milk that has been dried at low temperatures is the best source of protein. Roller-drying, the large-scale commercial method of drying milk, destroys certain amino acids. Store in a lightproof airtight container in a dry place because moisture and high humidity destroy some amino acids in dry milk powder.

I prefer skimmed milk powder to whole milk powder because of the lower calorie content; and noninstant to instant because it has almost twice as much protein per cup in the dry form (but it has the same amount of protein when reconstituted, because you use less noninstant per quart).

Noninstant milk is powdery and instant milk is granular. To reconstitute, combine ¼ cup noninstant or ⅓ cup instant milk powder with 1 cup of water. Whirl in a blender to dissolve, or shake in a jar. Undissolved milk powder will make white powdery lumps in the bread. When using the powder as a dry solid, dissolve it in the liquid or sift with a part of the flour to break up lumps and distribute the powder evenly.

A small amount of milk powder added to a dough or batter makes a fine, close-grained bread. More than ¼ cup for each cup of flour will make a bread dense and gummy. When there is a lot of milk powder in the batter or dough of a bread, lower the baking temperature by 25–50° to prevent burning. When cooking over direct heat use a double boiler.

Soured Milks

Soured milks are used for flavor, acidity, and the delicate crumb they create. Because of the lactic acid and soft curd of soured milks, breads made with them have a smooth texture and keep fresh for a long time. Soured milks are particularly good for quick breads served hot, like biscuits, and for fruit and nut breads, which mature after several days. Soured milks make yeast breads rise quickly.

Raw unpasteurized milk sours naturally in 2 days if unrefrigerated or after about a week in the refrigerator. Pasteurized, homogenized milk does not sour; it spoils.

HOMEMADE SOUR MILK: add 1 tablespoon of lemon juice or white vinegar to 1 cup of liquid milk. Let stand for a few minutes to curdle. It will look slightly thickened.

BUTTERMILK: originally the residue from the butter churn, today buttermilk is made by adding acid-producing bacteria to skimmed milk. The bacteria "culture" the buttermilk to a pleasant sour taste. To culture your own buttermilk, put about 2 tablespoons of buttermilk and 1 quart of skimmed milk into a large jar. Shake to mix. Let the jar stand at warm room temperature (for instance, near the pilot light of a stove) until curdled. It will take 4 to 8 hours depending on the temperature and the type of buttermilk bacteria used.

BUTTERMILK SKIMMED MILK-POWDER: dehydrated buttermilk. Can be used dry or reconstituted.

SOUR CREAM: originally made from soured sweet cream, now cultured by adding bacteria to cream to sour and thicken it.

YOGURT: a puddinglike curdled milk made by adding a yogurt culture (a type of bacteria) to milk. The tart taste and thick consistency make yogurt a perfect high-protein substitute for sour cream.

To make yogurt, combine a quart of warm water and 2 cups of milk powder. In a crock or casserole combine the milk and 2 tablespoons of plain yogurt. Cover the crock and wrap it in a towel to insulate it against cold. Place the crock in an oven that has been heated to 200° and then *turned off*. Try not to shake the crock, since yogurt is sensitive to being jostled. Let the milk curdle overnight.

To thicken yogurt or make yogurt cheese, drain the yogurt in a cheesecloth bag or in a paper-lined funnel.

Save the liquid (the whey) and use it in breads. The thickened yogurt is particularly good for toppings and fillings.

POWDERED YOGURT CULTURE: a dehydrated yogurt that will remain active for about 1 month once it is reconstituted. It will keep for about 6 months in its powdered form. There are no advantages to using the dry powder in breads because it is expensive, and buttermilk powder, which is less expensive, has the same taste.

CHEESE

Crumbly, moist, soft, semi-soft, and hard cheeses give new textures to breads. Goat's milk or sheep's milk cheeses, in particular, give new tastes. Grate hard cheeses into doughs and batters. Wet cheeses such as ricotta and cottage cheese make a moist loaf and are particularly good for high-protein toppings and fillings. Too much cheese will make the bread gummy. Use no more than ½ cup cheese for each cup of flour in the bread. Hard cheeses will moisten a loaf and make a close grain. Bake longer to prevent the sogginess of melted cheese.

CREAM CHEESE: an unripened cheese made from whole milk enriched with cream.

WHEY: the liquid drained from the curd when cheese is made.

INSTANT POWDERED WHEY: dehydrated whey can be used as a yeast-booster.

Leavening

CHEMICAL

BAKING SODA (BICARBONATE OF SODA): a white, alkaline powder. Baking soda and an acid ingredient act as a single-acting baking powder (see below).

BAKING POWDER: a white, powdery mixture of baking soda and an acid ingredient, usually tartaric acid. Some baking powders contain cornstarch and preservatives.

SINGLE-ACTING BAKING POWDER: baking soda with tartaric acid and perhaps cream of tartar. Single-acting baking powder gives off most of its leavening gas the moment the powder touches the liquid. The reaction is quick, so it is important to put the bread into a heated oven swiftly to retain the bubbles of air. Single-acting baking powder is not a good leavening for breads that are stored in the refrigerator or freezer before baking.

DOUBLE-ACTING OR COMBINATION BAKING POWDER: a combination of baking soda and several acidic chemicals that react more slowly than single-acting baking powder. When moistened, a portion of the leavening gives off carbon dioxide in the cold dough or batter, but there is another burst of gas released in the heat of the oven.

BIOLOGICAL

YEAST: requires special care because it is a living plant that needs food and water to grow, air to breathe, and warmth to flourish. Temperature regulates yeast growth; by changing the temperature of the ingredients you can control the growing yeast. Yeast is destroyed by very high temperatures and slowed to inactivity at low temperatures. Yeast begins to activate at about 50°, matures between 75° and 85°, flourishes between 90° and 110°, and begins to die at 120°. To illustrate, taste a piece of yeast dough as you prepare it. Because the temperature of the human body is a good one at which to incubate yeasts, the yeast in the dough will continue to multiply and grow in your stomach. Your body, therefore, is the best homemade thermometer to indicate the proper warmth for growing yeast. All ingredients that mix with yeast should be body temperature. Test liquids on your wrist or elbow. If they feel comfortably warm the temperature is right.

For a fine-grained loaf, the dough should rise slowly and evenly so that the flour and gluten can mature. For a quicker rising to save time or to make a very light-textured bread, increase the room temperature or use more yeast. Extra yeast, however, should be used sparingly since it may produce a porous texture and an unpalatable taste.

To activate yeast, mix it with a small amount of wrist-warm water. To test or "prove" the yeast, which shows that it is still alive, add a pinch or drop of sweetener to the dissolved yeast and wait until it bubbles. The yeast, if alive and active, will foam in 5 to 10 minutes.

ACTIVE DRY YEAST: dehydrated granules or small pellets of dormant yeast packed in 1-tablespoon foil packets, in bags, or jars of larger quantities. Some packaged yeast contains preservatives. The packets are dated to indicate when the yeast begins to lose activity. However, yeast will probably remain active long after the expiration date. Store dry active yeast in a moisture-proof container in the refrigerator or freezer.

COMPRESSED OR FRESH YEAST: a cream-colored cake of moist, pressed yeast that crumbles easily and breaks with a clean edge. Fresh yeast is sold in small ⅔-ounce foil-wrapped packages, in 2-ounce blocks, or in 1-pound bricks. Bakeries are often willing to sell compressed yeast to aspiring bakers. Refrigerated yeast will keep 2 to 3 weeks; frozen yeast, 2 to 3 months (with some loss of activity). Not-so-fresh compressed yeast is still usable if it crumbles easily. Spoiled yeast is foul-smelling and/or becomes soft and pasty. Brown spots of dried-out yeast on an otherwise good piece can be scraped off gently. Use a little extra if the yeast is more than 2 weeks old.

Many people who have had baking failures with dry active yeast succeed with compressed yeast because it dissolves more easily.

ADJUSTING LEAVENING FOR HIGH ALTITUDE BAKING

Baking adjustments are needed at high altitudes because, with less air pressure, carbon dioxide expands more quickly and exerts more leavening power—often too much for a batter or dough.

Begin all adjustments at three thousand feet.

In yeast breads use less yeast than the recipe specifies, or let the bread rise several times in the bowl. This gives the bread a finer grain to compensate for the coarse grain that results from quick rising.

In quick breads, use only three-quarters of the amount of baking soda or powder specified in the recipe. However, do not decrease the baking soda beyond

½ teaspoon for each cup of soured milk. The baking soda is needed to neutralize the acid.

For further information write for: Pamphlet #41, Colorado State University, Cooperative Extension Service, Fort Collins, Colorado.

Sugars

Not all sugars are interchangeable in a recipe because the weight, moisture, and sweetening power vary. Specifically, to substitute liquid sugars, like molasses or honey, for dry sugar, like granulated white sugar, you must compensate for the added moisture. Therefore, for each cup of liquid sugar used, reduce the liquid in the recipe by ¼ cup. In yeast breads, where there is a small percentage of sugar, sugars influence the taste of the bread more than the texture. In quick breads, the larger proportion of sugar makes a change in textures more noticeable when one sugar is exchanged for another. Liquid sugars increase the length of time a bread will stay fresh, since they retain moisture and keep the bread from drying out.

BEET OR CANE SUGARS

Sugar-refining boils, spins, filters, and separates sugar crystals from the black sticky molasses in sugar beets and sugar cane.

MOLASSES: a dark brown or black syrup with a strong sweet flavor. Molasses is available in a range of flavors and colors; dark molasses is stronger-tasting than light molasses. Store covered at room temperature.

BLACKSTRAP MOLASSES: a syrupy sugar that is the result of the third boiling of sugar cane to extract the last sugar crystals. I prefer blackstrap molasses because the flavor is strong and consistent from one jar to the next and the nutritive value is higher than other molasses. To mute the powerful taste, combine blackstrap molasses with a milder sugar like honey or maple syrup. Add ½ teaspoon baking soda for each cup of molasses used, to counteract the acidity. In breads that substitute molasses for white sugar, lower the baking temperature by 25–50° to prevent the crust from burning.

BROWN SUGAR: light or dark; it is made from refined white sugar with molasses added. The dark variety has more added molasses and therefore has a stronger taste. Store brown sugar with an orange rind or slice of apple, covered, in a dry place so that it does not dry and harden. If the sugar hardens, sprinkle it with a few drops of water and heat in a 200° oven for a few minutes.

Brown sugar makes a heavier, coarser cake than white sugar because of the extra moisture and syrup. It makes crisper cakes and quick breads than do honey and molasses.

"RAW" SUGAR: a coarse, squarish, beige crystal made by coating white refined sugar with a film of molasses.

TURBINADO SUGAR: made by a process that leaves sugar slightly unrefined and unbleached after the last molasses is removed.

WHITE SUGAR: the refined, bleached, crystalline residue after molasses is removed from sugar cane or sugar beets.

I do not usually use white sugar because it has an uninteresting taste, makes drier breads than liquid sugars do, and adds no nutrients besides calories. "Raw" and turbinado sugar are not very different, except that they are more expensive. I prefer to bake with brown sugar, which combines the crunchy texture of white sugar with the moisture and flavor of molasses.

HONEY

A thick golden syrup from pollinating bees. The flavor, color, and taste of the honey depend on the flower from which the bees take nectar. The darker the honey, the stronger the taste. Clover honey is mild; buckwheat honey is strong. Check to see if there are any local honeys in your area; they are likely to be most flavorful.

Honey gives breads a pleasant taste, a chewy texture, a brown color, and assures freshness for many days. Too much honey will make a quick bread or cake pasty.

To warm honey for easy mixing or to reliquify if it is crystallized, stand the honey jar in hot but not boiling water.

Since honey often makes breads brown fast, bake breads that substitute honey for white sugar at a baking temperature 25°–50° lower to insure thorough baking in the center before the crust burns. Store honey covered at room temperature.

MAPLE SWEETENERS

MAPLE SYRUP: an amber-colored and pleasant-tasting liquid made from the sap of the maple tree, boiled to evaporate most of the moisture. Store cans of maple syrup covered in the refrigerator to inhibit mold. If the syrup crystallizes, sit it in a hot water bath.

MAPLE SUGAR: made from granulated maple sap. Maple sugar has a strong, sweet taste. Because it dissolves slowly, it is best to grate or sliver it before adding to other ingredients.

CORN SYRUP

This is a thick, sticky liquid prepared from corn-starch. Dark varieties have a stronger flavor than light ones.

SORGHUM

This is a liquid sugar made from sweet sorghum cane. It has a thin consistency and a slightly tart flavor.

MALT POWDER OR MALT SYRUP

This is a beige powder or liquid made from fermented grain, usually barley. Malt is much sweeter than white sugar.

Oils and Fats

Any oil or fat can be substituted, one for another, in a bread. In yeast breads, where there is a small proportion of fat, substitutions make little difference. In quick breads, pastries, and cakes, however, the large proportion of fat makes a substitution more noticeable.

Since spoilage of oils and fats is more often caused by exposure to oxygen in the air rather than by bacteria, keep all oils and fats sealed tightly in containers.

BUTTER

Butter is used for taste. It is by law 80 percent fat. The remainder is water and milk solids, which contribute the small amount of protein found in butter. Butter must be fresh; rancid butter will be detected in the finished bread, since baking does not disguise it. Salted butter keeps longer than sweet butter. In the recipes in this book I have used unsalted butter, which, to me, has a fresher flavor. If you use salted butter, use less salt in the rest of the recipe to compensate. Use unsalted butter to grease baking tins, because salted butter leaves too strong a flavor on the crust of the bread. Store butter in a covered container in the refrigerator to prevent rancidity and to keep it from absorbing the odors of other foods.

MARGARINE

This is a solid shortening made by whipping hydrogen into refined vegetable oils and then adding some milk. Sometimes animal or dairy fats are added. Read the package for the contents. Most margarines are 80 percent fat, as is butter, and they are nutritionally enriched to equal butter. Margarine may be used in any recipe for butter; however, most margarines are salted, so use less salt when substituting margarine for sweet butter. Avoid greasing baking tins with margarine; the taste is too strong and salty. Store margarine covered in the refrigerator. It can be kept frozen indefinitely.

VEGETABLE OILS

These oils are pressed from seeds, nuts, fruit, or vegetables. Some are made from corn, cottonseeds, olives, soybeans, sesame seeds, sunflower seeds, walnuts, hickory nuts, and beechnuts, to name a few. Unrefined oils are cloudy, and each has a characteristic flavor and odor. To clear the cloudy oil, unrefined oils are bleached and deodorized, which makes all refined oils practically indistinguishable from one another.

Oil is 100 percent fat. When substituting a vegetable oil for butter use only $8/10$ of a cup of oil for each cup of butter in the original recipe. Use mild-flavored oils, like corn, cottonseed, or safflower, in quick breads, cookies, and cakes.

In quick breads and cakes, oils make a tender crumb. Mix well to maintain a light texture. A large proportion of oil in a batter will make a very crumbly texture.

Store unrefined oils in the refrigerator; they become rancid easily. Store refined oils covered in a cool place.

SOLID VEGETABLE SHORTENING: a white, soft fat made by whipping air into refined vegetable oil. Many people find it good for baking because it holds its shape when being creamed with a sweetener or cut into flour.

Nuts and Seeds

Nuts and seeds are sold in the shell (unhulled), shelled (hulled), broken into pieces, slivered, sliced, and ground into butters, meals, and flours. Nuts and seeds add flavor and a crunchy texture to breads. Flours, meals, and butters made from nuts and seeds bring flavor to the bread without the crunchy consistency. In the recipes in this book only unsalted nuts are used.

Nuts and seeds can be unroasted (raw), or roasted (toasted) to bring out the flavor. *To roast raw nuts and seeds at home,* shell 1 cup and mix with 1 teaspoon oil or melted fat. Spread the nuts or seeds on a baking pan and roast in a 350° oven for 5 to 15 minutes—depending on the size. Stir occasionally to assure even browning. To toast on the top of the stove, brown the nuts or seeds in a heavy frying pan, heating slowly and stirring until lightly browned. The retained heat in the nuts or seeds keeps them browning after they are removed from the heat, so try to avoid overbrowning.

Nuts with thick inner skins, like almonds, can be unskinned by placing the nuts in boiling water for a few minutes. This process is called *blanching.* The skin should slip off.

NUT FLOUR: Nuts and seeds can be ground into flour and meal by whirling them in a blender. Chill the nuts and seeds before and after grinding to prevent them from becoming oily. Watch the grinding carefully so the pulverized particles remain dry and do not become oily or mushy. Commercial meals and flours often have the oil extracted before grinding.

NUT BUTTER: To make a nut or seed butter blend 1 to 3 teaspoons of oil and ½ teaspoon of salt (if desired) with 1 cup of nuts or seeds, or grind the nuts through the nut butter blade of a meat grinder. Nut and seed butters make good shortenings for yeast breads if they are well dissolved in the liquid. In a bread where the shortening is a large fraction of the ingredients, nut and seed butters can be used for part of the shortening. Too much nut or seed butter will result in a mushy, sticky bread.

To chop nuts fine, put nut meats between two pieces of waxed paper or into a plastic bag, and roll with a rolling pin. Pulverize seeds in a mortar or bowl with a pestle to release the flavor. To sprout seeds, see page 319.

Most nuts and seeds remain fresh and retain nutrients longest if stored in their natural protection—the shell. This is impractical at times, however. Shelled nuts and seeds should be stored in an airtight container in a cool place to discourage their becoming rancid because of moisture and high temperature. Whole nuts keep better than chopped nuts. Refrigerate or freeze shelled nuts and seeds; they will keep for months. They do not have to be defrosted to be used. Store nut or seed butters in closed containers in the refrigerator.

NUTS

Most nuts are interchangeable in a recipe. The following are the most commonly used in breads, pastries, and cakes.

Almonds, butternuts, Brazil nuts, beechnuts, cashews, coconuts, hazelnuts (filberts), hickories, macadamia nuts, pecans, pignolias (pine or piñon nuts), pistachios, walnuts.

PEANUTS: In reality, peanuts belong to the bean and pea family. They grow from plants that flower and have tendrils that burrow into the soil. Peanuts can be treated as nuts for their baking qualities, but chemically, and therefore nutritionally, peanuts are more similar to dried beans. Peanut flour makes breads dark and heavy.

SEEDS

Use the following seeds whole or cracked—anise, caraway, celery, chia, cumin, dill, fennel, flax, mustard, poppy, turmeric. Use these grated or ground—allspice, cardamom, cloves, coriander, fenugreek, nutmeg, peppercorns.

COTTONSEED: this very high protein seed will soon be available as flour to home bakers. Scientists have recently deactivated the poisonous pigment in cottonseed—gossypol—without damaging the cottonseed protein. To enrich breads use about 2 to 4 tablespoons of cottonseed flour per cup of flour in the recipe. For quick breads, especially pancakes, as much as three-quarters of the flour can be cottonseed.

PUMPKIN SEEDS: cleaned and toasted from a fresh pumpkin or bought whole and hulled, called "pepitas."

WHOLE SESAME AND SUNFLOWER SEEDS: sprinkle on the surface of unbaked yeast bread, into a greased muffin or bread tin, or stir into the batter or dough.

SESAME AND SUNFLOWER MEAL: coarse ground seeds. Sesame and sunflower meal add moisture and fats to batters and doughs, making a heavy, moist bread that bakes quickly.

SESAME BUTTER (FROM RAW SESAME SEEDS) OR "TAHINI" (FROM TOASTED SESAME SEEDS): a thick, oily paste made from mashed sesame seeds. Use as a liquid or fat in breads. Tahini has a distinct flavor and is the basis of many Middle Eastern foods. It is available in international groceries and health food stores.

Dried Beans

Each dried bean has a characteristic flavor: common beans, mung, garbanzo (chick-peas or chichi), red or brown lentils, black-eyed, yellow and green split peas (not for sprouting), pintos. Any bean or bean flour can be used interchangeably without changing the texture of a bread. Use in small amounts; a bread with too much bean flour is dense, dry, and compact.

Soaked or cooked beans mashed to a pulp or paste can be added to breads to make a moist loaf. Toasted whole beans, while nutlike to eat plain, become soft in doughs and batters. Bean grits, if soaked before adding to a bread, make it chewy; if unsoaked, they make the bread crunchy. Water from soaking and washing beans makes a good bread liquid. Whole or ground bean sprouts remain crisp in baked breads.

To grow sprouts: Any unhulled, uncooked grain, bean, or seed will sprout. The sprouting method I find easiest and most successful is to soak the kernels overnight in a dish of water and then drain them, rinse them, and place them in a jar, bowl, or casserole. Cover with the lid or with a piece of cheesecloth, and put in a warm place. Check the kernels each day. Tiny kernels (like alfalfa seeds) simply rest and grow; larger ones (those large enough to hold comfortably between your fingers—like beans) should be rinsed with fresh water and drained every day. Small kernels will grow in three to four days; large kernels will grow in four to five days. Finished sprouts are green, have long tails, and have used the starch and protein supply in the kernel to make vitamins in the newly sprouted plant. Expect ¼ cup of kernels to grow into about 2 cups of sprouts.

CAROB

Carob is the inner flesh from the pod of the tamarind or Saint John's bread tree, which is milled to make powdery flour. Carob flour is sweet and is most frequently used as a flavoring. Some say that carob tastes similar to chocolate. It is often used as a substitute. Raw or toasted carob flour can be used in baking any breads and cakes. When adding carob flour to recipes, lower the baking temperature from the original suggested temperature because carob scorches easily.

CHOCOLATE

These are the dark-brown, strong-flavored products of the cacao bean that have been fermented, cured, and roasted. Begin with unsweetened (bitter) chocolate so that you can control the sweetness.

COCOA: powdered, partially defatted, and roasted cacao beans that give a strong, bittersweet taste to breads and absorb a lot of moisture. When adding cocoa to a recipe in which it was not included originally, expect to add less flour. Use unsweetened cocoa for baking.

CHOCOLATE: Baking chocolate is unsweetened. Semisweet, sweet, bittersweet, and milk chocolate are pleasant to add as tiny morsels to cookies and cakes. Substitute ¼ cup unsweetened cocoa and 2 tablespoons shortening for 1 ounce (1 square) of unsweetened melted chocolate.

SOY

Soy is a high-value vegetable protein that complements wheat protein in any bread. Soy products are raw or toasted. Toasted soy is called soya and has a pleasant nutty flavor; many find that untoasted soybeans have a bland, flat taste that benefits from extra salt and elaborate flavorings. Soybeans are available in a defatted or low-fat form (after soy oil has been pressed out) or a full-fat form.

ROASTED SOYBEANS: crispy half-beans that taste like bland peanuts.

SOY GRITS: coarse ground pieces.

SOY FLAKES: steamed and pressed whole soybeans.

SOY MEAL: rough-ground, somewhat floury.

SOYA GRANULES: toasted soy grits.

SOY OR SOYA FLOUR: a fine-milled powder. Soy flour helps blend ingredients with less separation of fats and liquids (as when adding eggs to creamed butter and sugar) and increases the length of time a bread will remain fresh by slowing the rancidity of fats.

In small amounts, soy flour makes moist, compact quick breads; too much makes the bread dense and dry. In yeast breads, use soy flour in combination with other flours, particularly gluten flour, because alone, soy flour makes a hard, bricklike loaf. In pancakes and cookies, soy flour can compose the major portion of the flour, making them light and moist.

To avoid lumping, sift or mix the soy flour with the other flours before adding it to the dough or batter. Mix full-fat soy flour with the liquids, or blend it with the shortening, to distribute it evenly. Breads with a large proportion of soy flour brown quickly, so reduce the baking temperature by 25–50° if soy flour is added to a recipe that previously had little or none.

SOY AND SOYA POWDER: very fine, pulverized soy flour; ¼ cup soy powder and 1 cup of water make soy milk, which can be substituted for cow's milk.

TOFU BEAN CURD OR SOY CHEESE: made from curdled soy milk and pressed into custardlike cakes. Tofu is mild and delicate and is usually used in Oriental dishes. It is particularly good sweetened and mashed in puddings and custards.

MISO: fermented soybeans and a grain, usually barley or rice. Miso makes a good sandwich spread when mixed with sesame butter.

SOY SAUCE: from fermenting soybeans and salt. Use as a salt substitute in breads that do not have a sweet flavor.

VANILLA BEAN

This is the cured, full-grown, but unripe seed pod of a fragrant orchid. To flavor a hot liquid, split the pod and soak it for 15 minutes. To flavor a batter or dough, scrape the insides of the pod into the mixture.

VANILLA EXTRACT: a concentrated liquid made from the oils of the vanilla bean, plus alcohol and water.

Fruit

Fruit, fresh or dried, are easily added to breads. Fresh fruit retain their shape when baked and have a more distinct flavor than canned fruit. When using a presweetened fruit or fruit juice, include less sugar in the rest of the recipe.

Dried fruit are dehydrated fresh fruit. Some commercial processes add sulfur to prevent darkening but the sulfur also leaves an acidic taste. Plump and soften dried fruit by soaking them in a hot liquid. For quick breads, toss chopped fruit in a few tablespoons of the flour with a little baking powder and stir the fruit in last. This insures that the fruit will not stick together and will be evenly distributed in the bread.

BANANAS: sweetest when overripe and the starch turns to sugar.

BANANA FLAKES: dried and pulverized whole bananas.

GREEN BANANA FLOUR: sun-dried bananas ground to a fine powder.

CRANBERRIES: fresh whole cranberries are tart, colorful, and retain their shape well after baking.

DATE SUGAR: dried, granulated dates.

DATE BUTTER: date purée.

Vegetables

Raw vegetables like pumpkins, beets, or carrots, grated into breads give them a crunchy texture and slightly sweet flavor. Vegetable juices, purées, cooked and mashed vegetables, cooking broth or soup stock all make good liquid additions to both yeast and quick breads.

TUBERS

Potatoes

Potatoes are rich in an enzyme that makes yeast very active. Breads made with potato ingredients rise well, have a large volume, a slightly coarse texture, and are slow to stale. Cooked and mashed potatoes added to yeast breads such as pumpernickel make a heavy, moist loaf.

POTATO MEAL: cooked and dried potatoes, ground to a granular meal; added to any bread, potato meal makes a crisp, crunchy texture.

POTATO FLOUR OR STARCH: a fine-ground potato meal. Potato flour is very powdery and tends to lump. To avoid lumping, blend it with other flours or blend it with the shortening. Potato flour makes very light cakes.

POTATO WATER: water drained from boiling potatoes. Used as the liquid in breads, potato water introduces the potato enzyme without the texture of mashed potatoes or potato flour.

Herbs and Spices

The following suggestions may help you to become more daring when confronted with dozens of small bottles of herbs and spices. Any herb or spice will make plain bread distinctive. Sift herbs and spices with the flour to distribute the flavor evenly:

ALLSPICE: sweet breads, fruit breads, and pies, especially apple

ANISE: sponge cakes, Swedish rye

BASIL: cheese breads

CARAWAY: rye breads

CARDAMOM: coffee cakes, sweet breads, fruit breads, and pies

CLOVES: sweet breads, fruit breads, and pies

CINNAMON: coffee cake, sweet breads, fruit breads, and pies

CORIANDER: fruit pies, especially apple, gingerbread

CUMIN: any plain bread or crackers

DILL: apple pie, cheese bread

FENNEL: fruit pies

FENUGREEK: any plain bread or crackers

GERANIUM: pound cake, custard and fruit pies

GINGER: gingerbread, fruit breads, coffee cake

MACE: fruit breads, sweet breads

MINT: with chocolate

MUSTARD: cheese breads

NUTMEG: with mace, sweet breads, coffee cake

ONIONS: cheese breads, sautéed on flat breads, and crackers

326

POPPY SEED: pound cake, coffee cake fillings, bread toppings

SAFFRON (for yellow color): challah, coffee cakes

SESAME: Danish filling, crackers, bread toppings

Brewer's Yeast

Brewer's yeast is a dehydrated yeast that was once a product of the brewery and is now cultivated commercially. It is an inactive yeast with no leavening power. The flavor is strong and distinctive; many people find it bitter. A range of flavors from medium to strong is available, and a particularly mild variety is cultured in buttermilk.

Brewer's yeast can be bought in tablets, granules, flakes, and powder. One to three tablespoons of brewer's yeast powder added to a dough or batter will not affect the texture and will fortify the nutritional value.

Index